Latin American Political Economy

Series Editors

Eduardo Moncada, Barnard College, New York, USA

Aldo Madariaga, Santiago, Chile

Sara Niedzwiecki, Santa Cruz, USA

Latin American Political Economy publishes new, relevant, and empirically-grounded scholarship that deepens our understanding of contemporary Latin American political economy and contributes to the formulation and evaluation of new theories that are both context-sensitive and subject to broader comparisons. Inspired by the need to provide new analytical perspectives for understanding the massive social, political, and economic transformations underway in Latin America, the series is directed at researchers and practitioners interested in resurrecting political economy as a primary research area in the developing world. In thematic terms, the series seeks to promote vital debate on the interactions between economic, political, and social processes; it is especially concerned with how findings may further our understanding of development models, the socio-political institutions that sustain them, and the practical problems they confront. In methodological terms, the series showcases cross-disciplinary research that is empirically rich and sensitive to context and that leads to new forms of description, concept formation, causal inference, and theoretical innovation. The series editors welcome submissions that address patterns of democratic politics, dependency and development, state formation and the rule of law, inequality and identity, and global linkages.

Sebastián Carrasco

From (De)regulation to Industrialization?

Chilean Lithium Policy in Comparative Perspective

palgrave
macmillan

Sebastián Carrasco
School of Government
Universidad San Sebastián
Santiago, Chile

ISSN 2945-7076 ISSN 2945-7084 (electronic)
Latin American Political Economy
ISBN 978-3-031-77129-3 ISBN 978-3-031-77130-9 (eBook)
https://doi.org/10.1007/978-3-031-77130-9

This Palgrave Macmillan imprint is published by the registered company Springer Nature Switzerland AG
The registered company address is: Gewerbestrasse 11, 6330 Cham, Switzerland

Acknowledgments

The journey of a researcher is often a solitary one, particularly during the writing of lengthy documents, which can lead to a sense of isolation. This was especially true in the context of the COVID-19 pandemic, which affected everyone, including the research, that began during this period. Fortunately, despite the challenges, this book benefited from the support of various colleagues, institutions, and friends, all of whom deserve my deepest gratitude.

First and foremost, this book would not have been possible without the guidance and support of Aldo Madariaga and Mayarí Castillo. The book is largely the result of my doctoral thesis at Universidad Mayor, where Aldo and Mayarí served as my advisors, providing me with invaluable advice and companionship throughout the entire process. Aldo greatly contributed to my theoretical foundation in political economy and provided me with the astounding opportunity to travel to Germany to complete this project. Mayarí, in her dual role as both tutor and director of the doctoral program, ensured that deadlines were met and demanded the rigor necessary to complete the first draft of what is now this book.

Secondly, I would like to express my special gratitude to Antoine Maillet, who not only encouraged me to pursue a path in research but also instilled in me a passion for environmental issues, which have been a constant source of inspiration for my work. His unwavering support and words of encouragement during moments of uncertainty were crucial in helping me find my way. Even up to the final stages, Antoine assisted me in deciding the final title of this book.

On an institutional level, I extend my appreciation to the academic authorities who provided the necessary support for this project to come to fruition: Juan Carlos Arellano, Director of the Department of Sociology, Political Science, and Public Administration at the Catholic University of Temuco, and José Miguel Cabezas, Director of the School of Government at San Sebastián University, for their leadership and guidance. I am also thankful to the Max Planck Institute for the Study of Societies, and its Director, Lucio Baccaro, where I was able to complete the first full draft of this work.

To the Free University of Berlin, I owe my deepest gratitude for the invaluable feedback, unwavering support, and enriching discussions with Bettina Schorr, which have been instrumental in the progress of this work.

At the Max Planck Institute for the Study of Societies, I also wish to thank Ariana Tassinari and Fabio Bulfone for their contributions and suggestions, whose ideas and constructive critiques have been immensely helpful in the completion of this project.

This intellectual journey would not have been the same without the company and encouragement of various colleagues. I am especially thankful to Alejandro Olivares, Javier Hernández, Rodolfo Disi, Francisco Fernández, Gonzalo Delamaza, Maritza Paredes, Teresita Rocha-Jiménez, Nicolás Montalva, Álvaro Castillo, Rodrigo Pérez-Silva, Carolina Acevedo, Jorge Atria, Emilio Moya, Rodolfo de Camargo, Camila Mella, Bruna Fonseca, Lihuen Nocetto, and finally to José Carlos Orihuela, who served on my doctoral thesis committee and provided crucial feedback at key moments in this research.

My gratitude also extends to the research assistants, Valentina Cariaga, Daniela Tapia, and Matías Otth. Without their dedication and collaboration, this project would not have been possible. They are outstanding professionals who carry out their work with rigor and impeccable attention to detail. I have learned a great deal from them. I also want to express my gratitude to Cesar Morgado for his support throughout the process and his help with key aspects, such as transcribing interviews with stakeholders and reviewing the final manuscript, and to Paula Collio for her assistance in editing this book in English.

A special thanks goes to the anonymous reviewers of the book, whose valuable comments greatly enhanced its content.

Finally, I would like to thank the Fondecyt project 11241196, "Towards a New Development Model? Institutions, Actors, and Conflict around Lithium Policies in Chile," from the National Agency for Research and Development (ANID) in Chile, for providing the necessary resources to complete this research. I also extend my thanks to the Max Planck Partner Group "Challenges of Green Growth" for their support.

I cannot fail to mention my family and friends, whose support has been a cornerstone throughout this journey. I am especially grateful to my parents, Alejandro and Rosa, for their unwavering support and understanding. To my lifelong friends who tolerate me and offer words of encouragement when needed. Last but not least, to María Elena, my partner, who has stood by me through both the good times and the bad. Her love and understanding have been key to bringing this book to fruition.

Contents

1 **Introduction** 1
The Empirical Puzzle of the Lithium Political Economy 5
The Theoretical Puzzle: State-Business Relations and Green Industrial Policy 7
State Capacity and Business Power: Gaps in the Literature and Contributions of the Book 8
State–Business Relations: Toward a Typological Proposal 11
The Methodological Puzzle 13
Typological Theory and Process Tracing 14
Research Techniques 15
Plan of the Book 16

Part I State, Business and Green Industrial Policy

2 **Green Industrial Policy: A Theoretical Perspective** 21
Introduction 21
Lithium, Climate Change, and Green Industrial Policy 22
The Discussion on Climate Change, Energy Transition, and Green Growth 22
The Debate on Green Industrial Policy 24
Industrial Policy in Latin America 26
Toward a Typology of Green Industrial Policy (GIP) 27
Explanatory Factors of Green Industrial Policy 32

State–Business Relations in the Context of Green Industrial Policy 32
State–Business relations in the literature on Developmental State 34
State–Business Relations for a New Green Development Model 38
Industrial Policy in Context: Lithium Extraction and Socio-Environmental Conflicts 40
Extractivism, Socio-Environmental Conflicts, and Green Industrial Policy 41
Socio-Environmental Impacts of Lithium Extraction in Latin America 42

3 Operationalizing State–Business Relations for the Study of Green Industrial Policy 45
Introduction 45
State Capacity 46
Operationalizing State Capacity for Industrial Policy 46
State Capacity from a Relational Perspective 49
Business Actors 55
Business Strategies in Green Industrial Policy 55
Business Preferences in Green Industrial Policy 60
State–Business Dynamics in the Context of Global Value Chains (GVCs) 64
Toward a Typology for Studying State–Business Relations 66

4 Contextual Analysis of Lithium Policies in the Latin American Context 69
Introduction 69
Climate Change, Energy Transition, and Lithium Extraction 71
Socioeconomic Dynamics of the Lithium Industry 73
Global Economic Dynamics in Lithium Extraction 73
Economic Challenges of the Lithium Industry 78
Institutional Context of the Latin American Lithium Policies 80
Socio-Environmental Dynamics of the Lithium Industry 82
Socio-Environmental Conflict in Chile 84
Socio-Environmental Conflict in Argentina 86
Socio-Environmental Conflict in Bolivia 89

Part II The Configuration of Lithium Policies in the South American Context

5 State Capacity in Chile's Lithium Policy 93
Introduction 93
The Institutional–Legal Dimension of Lithium Extraction in Chile 94
Historical Background of Lithium Policy 94
Institutional Framework for Lithium Exploitation in Chile 96
Renewed Interest in Lithium in the New Century 101
The Political Dimension of State Capacity in Chile's Lithium Policy 104
Piñera Administration (2010–2014) 104
Bachelet Administration (2014–2018) 109
Administrative Dimension of the State Capacity in Lithium Policy 112
The Role of Experts: Presidential Lithium Advisory Commission 112
Conclusions 120

6 The Role of Business in Chile's Lithium Policy 123
Introduction 123
Instrumental Business Power in Chile's Lithium Policy 125
The Original Sin: Corruption Cases in the Lithium Sector 125
Legal Conflicts, New Contracts, and Lithium Industrialization 130
Lithium Preferential Prices 133
The Controversial Progress of the Clean Technologies Institute 136
Structural Business Power in Chile's Lithium Policy 139
The Marginal Role of State-Owned Enterprises 143
Business Preferences 146
Advancing the Lithium Agenda? Gabriel Boric's Strategic Shift 147
Conclusion: Conflictual State–Business Relations and Selective Industrial Policy in Chile 149

7 **Closing the Lithium Triangle: Public Policies in Argentina and Bolivia** 153
Introduction 153
The Argentine Case 155
Lithium Exploitation in Argentina: A Contextual Analysis 155
State Dynamics and Lithium Policies in Argentina 158
The Role of State-Owned Enterprises (SOE) 160
Business Dynamics and Lithium Policies in Argentina 161
The Bolivian Case 163
Lithium Policy in Bolivia 163
State Capacity and Business Dynamics in Bolivia 165
Socio-Environmental Dynamics and Lithium Policy in the Triangle 169

8 **Divergent Trajectories of Lithium Policies: Some Conclusions** 173
Revisiting the Argument: The Role of the State and Business in Shaping Lithium Policies 173
Advancement of Lithium Industrial Policies in Latin America 173
Lithium Policy and Capitalist Dynamics 177
Implications for Decision-Making Processes and Public Policies 181

Appendix 1. List of Interviews 185

Appendix 2. Key Characteristics of Major Companies in the Lithium Industry 187

References 191

Index 217

About the Author

Sebastián Carrasco is Assistant Professor at the School of Government, Universidad San Sebastián, Chile and an Associate Researcher with the Max Planck Partner Group "Challenges of Green Growth." He holds a Ph.D. in Public Policy and an MA in Political Science. Previously, he served as a professor of Public Administration at Universidad Católica de Temuco (Chile), and as a visiting researcher at the Max Planck Institute for the Study of Societies (Germany) and at the Free University of Berlin (Germany). He is the principal investigator of the Fondecyt project 11241196 and a co-investigator of the Fondecyt project 1240892, both funded by the National Agency for Research and Development (ANID) in Chile. His work has been published by *The Extractive Industries and Societies*, *Competition & Change*, among others.

List of Figures

Fig. 1.1	State–business relations and industrial policy outcomes. *Source*: Own elaboration	13
Fig. 2.1	Types of green industrial policy in lithium. Source: Own elaboration	31
Fig. 2.2	Lithium Value Chain and Industrial Policy Outcomes. Source: Own elaboration	32
Fig. 4.1	Major lithium resources in the world. Source: Own elaboration based on U.S. Geological Survey, Mineral Commodity Summaries 2004–14-24	74
Fig. 4.2	Major Lithium Reserves in the World. Source: Own elaboration based on U.S. Geological Survey, Mineral Commodity Summaries 2004–14-24	75
Fig. 4.3	Million Tons of Lithium Carbonate Exported by Leading Exporters Worldwide. Source: Own elaboration based on data from the U.S. Geological Survey, Mineral Commodity Summaries	76
Fig. 4.4	Value Chain of Lithium-Ion Batteries. Source: Own elaboration based on Irarrazaval and Carrasco (2023)	76
Fig. 4.5	Market share of lithium carbonate exports by major global exporters. Source: Own elaboration based on data from the U.S. Geological Survey, Mineral Commodity Summaries	77
Fig. 4.6	Leading Lithium-Importing Countries in 2021 (import values in thousands of USD). Source: Own elaboration based on data from WITS	78

Fig. 4.7 Government Effectiveness Index in Lithium Triangle Countries. Source: Own elaboration based on World Bank data 80
Fig. 4.8 Ease of Doing Business Index in Latin America, Lithium Triangle, and Major Global Regions (2020). Source: Own elaboration based on data from the Ease of Doing Business Index 82
Fig. 4.9 Lithium Projects by Region in the Lithium Triangle. Source: Own elaboration based on the Ministry of Mining of Chile, the Secretariat of Mining of Argentina, and YLB data 85
Fig. 5.1 Timeline of the history of SQM and Albemarle. Source: Own elaboration 101
Fig. 5.2 Key Components of the Lithium Policy and Governance of the Salt Flats. Source: Own elaboration based on empirical evidence collected 103
Fig. 5.3 Main topics in the public discussion on Lithium. Source: Own elaboration based on press analysis 110
Fig. 5.4 Constitutive elements of political capacity in Chile's lithium policy. Source; Own Elaboration 113
Fig. 6.1 Timeline of the lithium bidding process during Piñera I Administration. *Source* Own elaboration 128
Fig. 6.2 Chilean copper and lithium exports (2010–2023) (in millions of US dollars). *Source* Own elaboration based on Central Bank of Chile database 146
Fig. 6.3 Causal narrative explaining the establishment of lithium policy in Chile. *Source* Own Elaboration 151

List of Tables

Table 3.1	Dimensions of state capacity	48
Table 3.2	Operationalization of state capacity	49
Table 3.3	Areas of State Capacity According to Christoff (2005)	50
Table 3.4	Operationalization of business power	59
Table 3.5	Typology of State–Business Relations and Types of Industrial Policy	66
Table 5.1	Lithium mining holdings by type of actor	95
Table 5.2	Formation of SQM and Albemarle from the 1980s privatization process	97
Table 5.3	Members of the National Lithium Commission	107
Table 5.4	Empirical findings on state capacity in lithium policy in Chile	122
Table 6.1	Main agreements reached in the negotiation between CORFO and SQM. *Source* Own elaboration based on Ciper (2018)	132
Table 7.1	Typology of state–business relations, types of industrial policy and cases	154
Table 8.1	Summary of changes in lithium actions and policies by government	175

CHAPTER 1

Introduction

Elon Musk is one of the wealthiest people in the world. He is also the founder of major companies such as SolarCity and Tesla Motors, which aim to contribute to the global energy transition using renewable energy in technological innovations, particularly by manufacturing electric vehicles. In 2017, this billionaire entrepreneur arrived in Chile with the goal of negotiating with a Chilean capital company, one of the largest producers of lithium salts worldwide, to invest in the supply of this mineral. At the time, there were even rumors that Tesla might build a lithium processing plant in the country (El Mostrador, 2018).

Lithium is a non-metallic mineral found in high concentrations in only a few countries, with Chile, Argentina, and Bolivia being major exporters and holding some of the largest global reserves. This mineral has various industrial uses, but in recent decades, demand has increased exponentially due to its use in the technology sector (Zícari et al., 2019). Lithium is a crucial component for the development of batteries that store energy from renewable sources—namely, lithium-ion batteries. Among its many uses, these batteries are essential for the operation of electric vehicles, such as the high-end models produced by Tesla Motors.

Lithium plays such a critical role in Tesla's electric vehicles that Elon Musk himself traveled to Chile to negotiate contracts with local lithium companies and obtain the mineral's future supply, a goal that ultimately

S. Carrasco, *From (De)regulation to Industrialization?*, Latin American Political Economy, https://doi.org/10.1007/978-3-031-77130-9_1

was not achieved. Musk was unable to secure a stock for his companies and subsequently announced that he would source lithium from the United States to avoid reliance on the Chilean market (O'Ryan, 2020). Furthermore, he indicated that he would start applying new technologies to reduce dependence on lithium, which caused a decline in the stock price of Sociedad Química y Minera de Chile (SQM) (San Juan & Gac, 2020).

Despite these threats, a couple of years later, in response to a comment suggesting that the United States had orchestrated a coup in Bolivia to secure lithium for Tesla, Musk said on Twitter (now X): "*We will coup whoever we want! Deal with it.*" Regardless of whether his comment was meant ironically or not, this episode highlights the continued significance of lithium for Musk and the opportunities it presents for Latin American countries. Currently, Musk's attention has shifted to Argentina, where he has already held meetings with the governor of Catamarca to extract lithium from that region of the country (Clarín, 2022).

How can it be explained that Elon Musk, one of the most prominent businessman in the world, was unable to engage in the exploitation of a mineral in an extractivist and free-market economy like Chile's? Why is he interested in exploiting the political crisis in Bolivia to secure lithium? And what explains his eventual success in making deals in Argentina to extract the mineral? The explanation seems to lie in the divergent trajectories that lithium policies have taken in these Latin American countries, based on the relationships between the state and business in the Region.

Recently, public policies on lithium in South America have been debated between industrial development and free-market approaches, aiming to enhance markets and increase exploitation quotas while advancing the value chain. Thus, the potential of lithium for electromobility has led to the construction of imaginaries around the creation of new development models for South American countries (Barandiarán, 2019). In practice, this has been reflected in various attempts to progress toward the production of higher value-added lithium products in the lithium triangle countries.

Nevertheless, the outcomes of public policy have varied among the three countries, achieving different degrees of progress regarding the configuration of industrial policies in this area. Bolivia has established an ambitious industrial policy that, under state control, aims to advance toward the production of complex lithium-based products within the country, but in practice, it has not progressed beyond the pilot phase.

On the other hand, Argentina has made some attempts to add value to lithium, but these have not succeeded. Instead, there has been a recent intensification of low-value-added extractive activities, increasing the number of raw lithium exploitation projects. Finally, Chile has advanced in designing lithium industrialization policies to develop complex products and integrate science and technology into production. However, the implementation of these new regulations has been uneven, making progress in some areas while failing in others.

Considering these factors, this research seeks to explain the different trajectories that lithium policies have taken in Latin America, exposing how industrial development and scaling up in the value chain of extractive activities are possible in certain institutional contexts. To achieve this, this book analyzes the case of Chile, complemented by the study of Argentina and Bolivia as shadow cases, thereby enhancing the validity of the results. The book proposes the existence of types of public policy based on an explanatory framework that focuses on the strength/weakness of the State, on the one hand, and the level of opposition/support from companies to the policies, on the other. This reseacrh thus aims to demonstrate how the relationship between the State and specific companies involved in lithium extraction impacts industrial policies and value-added processes.

Using theories on state capacities (Cingolani, 2013) and those from business strategies in public policy (Meckling, 2015), I argue that transformations in public policies on this matter depend not only on a more or less active role of the State—as primarily studied in the literature—but also, to an equal extent, on the position of the company regarding these policies. After all, private companies play a crucial role in mineral exploitation and are central to the discussion on industrial policy (Bulfone, 2022).

Thus, the analysis progresses toward a theoretical proposal on state–business relations in dialogue with discussions on industrial policy articulated within comparative political economy, while contributing to the development of an original perspective on the matter. In this regard, throughout the book, I explain how different state–business relationships impact the outcomes of lithium policies. The divergent experiences of lithium policies in Chile, Bolivia, and Argentina raise central questions about the process of value addition to the Latin American industry and, more broadly, about the development models articulated in the region.

Empirically, the research demonstrates that building ad hoc state capacities is a necessary condition for advancing value addition processes related to lithium, despite being a factor typically discussed in the literature focusing on developed countries. At the same time, I argue that these capacities are relational, as they depend on support from business actors to make significant progress in policies that add value to the production process. In particular, the Chilean case reflects a process of constructing different institutional structures, renegotiating contracts with lithium-extracting companies, and establishing various innovation and development initiatives to add value to lithium. However, opposition from lithium-related companies at specific times has impeded decisive progress in implementing these measures, resulting in a selective industrial policy. The current government of President Gabriel Boric (2022–2026) has introduced a new lithium public policy strategy that incorporates several elements from the Bachelet administration's policy, though the results remain uncertain.

The study is complemented by the cases of Argentina and Bolivia. Bolivia lacks the technical knowledge and capacities, but at the same time, it has the support of international companies, and a state-owned enterprise created specifically to manage the lithium production process. The inherent state weakness results in a low-intensity relationship, leading to the establishment of industrial policy instruments that have not been successfully implemented. To date, the Bolivian state has not managed to achieve large-scale production, resulting in a stagnated industrial policy. In contrast, Argentina's federal state structure, combined with the significant autonomy of provinces in controlling mining (including lithium), and weaknesses in federal enforcement, means that central political directives are not realized. Moreover, the influence exerted by companies and their opposition to industrialization projects results in a relationship dominated by businesses, where political actors benefit from short-term lithium rents. Thus, liberal approaches to lithium exploitation persist, promoting the establishment of low-value-added lithium extraction and export projects. Currently, Argentina has 50 lithium projects in the pipeline, 6 under construction, and 4 in operation. The Argentine case reflects a non-industrial policy approach.

The Empirical Puzzle of the Lithium Political Economy

In the early 2000s, Latin America experienced a commodities boom that significantly boosted the economic growth of the region's countries, while at the same time, increased environmental degradation and led to various social conflicts related to mining activities (Amengual & Dargent, 2020; Fernández-Milmanda & Garay, 2020). In Chile, the rise in international copper prices—the country's primary export commodity—allowed for an increase in fiscal revenues (Sater, 2021 p. 448) and, consequently, for the expansion and deepening of social policies and programs that had been developing for decades (Farías, 2019). However, this economic growth was accompanied by a rise in socio-territorial conflicts (Delamaza et al., 2017), socio-ecological inequalities (Castillo-Gallardo, 2016), and the emergence of local resistance to extractive activities (Valenzuela-Fuentes et al., 2021).

Currently, Chile faces a new boom, this time centered on a recently recognized crucial commodity: lithium. This mineral, found in high concentrations in only a few countries, makes Chile one of the largest global exporters and the leading exporter in Latin America [followed closely by Argentina and more distantly by Bolivia] (Fornillo, 2015; Gonzalez & Snyder, 2020). Lithium has various industrial uses, but in recent years, demand has exponentially increased due to its role in the technology sector (Zícari et al., 2019). Lithium is a key component in developing batteries that store energy from renewable sources—namely, lithium-ion batteries—which are essential for the operation of electric vehicles and other energy-storage devices (World Bank Group, 2017). As such, lithium is considered a mineral that could contribute to the global energy transition and promote green growth for the countries that exploit it (Barandiarán, 2019).

In the 1990s, Chile established its lithium management system, placing exploitation in the hands of two private companies—SQM and Albemarle—leaving minimal control mechanisms for the State. However, during President Michelle Bachelet's second term (2014–2018), a lithium policy and governance strategy for salt flats was formulated, aimed at increasing value addition around the mineral. Specifically, the new policy had three main objectives: (a) to expand the local market with increased regulation, addressing long-standing regulatory issues; (b) to advance the production of higher value-added lithium products by involving both public and private companies to foster technological innovations and fund research centers in the field; and (c) to implement measures for environmental protection and the welfare of communities living near the salt flats where the mineral is extracted. This public policy envisioned the development of applied lithium research through funding research centers, new contracts to ensure a better position for the State against extractive companies, promoting greater public and private investment in productive linkages, establishing a new dynamic of engagement with communities and the environment, and even state exploitation of the resource through a public company: CODELCO.

This marked a turning point in the configuration of public policies in Chile, which since the 1990s have predominantly focused on market regulation (Maillet, 2015a), with attempts at industrial policy changes in certain periods being resisted by entrepreneurs, who have inhibited value addition processes in other areas of the economy (Bril-Mascarenhas and Madariaga, 2019). The relatively swift establishment of this policy signifies a turning point in the dynamics of industrial policy formulation.

Institutional norms began to be implemented at various levels. However, at a certain juncture in the institutional trajectory, the newly established rules failed to effectively alter the behavior of actors involved in lithium governance. Consequently, specific institutional arrangements emerged where business actors partially adhered to the established norms while directly violating some of their provisions. This led to selective compliance with regulations, favoring the institutionalization of informal practices that allowed rules to be adapted to business interests. In this context, how can we account for the swift formulation of a public policy aimed at industrializing a sector—an achievement not seen since the return to democracy in 1990—despite the various implementation challenges it later faced?

To this, we can contrast the trajectories of Bolivia and Argentina. Bolivia has developed a state-led industrial policy regarding lithium, establishing a state-owned company, YLB, and negotiating with various transnational companies over the years for the development of complex lithium products. Despite these efforts, Bolivia has achieved marginal results, and the departure of Evo Morales from power has negatively impacted the progress of the industrialization process. Meanwhile, Argentina has launched several initiatives aimed to increase value addition in the lithium industry, but these measures have been unsuccessful. Instead, liberal dynamics have intensified in recent years, promising that

Argentina could become the world's leading lithium exporter in the future.

Thus, it is observed that lithium policies in Latin America oscillate between liberal dynamics and value addition in lithium exploitation, with varying degrees of applicability. Given this, my central research question is: What institutional factors explain the divergent trajectories of lithium policies in Latin America, and how do these factors operate? The explanation, I argue, lies in the state–business relations and how these have evolved concerning lithium.

The Theoretical Puzzle: State-Business Relations and Green Industrial Policy

The literature has suggested that economic growth based on natural resources, at various times, has promoted the establishment of nationalist public policies focused on industrialization and the diversification of the productive matrix (Chua, 1995; Obaya, 2021). This book posits that the specific characteristics of lithium as a key mineral for advancing energy transition make an industrialization process possible. Indeed, given lithium's importance as a crucial component for combating climate change, development and industrialization discourses regarding the management of this mineral have become central in the collective imagination of Latin American countries (Barandiarán, 2019). However, placing the issue on the public agenda—and its consequent promotion—is not sufficient for the development of industrial policies.

On the one hand, comparative literature has demonstrated the importance of the capacity of bureaucratic institutions and the actors within them [bureaucrats and politicians] to drive processes of change and implementation of public policies (Brinks et al., 2020; Cingolani, 2013). Nevertheless, the growing body of literature on industrial policies has not addressed the political conditions necessary for the implementation of these policies (Mazzucato, 2011; Rodrik, 2014), highlighting the need for further research in this area.

Additionally, in the realm of industrial policies, different actors gain relevance for understanding policy configuration: entrepreneurs. Unlike other areas of public policy, industrial policy is inherently a space where the central actors are entrepreneurs and specific companies upon which the government directly intervenes to improve the performance of the company or the economic sector (Bulfone, 2022; Warwick, 2013). Thus, entrepreneurs are not merely one actor among many but possess power and resources that afford them a privileged position in relation to such policies (Bril-Mascarenhas & Madariaga, 2019). This is particularly true in the case of lithium, where extractive activities are concentrated in specific geographical locations and few companies have the necessary technical expertise to carry out these activities (Kazimierski, 2018).

In this context, the aim of this research is to analyze how state–business relations, established at specific moments, influence lithium policies. Understanding these relationships as dynamic processes allows for a deeper insight into how lithium policies are shaped in Latin America. Additionally, I propose that these configurations are not static but are subject to change. Therefore, instead of viewing public policies as fixed outcomes, this study observes them as ongoing processes that are sensitive to shifts in actor relationships.

State Capacity and Business Power: Gaps in the Literature and Contributions of the Book

In recent years, there has been a growing academic interest in the socio-political and economic dynamics associated with lithium at various analytical levels. Locally, research has focused on the socio-environmental impacts and inequalities resulting from lithium extraction (Agusdinata et al., 2018; Liu & Agusdinata, 2020; Marina & Cueto, 2013), particularly concerning the industrial use of water at the expense of community consumption (Jerez et al., 2021), which has led to various conflictual dynamics between communities and companies (Gundermann & Göbel, 2018). On a global scale, research has concentrated on the global dynamics and networks of lithium (Obaya & Céspedes, 2021), especially concerning the rising demand and increasing prices in international markets (Martin et al., 2017), the geopolitical relevance of the mineral for Latin America (Fornillo, 2019), and the challenges it poses for national development and energy transition processes (Dorn & Ruiz-Peyré, 2020; Obaya et al., 2021).

Thirdly, national studies on lithium focus on two main analytical areas. One group of studies has concentrated on the discourses and imaginaries constructed around lithium, examining how these narratives justify and legitimize extraction by introducing the 'green' component as a distinguishing factor from traditional mining activities (Barandiarán, 2019; Voskoboynik & Andreucci, 2022). Conversely, other analyses have addressed the governance of lithium in the region (Obaya & Pascuini, 2020), detailing existing legislation and the functioning of the industry in Latin American countries (López et al., 2019).

My research aligns with national studies on lithium but introduces a novel analytical perspective: the study of public policies that, to varying extents, promote industrialization around lithium. While some limited research has addressed comparative analyses of lithium policies in Latin America, considering public policy as an independent variable, such as Lunde (2020), who examines how existing policies in the lithium triangle affect industry development, this research proposes studying public policies as a dependent variable. This perspective has not yet been incorporated into lithium studies and would contribute to the discussion on the formulation and implementation of public policies.

The countries of the lithium triangle share certain geographic and historical characteristics concerning this mineral. However, in recent years, their public policies have developed distinct and differentiated trajectories, driven by political projects aimed at scaling up the lithium value chain. The research aims to explain how these divergences in public policy arise.

On the other hand, studies analyzing the dynamics between public actors and private companies generally focus on lithium governance (León et al., 2020; Obaya & Pascuini, 2020; Poveda, 2020). However, this perspective is based on the premise of a certain horizontal relationship among the actors involved in managing a public good, such as lithium in this case (Maillet & Carrasco, 2019). I argue that this assumption obscures the conflictual nature of the relationship between entrepreneurs and bureaucratic and political actors within the framework of a capitalist democracy (Lindblom, 1982), as highlighted by a growing body of literature on business influence in public policy processes (Hacker & Pierson, 2002).

This is particularly relevant in the case of industrial policies, where the target of state intervention is specific companies and entrepreneurs (Bulfone, 2022). Based on this, I propose a theoretical approach to the research problem that integrates the literature on state capacity and business power, situating the discussion within the broader debate on the role of the state in development (Evans, 1996). This aims to illuminate how these two types of actors interact in a relatively unexplored area such as green industrial policy in developing countries, in contrast to European or Global North countries.

I argue that studying the relational dynamics of these factors is key to understanding industrial policy and that this approach is relatively novel for two reasons. First, the green industrial policies developed globally in recent years have been insufficiently explored from a political perspective that can explain their variations, successes, and failures. Instead, the focus has been on the economic and technological dimensions of industrialization (see Mazzucato, 2011). Industrial policies have shown success in some contexts but have failed in others during the twentieth century (Lall, 2001; Willem te Velde, 2003). The same is true today for new green industrial policies promoting energy transitions and sustainable development models (Rodrik, 2014). Thus, my research seeks to understand the political and institutional conditions that enable value-adding processes.

In recent decades, industrial policy has emerged as a viable development strategy to achieve various political goals, such as equity and social justice (Schneider, 2015), as well as environmental objectives, as it facilitates the socio-productive transformations necessary to face climate change (Ambec, 2017). Even today, international institutions like the World Bank, are providing public policy recommendations in this direction (Altenburg & Rodrik, 2017). Nevertheless, it is unclear under what conditions these transformations can occur. On the one hand, it is necessary to understand how the State organizes to achieve its objectives and the political support for such measures (Schneider, 2015). On the other hand, it is crucial to understand the interests of companies, which, depending on technological and economic circumstances, may support or oppose these measures (Breetz et al., 2018; Meckling, 2015).

This is particularly significant in the Latin American context, where many countries are in a middle-income trap (MIT) (Doner & Schneider, 2016). In this situation, middle-income countries like Chile and Argentina, cannot compete on wages with low-income countries, nor can they compete on technological development with high-income countries that have decades of technological innovations and strong positions in the global market. Thus, minerals like lithium present a new opportunity for stagnated countries, offering development alternatives that could help them position themselves internationally in the pursuit of energy transition processes.

Finally, this research aims to refine the understanding of value-adding processes in the Latin American context, where the discussion on development has traditionally focused on structural factors. In this regard, I align with Orihuela's (2013) argument that the political economy of development emphasizes structural factors and initial conditions to explain institutional performance and the potential to escape the resource curse. However, institutional change and overcoming the resource curse can occur through various pathways and involve different actors, beyond structural issues (Schorr & Damonte, 2021a). This book seeks to contribute by analyzing how different institutional pathways for lithium policies have emerged within the Latin American context, driven by the interaction among actors and their evolving strategies and interests, beyond the macrostructures affecting developing countries.

State–Business Relations: Toward a Typological Proposal

To explore the theoretical aspects of State–business relations and their role in shaping industrial policy, I first use perspectives from political economy to analyze green industrial policies, a field that remains underexplored in the discipline, particularly due to the decline of industrialization in public debate and the rise of liberal policies over recent decades in the Western world (Bulfone, 2022). Second, I synthesize various approaches from political economy concerning the influence of businesses on public policies (Hacker & Pierson, 2002), organizational strategies of firms in response to state regulations (Vaughan, 1982), and state capacities (Cingolani, 2013), with a particular focus on the development of industrial policies (Katzenstein, 1985).

The literature on developmental states in the twentieth century has highlighted the complexities in State–business relationships (Evans, 1996). Since the 1980s, development studies have sought to understand capitalist dynamics through State–business relations (Schneider, 2015), within different institutional contexts (Hall & Soskice, 2001). The conclusions have varied, indicating that a virtuous relationship between government and businesses can lead to increased production (Evans, 1996), greater economic growth (Amsden, 1991), and investment (Schneider, 2015); however, such dynamics can also result in corruption, undue influence, and the deepening of economies dependent on natural resource exploitation (Etchemendy, 2011; Krueger, 1974; Ross, 2015). Thus, there is an ongoing debate regarding the role of the State and private actors in the economy and how these interactions can lead to new models of development.

The case of lithium is particularly relevant for analyzing this dynamic. There remains significant uncertainty about the future of lithium, its role in the energy transition, and the new technologies emerging for energy storage and renewable energy expansion. Additionally, the lithium market is characterized by a limited number of global suppliers—though their number have grown rapidly in recent years—and technical knowledge remains concentrated in a few firms. In Chile, lithium extraction benefits from low costs, but the global value chains associated with the mineral are far removed from the extraction sites.

In this regard, my argument focuses on how different types of relationships between the State and businesses affect the configurations of lithium policies in the Global South. Given the prevailing structure in the modes of production and specialization of lithium, any significant progress in industrialization requires high state capacity coupled with business support, to develop cutting-edge policies that promote the transformation of certain productive sectors, focusing on the promotion of national champions. Conversely, a State with high state capacity that promotes value-adding processes may encounter opposition from business actors. Especially in sectors where companies engage in low-value-adding extraction activities, incumbent actors may lack incentives to alter their production strategies. In this case, given the importance of the lithium sector for energy transition processes, my argument is that the State can still advance in developing industrial policies, even in the face of business opposition, resulting in selective industrial policy. Among other things, despite business opposition, the State can establish research centers and create instruments for developing new technologies, among other value-adding measures.

In a context of low state capacity but with business support, some instruments can be implemented, where the State assists companies in resolving specific coordination issues. However, without strong capacities, significant value-adding processes that transform the productive sector cannot be achieved. Under these conditions, pilot programs and innovations may be implemented, but at a non-commercial level. This leads to a stagnant industrial policy, where policies aimed at increasing lithium value-adding are developed, specific changes are made, but the results do not have significant effects on economic aggregates. Finally, a favorable climate for industrialization may be created, with political actors promoting industrialization processes. However, without state capacities and with opposition from incumbent business actors, an industrial policy

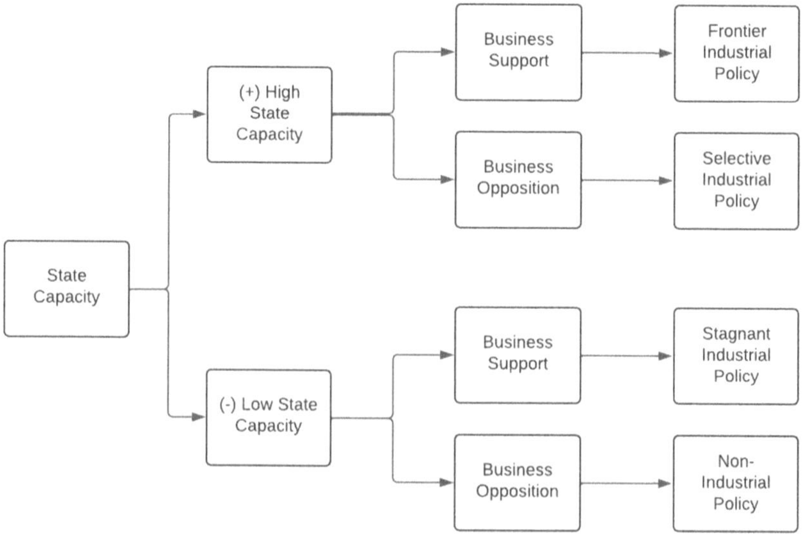

Fig. 1.1 State–business relations and industrial policy outcomes. *Source*: Own elaboration

may not be generated, exacerbating a liberal logic in mineral exploitation and maintaining traditional extractivist practices (Fig. 1.1).

The Methodological Puzzle

Methodologically, the study will conduct a case study on lithium policy in Chile. Generally, it proposes a classic research strategy in Political Science involving an in-depth examination of cases analyzed through case studies, which are then compared using a comparative methodology (Landman, 2017). Thus, this research not only aims to describe a phenomenon but also to explain it by establishing a link between explanatory factors and a specific outcome (Brady & Collier, 2004). Specifically, the case of lithium policy in Chile will be analyzed in depth from the presidency of Michelle Bachelet (2014–2018) to the recent developments under the government of Gabriel Boric (2022–2026). The Chilean case will be contrasted with the experiences of Argentina and Bolivia.

In general terms, a case study refers to the intensive study of a single unit, with the goal of generalizing about a larger set of units

(Gerring, 2004). Methodological developments in small-N studies distinguish different analytical approaches for handling cases (Blatter & Blume, 2008). Specifically, political science literature differentiates between co-variation analysis, process-tracing, and congruence analysis as methodological designs for conducting such studies (George & Bennett, 2005). However, studying a case within a national context may lead to issues of external validity and others related to the endogeneity of results.

To address some of these issues, small-N researchers use auxiliary cases to assess a more general validity of the findings (Soifer, 2020). One of the most used techniques in auxiliary cases involves the development of "shadow cases," characterized by the analysis of a case using the techniques of a case study but conducted peripherally to the central case (Soifer, 2020). Thus, the shadow study shifts the focus from the individual case to a sample of cases (Gerring, 2006). Soifer (2020) identifies three central characteristics of shadow cases: 1) there is an intensive analysis of one case; 2) it is auxiliary to a central case; and 3) it occupies a subsidiary role within a general project. Consequently, shadow cases provide greater generalizability to the analysis conducted on the central case, though without the same depth.

In this study, in addition to conducting an in-depth case study of lithium policy in Chile, I propose implementing shadow case strategies to analyze lithium policies in other Latin American contexts. Specifically, the research aims to conduct shadow case studies on Bolivia and Argentina, creating a general mapping of lithium policies in Latin American. This region hosts the world's largest lithium reserves (COCHILCO 2018). Chile, Argentina, and Bolivia form the so-called "lithium triangle," a contiguous geographical area among the borders of these countries, where significant salt flats from which the mineral is extracted are located. Analyzing these countries allows for a study of all existing cases in the region and, methodologically, an examination of the various types of industrial policies developed within this typology. Analyzing the three cases enables an understanding of the divergent trajectories that lithium policies take in different South American countries.

Typological Theory and Process Tracing

To analyze our cases in depth, the methodology proposes two approaches. First, a typological theory (George & Bennett, 2005) is established, which categorizes different types of State–business relations that produce various policy outcomes and are tested in the case studies. Specifically, typological theory involves developing a theory that specifies independent variables and categorizes them into certain types created by the researcher, which are used to measure outcomes (George & Bennett, 2005). The strength of this approach lies in its ability to elucidate how different configurations of independent variables affect the dependent variable (George & Bennett, 2005). Additionally, it helps identify which cases are most suitable for comparison.

Secondly, the methodology is complemented using process tracing (Beach & Pedersen, 2019), a causal inference technique that allows for the examination of event sequences within a case to test hypotheses about mechanisms explaining the relationship between two variables (Bril-Mascarenhas et al., 2017). Combining different approaches strengthens the study in several methodological aspects, such as enhancing the internal validity of descriptive and causal inferences (Blatter & Haverland, 2012) and identifying causal mechanisms between variables (George & Bennett, 2005). In particular, the typological theory will be developed in the first stage, and in the second step, process tracing will be added to empirically test how different categories within the typology impact lithium policy outcomes.

Research Techniques

The methodology is supported by diverse and extensive empirical evidence obtained from various sources: systematic press review, with 909 articles classified and analyzed according to categories; analysis of legal and governmental documents; 40 interviews conducted with key actors involved in the process; and non-participant observation of 6 lithium forums. The use of these different techniques allows for data triangulation, resulting in analyses with a high degree of internal validity, a central element in qualitative research development. The proposed approach is tested through in-depth analysis of the Chilean case and subsequently refined through the discussion of other Latin American cases where lithium is a significant mineral for national development strategies.

Regarding documents, various government reports on lithium activities in Chile were analyzed. Specifically, laws and other legal frameworks that establish and delimit lithium public policies were examined, along with legislative records and other related documents. Government reports assessing the implementation of these measures, environmental studies, and bidding instruments were also reviewed. Content analysis of these texts was conducted to achieve a detailed description of lithium policies and the progress of their implementation.

Secondly, a press analysis was conducted to gather information on major controversies and measures related to the national lithium policy in Chile. A qualitative database was compiled by reviewing 909 newspaper articles from *La Tercera*, a Chilean newspaper, published between 2009 and 2024. These articles were selected using the keyword "lithium," ensuring that only those explicitly mentioning the topic were included. This period encompasses the formulation of lithium policies in Chile and their subsequent implementation up to the present. This allowed for the reconstruction of key milestones and political, social, and economic conflicts that occurred during this period concerning lithium public policies. Information treatment involved content analysis, which was systematized through the creation of a qualitative database stored in Excel. The information gathered, synthesized, and discussed is validated through triangulation with interview data.

Finally, semi-structured interviews were conducted with 40 key actors involved in lithium policies in Chile, Argentina, and Bolivia. The decision to use semi-structured interviews is based on the complexity of the issue, which renders highly unpredictable responses (Corbetta, 2007, p. 352), ensuring the necessary freedom to address relevant topics in depth and collect important information. The interviews were carried out following a varied qualitative sampling approach that incorporated perspectives from different business, states, and social actors involved in lithium policy processes in Chile, Bolivia, and Argentina (see Appendix 1).

Plan of the Book

Following this introduction, the study is structured as follows. Chapter 2 presents the theoretical and conceptual foundations guiding the research. Specifically, this chapter focuses on characterizing the dependent variable, namely green industrial policy, highlighting the main aspects established by the literature. Secondly, it reviews the literature on the developmental state, arguing its relevance for the analysis of industrial policies. Finally, it theorizes the role of socio-environmental conflicts in the lithium industry, proposing that these constitute a significant contextual variable for analyzing industrial policies.

Chapter 3 operationalizes the relationship between the state and businesses to analyze green industrial policy. Particularly, it discusses the role of state and business actors in shaping public policies, with particular emphasis on the dynamics surrounding industrial policies. In the same vein, it explores the strategies of business and state actors in the specific context of lithium extraction in Chile, Argentina, and Bolivia. Finally, it establishes a typology of state–business relations, explaining how different relational configurations account for industrial policy processes.

Chapter 4 provides empirical background to contextualize the dynamics surrounding lithium extraction and its economic, political, and social implications. It describes how lithium fits into global economic dynamics for battery production and existing demand projections. It details how the lithium market has evolved, including commercial dynamics, price volatility, and other factors. Additionally, it addresses the socio-environmental issues arising from lithium activities. The integration of these aspects helps to illustrate the empirical problem of configuring a lithium industrial policy in Chile and in the Global South context. On the one hand, it observes the global market increase for the mineral due to its importance in producing technological products that aid in energy transition (replacing fossil fuels) and combating climate change (reducing pollution). Thus, with this background, it is possible to contextualize state–business relations concerning lithium, its exploitation, and policies.

Subsequently, Chapter 5 establishes the first analytical chapter of the book. Here, I analyze the development of state capacities in Chile and examine how various capacities are built to advance in lithium value addition. Initially, it discusses the prevailing political discourses on promoting lithium value addition processes. Next, it analyzes the political will, particularly of President Bachelet, who mobilized numerous experts to design the policy in coordination with various political authorities. During this period, legislators from across the political spectrum pressured the government to advance in lithium industrialization. Finally, it describes the establishment of public institutions for managing lithium policy.

Following this logic, Chapter 6 examines the role of business actors in the policy. In this sense, I argue how companies use different strategies to oppose specific policy instruments. Despite the deployment of various state capacities (bureaucratic, political, and technical), companies at this stage use various power resources to prevent effective policy implementation. During this period, companies breach new contracts, deter foreign companies from engaging in R&D, place private actors in key government positions, and pressure government officials to avoid certain measures. They leverage their specialized knowledge and existing capabilities to resist various regulations. Thus, I argue that the articulation of state capacities with business opposition results in a type of selective industrial policy.

Chapter 7 contrasts lithium policy in Chile with policies developed in other South American countries with reserves of this mineral, specifically Bolivia and Argentina. The comparative analysis provides perspectives that better test the typology developed to understand lithium policy configuration and how different trajectories are followed in the establishment of such policies. The findings allow for a discussion on the potential to advance industrial policy in Latin America and the possibility of effective management of capitalist dynamics in the Global South.

Finally, Chapter 8 synthesizes the findings of the book, highlighting its contributions to both the literature and the field of public policy analysis. By examining the intricate dynamics between state capacity, business influence, and the implementation of lithium policy in Chile in a comparative perspective, this work offers a nuanced understanding of how these factors interact in the policy process.

PART I

State, Business and Green Industrial Policy

CHAPTER 2

Green Industrial Policy: A Theoretical Perspective

Introduction

In this chapter, I develop a theoretical explanation of how public policies on lithium are configured in Latin America. To this end, the discussion is structured as follows. First, I discuss the resurgence of the debate on industrial policies in recent years, particularly in relation to their "green" components, which aim to advance toward new development models and facilitate energy transitions to address global environmental phenomena such as climate change. I argue that the specific characteristics of the lithium market have strongly introduced the debate on green industrialization in Latin American countries that exploit this mineral, although with varying emphases and approaches to achieving these value-added processes. Beyond technical aspects, these discussions respond to institutional contexts, as well as specific ideas and interests of the actors involved in the mineral's value chain. Finally, I present a typology of the different forms that industrial policy can take to guide the subsequent empirical analysis.

In the second section, I review the literature on the developmental state and argue its utility for studying industrial policies. While acknowledging the relevance of lithium for both economic development and addressing the climate crisis, my theoretical position is that the practices of lithium value addition depend on the types of relationships articulated between the State and business actors. This section highlights the

S. Carrasco, *From (De)regulation to Industrialization?*, Latin American Political Economy, https://doi.org/10.1007/978-3-031-77130-9_2

need for a strong State, coordinated with the business sector, to carry out productive transformation processes through the establishment of industrial policies. I argue that this is particularly relevant in the Latin American context, where there are various issues with state capacity and generally large business groups with significant power resources due to market concentration. Lithium presents a new opportunity to rethink these dynamics and strategies for development and energy transition.

Thirdly, I discuss the socio-environmental implications of lithium extraction. I note that, in studies on lithium, social sciences have shown a marked preference for analyzing the social dimensions associated with extraction. I argue that, although not the primary focus of this work, the perspective on socio-environmental conflicts provides a referential framework that enhances the understanding of state–business relations regarding public policies. Social dimensions can mediate and constrain the type of relationship the State can form with businesses concerning a particular policy. Hence, the importance of such framings in public policy analysis.

Lithium, Climate Change, and Green Industrial Policy

The Discussion on Climate Change, Energy Transition, and Green Growth

Climate change presents an unprecedented challenge that has compelled both States and businesses to seek various solutions for mitigating and adapting to the impacts of greenhouse gas accumulation. Countries have adopted different strategies to address this issue; some impose penalties for emissions, while others continue to subsidize fossil fuels (Colgan et al., 2021). Despite these varied approaches, since the 1990s, a prominent mechanism endorsed by international organizations has been carbon pricing. This system enables businesses to internalize negative externalities, creating incentives for polluters to alter their behavior, thereby promoting "greener" production processes (Green, 2021).

Economists generally view certain carbon pricing instruments, such as carbon taxes, as effective means to tax and reduce emissions. However, these mechanisms are often constrained by political economy factors that influence their implementation (Jenkins, 2014). Notably, industrial sectors with high specificity—such as energy-intensive industries, mining, heavy manufacturing, and chemicals—have strong incentives to oppose optimal carbon pricing due to the potential risks of devaluation (Jenkins, 2014; Murphy, 2002). According to collective action theory (Olson, 1989), large firms, which hold significant market power, face substantial risks if they implement significant carbon pricing measures, while smaller firms benefit more from collective action (Jenkins, 2014). Consequently, many businesses resist such policies. Empirical evaluations of carbon pricing initiatives have shown that these measures often result in only minimal reductions in greenhouse gas emissions, ranging from 0 to 2% annually (Green, 2021).

Generally, climate change policies are framed as global collective action problems with concerns about free riders. However, from a political science perspective, the central issue is not merely collective action but the distributive conflicts that emerge (Aklin & Mildenberger, 2020). The dynamics surrounding climate change policies are shaped by the distribution of power and different types of capital (Colgan et al., 2021). Climate change represents a large-scale distributive problem, where influential interest groups strive to mitigate the significant political and financial losses resulting from climate-friendly policies (Colgan et al., 2021). Some aspects of the energy transition involve costs but also present opportunities—such as the recent growth in green hydrogen industries—that are valued differently by various stakeholders. Many actors have short and medium-term incentives that overshadow the long-term benefits of transforming their business models to achieve environmental gains.

Today, it is no longer sufficient to merely identify the instruments and measures required to address climate change; it is also necessary to consider the political and economic conditions that make these changes possible. While we can determine the goals we aim to achieve, it is essential to pave the way to reach them. The current climate crisis has revitalized the debate on the implementation of state-led industrial policies as a partial solution to environmental problems, particularly regarding the use of fossil fuels. Such measures not only address environmental issues but also foster the creation of new markets, a phenomenon referred to as green growth.

The argument presented is that green growth necessitates green energy, where industrial policy becomes a key component in developing the technologies required for energy transition, thereby adding value to the production process (Rodrik, 2014). Given the strategic role of lithium as a component in batteries that promote electromobility, countries exporting this mineral have prioritized sociotechnical imaginaries in its exploitation (Barandiarán, 2019). These countries are currently promoting a productive transformation in the lithium sector to create processes with greater value addition by developing more complex products through research and development. Therefore, in the discussion about the planet's climate future, the lithium industry has become a central component.

The Debate on Green Industrial Policy

The debate on industrial policy has been characterized by various disagreements regarding its definition, which have even led to some antagonism toward the concept from economists and policymakers (Naudé, 2010). However, the concept of industrial policy discussed in the latter half of the twentieth century differs significantly from the current discourse, particularly with the incorporation of environmental considerations into production processes, especially concerning energy transition and the development of clean energy. In this regard, Naudé (2010) identifies three main periods in the debates on industrial policy.

The first stage, following World War II, viewed industrialization as a necessary condition for development, achievable through local industry protection, public enterprises, and a coordinating role of the State. The second stage began in the 1970s, marked by economic liberalization, where industrial policy was seen as undesirable, based on the premise that government interventions were worse than market failures, leading to rent-seeking and other negative effects on economic functioning (Krueger, 1990). However, due to the shortcomings in implementing the liberal measures of the Washington Consensus, a third stage emerged in the 2000s, characterized by a resurgence in the discussion of industrial policy, but with a different focus. Unlike the original perspectives, the new industrial policy aims primarily at innovation and technological improvement, promoting innovation systems (Naudé, 2010).

Today, industrial policy refers to government actions that alter the structure of an economy by directing resources toward sectors perceived as desirable for future development (Altenburg & Rodrik, 2017). Such policies involve selective government interventions that modify the production structure of specific economic sectors with the expectation of generating greater economic development than would occur in the absence of such intervention (Pack, 2006), thus moving away from Marxist perspectives on the State's planning role in the economy.

Empirically, industrial policies have been very successful in some countries, leading to structural changes and the development of new industries (Rodrik, 2014). For example, Mazzucato (2011) argues that many contemporary technological developments—such as the iPhone—have benefited from public funding allocated to research and development, which in the case of the U.S. is linked to the military industry. Similar observations have been made about the industrial development of various Asian countries and their accelerated industrialization process starting in the 1980s (Amsden, 2004). However, in some countries, industrial policies have led to white elephants and failed strategies.

In general, there are two principal criticisms of industrial policies: first, that governments often lack the necessary information to make informed decisions about which industries or sectors to support, and second, that once industrial policies are established, their decisions tend to be driven more by political motivations than by economic considerations (Rodrik, 2014). However, as Schneider (2015) notes, rather than debating the merits and drawbacks of industrial policies, it is more important to understand why different policy outcomes occur. The answer likely lies in the institutional factors related to policy design that facilitate these transformations (Rodrik, 2009, 2014).

Traditionally, industrial policy has been associated with enhancing productivity as a means to increase returns on capital and labor, thereby fostering greater economic growth (Altenburg & Rodrik, 2017). Furthermore, conventional economic views argue that economic development leads to ecosystem degradation and pollution, while stricter environmental regulations are believed to raise business costs and hinder growth. However, contemporary perspectives in political economy challenge these notions, suggesting that the additional costs associated with environmental protection can provide comparative advantages for companies engaged in industrialization processes (Ambec, 2017).

According to the United Nations (2015), promoting sustainable industrialization is essential for achieving sustainable development goals. Green industrial policies can play a crucial role in creating various pathways to enhance business productivity (Ambec, 2017, p. 1). In particular, 1) green standards and certifications can help companies produce differentiated products in the market; 2) companies can generate revenue from selling and adopting green technologies; 3) investing in green technologies can boost productivity beyond the costs of these new technologies; and 4) green industrial policies can increase productivity through knowledge spillovers in the innovation process. In this context, Dechezleprâtre et al. (2014) show that innovation in clean energy results in significant knowledge spillovers, with clean energy patents cited 43% more frequently than dirty patents.

Thus, although it once seemed that industrial policy had become obsolete, recent years have witnessed a resurgence in discussions about the industrialization of countries as a central development strategy to achieve various political and social goals based on principles of equity and social justice (Schneider, 2015). This renewed focus is reflected in recommendations from international organizations, such as the World Bank. Emerging green development perspectives have complicated these dynamics, placing industrialization at the heart of the debate—not only for advancing economic development but also for the socio-productive transformations necessary to address climate change and its impacts (Ambec, 2017; Rodrik, 2014; Altenburg & Rodrik, 2017).

Industrial Policy in Latin America

Literature indicates that high-income and upper-middle-income countries offer distinct opportunities for developing new green products and services, which can be enhanced through industrial policies. This includes advancements in renewable energy technologies, such as high-tech components for photovoltaic panels, energy storage via lithium-ion batteries, electric vehicles, carbon capture technologies, and high-performance building facades. For services, it involves intelligent transportation systems, energy management systems, eco-industrial parks, and systems designed to improve environmental performance across value chains (Altenburg & Rodrik, 2017).

In contrast, Latin America, with its middle- and lower-middle-income countries, does not compete at the same level in producing eco-industrial goods and services as developed nations (Doner & Schneider, 2016). Nonetheless, recent years have opened new opportunities due to the concentration of minerals crucial for many of these products, particularly lithium (Fornillo, 2018). However, these processes have not been without challenges. Within the global value chain, lithium industrial policy faces at least two significant challenges: one pertains to spatial issues, as the extraction of raw materials for green technologies often leads to pollution and environmental damage at the extraction sites (Dorador et al., 2020). Additionally, lithium is extracted in locations far from the rest of the production process, which is increasingly centralized in certain conglomerates dominating much of the value chain [such as the Chinese automotive industry or Tesla Motors] (Moreno-Brieva & Marín, 2019). This situation requires careful definition of existing opportunities to enhance the value-added process in Latin America.

The idea of prioritizing growth and addressing environmental concerns later rests on weak empirical foundations (Padilla, 2017), as environmental degradation undermines the future growth potential of developing countries. Environmental concerns about development have shifted the discussion on industrialization toward the necessity of green industrial policies—policies that facilitate the transformation of economic structures to tackle climate change while promoting growth. Specifically, green industrial policies, such as those related to lithium, have become increasingly appealing across various contexts and under different governments (Rodrik, 2014).

In over 50 developed countries, practices and standards have been established to promote green technologies (Steer, 2013). China, the United States, and Germany serve as notable examples of green industrial policy development. These dynamics are particularly relevant for Latin America, where manufacturing industry productivity remains stagnant (Altenburg & Rodrik, 2017). In this context, lithium has emerged as a promising opportunity to shift from natural resource extraction to the production of complex products with intensive R&D involvement (Fornillo, 2018), potentially enabling Latin American countries to develop new models of growth (Kazimierski, 2018).

Toward a Typology of Green Industrial Policy (GIP)

Policies aimed at promoting renewable energy do not automatically ensure the development and consolidation of the industry. As a result, two complementary types of policies can be distinguished: first, those that enhance development capacities through supply and/or demand-side incentives, and second, those specifically designed to establish a green industry (Lewis, 2021). The latter is what is referred to as green industrial policy. Although the array of instruments may be similar across different types, the critical distinction lies in how effectively these policies facilitate the development of a new industry (Lewis, 2021).

Lewis (2023) points out that certain measures, such as fostering R&D innovation, generally enjoy broad acceptance. In contrast, protectionist measures designed to bolster domestic production—such as those addressing imports and exports—tend to be more controversial. Implementing industrial policies with protectionist elements requires government intervention in international trade flows. Lewis highlights the tension that arises between industrial policy objectives and the international trade regime, particularly concerning trade agreements that mandate non-discrimination and equal treatment of trading partners (Lewis, 2014). Various renewable energy sectors have encountered trade sanctions in response to industrial policies that promote them (Lewis, 2014; Hughes & Meckling, 2017), with implementation in emerging economies like China and India being particularly contentious (Lewis, 2021). This underscores the importance of understanding the variety of policy instruments available, depending on their objectives and the implications of their implementation.

In the realm of industrial policies, a wide range of instruments is employed in coordination to drive productive change [value addition] in specific economic sectors. These instruments include workforce training, tax reductions, subsidies, R&D investment, and the promotion of cooperative dynamics among firms, among others (UNIDO, 2015). As a result, both academic research and international organizations have developed various typologies to organize these instruments into a coherent framework. Some typologies categorize instruments based on the complexity of the economy, distinguishing between early-stage, mid-stage, and late-stage industrial policies (UNIDO, 2015).

Given that the industrialization of lithium in Latin America is still in its early stages compared to prevailing economic development modes, the typology of industrial policies based on developmental stages is not the most suitable for this research. Other typologies focus on specific instruments, such as cluster policies, investment promotion, and public procurement practices (Kattel & Lember, 2010; Warwick, 2013). However, this research requires an approach to industrial policy that emphasizes public policy orientations rather than specific instruments. This approach aligns with the focus of the book on the political-institutional level at which these orientations are defined.

Regarding policy orientations, some proposals generally distinguish between horizontal and selective policies (Warwick, 2013). Horizontal policies benefit companies broadly by promoting competition, reducing certain regulations, and even establishing specific taxes. These policies acknowledge the need for economic complexity but maintain that instruments and incentives should not undermine comparative advantages (Crespi et al., 2014; Lavarello & Sarabia, 2017). In this regard, the State does not directly intervene in market prices or protect specific industries. In contrast, selective policies deliberately favor a particular industry or sector of the economy. Recent perspectives in political economy have further refined this typology by incorporating additional types of industrial policy into the framework. Thus, four types of industrial policies are now distinguished: horizontal, facilitative, selective, and frontier policies (Lavarello & Sarabia, 2017; Primi & Peres, 2009; Yoguel et al., 2007). Facilitative policies are an extension of horizontal policies but place greater emphasis on gradual structural changes. Specifically, these policies address coordination problems within value chains by supporting companies in solving technical, economic, and regulatory issues. Frontier policies, on the other hand, aim to induce structural changes through large-scale projects that focus on national champions and promote cutting-edge technological developments, including measures such as nationalization of companies.

These different types of policies can be understood as forming a continuum, ranging from general and less complex instruments to more selective and sophisticated ones. Complexity here primarily refers to the level of value addition within the industry's value chain and, consequently, the degree of orientation toward structural change. While there may be differences in specific aspects, these typologies of industrial policy, which focus on policy orientations, have proven to be heuristically useful in other studies on Latin America (Madariaga, 2016; Primi & Peres, 2009), affirming their validity as an analytical framework. In this context, I argue that, although horizontal policies are sometimes included within the scope of industrial policy, they should not be categorized as such. Horizontal policies, which provide general incentives and are not directed at specific sectors, do not align with the core objective of sector-focused industrial policy. According to Lewis (2021), industrial policy is defined by its intentional focus on developing particular industries. Therefore, from my theoretical perspective—primarily concerned with Green Industrial Policy (GIP)—horizontal policies do not qualify as industrial policies.

GIP aims to promote specific sectors that are directly linked to the energy transition. In contrast, horizontal policies often reinforce traditional extractive practices, such as the export of raw lithium, without significantly contributing to value creation in critical sectors for a green transition. Thus, horizontal policies represent a deficiency in genuine industrial policy.

For the purposes of this book, I propose a framework that allows for the understanding of the different stages that green industrialization strategies can reach, depending on the extent of public policy instruments employed. In this context, GIP is applied to traditionally extractive sectors, with the goal of advancing within the value chain. Consequently, industrial policy categories can be understood in terms of their progression along the value chain and, therefore, the level of industrialization they achieve. In this regard, frontier and selective policies are particularly relevant and align with GIP perspectives in the development of the lithium sector. However, some policies may aim for advancement in the value chain without necessarily effecting significant change. Similarly, there can be a negative outcome where industrial policy is absent. Ultimately, it is possible to focus on raw lithium extraction with minimal value addition, adhering to traditional extractive practices, even if there are intentions to drive productive transformation (Fig. 2.1).

In this context, it can be established that industrialization policies can be associated with different stages of the lithium battery value chain, representing the type of industrialization that might be pursued within the Latin American context. Broadly, as outlined by Irarrazaval and Carrasco (2023), three stages can be identified in the value chain.[1]

The first one involves the exploration and extraction of raw lithium. This phase encompasses traditional extractive activities that have historically characterized Latin American economies. Consequently, this stage aligns with what I categorize as a non-industrial policy. The second stage entails increased complexity, advancing to products with higher added value, such as cathodes and anodes—critical components of lithium batteries—alongside applied research for innovation and value addition in lithium-based products. The third stage focuses on the production of battery cells, which involves a higher degree of complexity and constitutes a major component of batteries. This phase requires additional materials,

[1] For a more detailed description of the lithium value chain and economic dynamics, see Chapter 4.

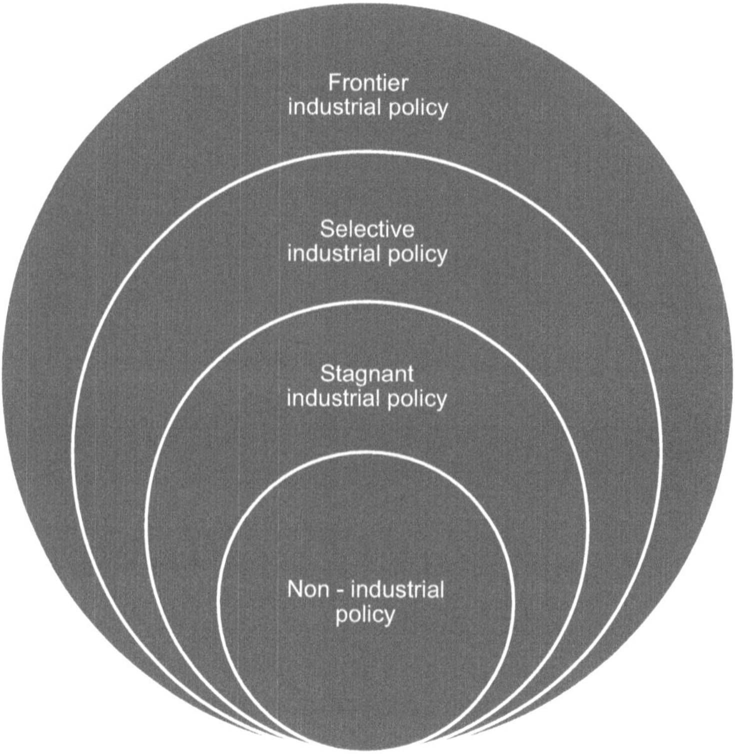

Fig. 2.1 Types of green industrial policy in lithium. Source: Own elaboration

suppliers, and market integration for its production. For instance, the development of industrial clusters and a significantly expanded industry could foster progress at this stage. This phase aligns with what can be described as frontier industrial policies.

Finally, there may be policies aimed at advancing the lithium value chain through its various stages that become stalled due to multiple challenges. These policies, which emphasize scaling the value chain, often fail to make significant progress in extractive strategies, as there are insufficient incentives or efforts to develop this area. As a result, industrialization is prioritized, but substantial outcomes remain limited to pilot projects. Figure 2.2 illustrates a framework that links the stages of the value chain with the corresponding categories of industrial policy developed.

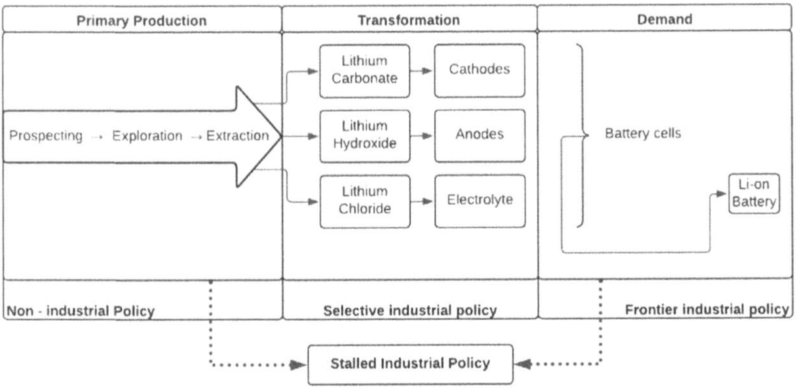

Fig. 2.2 Lithium Value Chain and Industrial Policy Outcomes. Source: Own elaboration

In this context, it is pertinent to question the specific circumstances that facilitate the emergence of one type of policy over another within the economic activities related to lithium. The following section will discuss these institutional dynamics in detail.

Explanatory Factors of Green Industrial Policy

State–Business Relations in the Context of Green Industrial Policy

The discourse on industrial policy has evolved from questioning its necessity to focusing on its effective implementation. This shift has moved from a focus on the policy content itself to the factors that facilitate successful implementation. This section explores the various dimensions of state–business relations and examines their impact on the development of industrial policies.

For green industrial policy, traditional economic theory highlights two key factors in the industrialization process for energy transition: price and quantity. These factors are captured through learning curves, which have advanced rapidly in recent years, particularly in the areas of batteries, solar energy, and wind energy, with lithium playing a pivotal role. However, policy is the less visible yet crucial aspect of these technology learning curves that influences their progression (Breetz et al., 2018). Thus, my argument is that understanding clean energy transition processes requires an appreciation of the co-evolution of technology, public policy, and politics (Breetz et al., 2018)—aspects not typically covered in classical economic discussions of industrial policy but essential for understanding value-adding processes involving natural resources, such as lithium.

This is especially pertinent during the initial stages of upgrading from raw material extraction to the production of complex products, as has been the focus in the lithium sector in recent years (Fornillo, 2018). Therefore, my argument is that the political dimension has been insufficiently explored in the literature on industrialization and value addition processes related to lithium. However, this dimension is crucial for explaining the observed public policy outcomes in Chile, as well as in Argentina and Bolivia.

The need for a political perspective in analyzing lithium policies becomes even more apparent when considering the specific dynamics of value addition processes in this industry. As discussed in earlier sections, industrial policy is grounded in shared visions of productive areas deemed important for achieving a desirable future (Altenburg & Rodrik, 2017). In the case of lithium, empirical research has revealed the prominence of certain socio-technical imaginaries held by key actors, underscoring the necessity of developing value-adding processes in the production chain and coordinating efforts between the public and private sectors (Barandiarán, 2019).

Nevertheless, the establishment of a shared discourse alone is not sufficient to advance transformations in the productive structures of specific sectors. As Breetz et al. (2018) argue, when the costs of new technologies exceed those of existing ones, energy transition processes necessitate a political coalition willing to support and foster these new technologies and their initial commercialization. This is particularly relevant in the lithium value chain, given that extraction sites are geographically distant from the companies involved in battery manufacturing (Martin et al., 2017). This distance complicates the market entry of new, value-added products, such as battery cathodes, from the Global South. Moreover, as new technologies become economically competitive, energy transitions are increasingly contested, with resistance emerging from incumbent industries that fear becoming economically disadvantaged (Breetz et al., 2018). It is also important to acknowledge that companies have varying interests; while some may aim to maintain raw lithium extraction, others will seek to advance toward the production of more complex products.

Therefore, despite a common horizon among the various actors involved in lithium governance (Poveda, 2020), my theoretical stance is that value-added practices can be contested by these same actors. Within the institutional framework in which they operate, these actors possess differing resources, strategies, and short- and long-term interests that impact the outcomes of industrial policy. My objective is to understand the extent to which industrialization practices related to lithium are contested by state [both political and bureaucratic] and business actors, and how these dynamics influence public policy outcomes.

To develop this argument theoretically, this section revisits classic discussions on state–business relations within the context of developmental state processes in the twentieth century and analyzes them considering the unique characteristics of contemporary green development proposals. These proposals, focused on value-added processes with environmental and economic objectives, as exemplified by the case of lithium, underscore the heuristic potential of this perspective for analyzing current public policies.

State–Business relations in the literature on Developmental State

The literature on the developmental state in the twentieth century has illuminated the complexities inherent in state–business relations. As Max Weber noted, the intersection of bureaucracy and capitalism has resulted in a deep-seated connection between these two spheres (Weber cited in Evans, 1992). This interconnection has led contemporary capitalist societies to grapple with a central dilemma: on the one hand, how to maximize the benefits for business actors, and on the other, how to prevent them from abusing their economic power at the expense of the broader population (Schneider, 1995). Since the 1980s, development studies have increasingly sought to understand capitalist dynamics through the lens of state–business relations (Schneider, 1995) and within various institutional contexts (Hall & Soskice, 2001), resulting in diverse outcomes, particularly with regard to industrial and economic policies.

Different studies have reached varied conclusions. Amsden (1989) argues that increased reciprocity between government and businesses leads to greater economic growth. Similarly, Evans (1996) identifies the system of state–business relations as crucial for enhancing production and investment through what he terms 'embedded autonomy.' This concept entails maintaining a degree of bureaucratic autonomy while ensuring that the State is not isolated from social preferences, thereby necessitating that the State forges strong ties with businesses while retaining its autonomy to express preferences in public policy (Schneider, 1995).

In general, the beneficial relationship between bureaucracy and businesses is attributed to the increased flow of information between public officials and strengthened investor confidence (Schneider, 1995). However, the literature also highlights potential drawbacks of a more active state role in the economy, such as the capture of authority by private interests (Stigler, 1971), corruption, undue influence of private actors on public officials (Etchemendy, 2011; Krueger, 1974), and the resource curse (Ross, 2015).

This is also evident in the realm of industrial policies. While such policies have been successful in some contexts, such as Southeast Asian countries (Willem te Velde, 2003), they have proven to be failures in others, such as Tanzania (Lall, 2001). Doner (1991) emphasizes that variations in state–business relations are crucial for understanding sectoral dynamics and the role of industrial policies in these contexts. Accordingly, in line with this perspective, there is a need for industrial policy analysis to focus more on businesses. This entails looking beyond the quality of policies and government agencies to examine the nature of state–business interactions more deeply.

A key question that arises from the above discussion is what constitutes the optimal relationship between the State and businesses for achieving virtuous processes. Initially, it appears that this relationship varies depending on the type of public policy in question. According to Schneider (1995), in macroeconomic policies, the ideal relationship between businesses and the State is achieved through consensus among actors, whereas in redistributive policies, negotiation is central. However, for industrial policies, their effective implementation relies on collaboration between State and business elites to add value in productive processes (Schneider, 1995).

Unlike other areas of public policy, industrial policies require close collaboration between these diverse actors to succeed. Therefore, the success of industrial policies hinges on coordination among private sector actors, as well as between public and private actors (Sabel, 2012). Specifically, critical elements for achieving effective public–private collaboration include genuine information exchange between public and private actors and the authority to align economic production and address rent-seeking behaviors (Schneider, 2015). Additionally, strong political will and support from the highest levels of government are essential for successful public–private collaboration (Rodrik, 2007; Schneider, 2015).

There is an ongoing debate in social theory regarding whether the private or public sector should lead economic activity—and by extension, growth and productive change. Structuralists of the 1950s emphasized the importance of developing the manufacturing industry and import substitution as the central path to development (Prebisch & Cabañas, 1949). The failures of these policies led to market liberalization and deregulation, which were consolidated into a coherent policy framework following the Washington Consensus of the 1990s (Lin, 2012). This paradigm remained dominant for at least the following two decades. However, a minimal role of the State, aimed at addressing market failures, has shown various limitations. Currently, one of the major challenges is how to address the most significant "market failure"—climate change—without considering an active role for the State in driving the necessary productive and energy transformations.

New developmentalism provides valuable insights into the roles of state and business actors, particularly within the context of industrial policies. First, it is important to recognize that contemporary dynamics of development have shifted opportunities for industrial policy to more decentralized arenas (Block, 2011; Schneider, 2015). Secondly, a new role for the State in these processes is emerging.

In line with this perspective, Altenburg and Rodrik (2017) argue that the role of governments today is to direct and accelerate structural changes in the economy for two main reasons. First, structural change that reallocates capital and labor from low- to high-productivity activities is crucial for enhancing productivity and income levels. Second, the overexploitation of natural resources necessitates the design of techno-institutional systems that decouple economic development from resource depletion and waste production (Altenburg & Rodrik, 2017). In the case of lithium, while most technologies already exist, government intervention is required to realign incentives and shift away from unsustainable technological patterns, thereby facilitating value addition processes. In this way, green industrial policies can stimulate demand and incentivize investment in R&D, fostering technological innovation (Ambec, 2017).

Moreover, some argue that the development of green energy, unlike other economic sectors, should be managed by the State for various reasons. Green technologies, while generating positive spillover effects, are also prone to failure due to the high risks involved. Additionally, government intervention is necessary to support green technologies because greenhouse gas emissions from industries are not appropriately priced. Taxes or regulatory mechanisms have failed to internalize climate change risks within businesses, leading to a discrepancy between the private returns of green technologies and the social benefits they promise. From an economic standpoint, subsidizing green technologies is seen as a preferable approach to address market failures (Rodrik, 2014). Ultimately, new developmentalism envisions the State as a facilitator of development, linking local industries with global technological and financial networks in ways that cannot be achieved by businesses alone (Ansell, 2000; Meckling & Nahm, 2018). Thus, a key aspect of studying these phenomena involves understanding the state's capabilities to implement value addition processes in critical areas necessary for advancing toward a green economy.

The design of industrial policy must also account for corporate policy patterns, as well as business strategies and capacities. Since industrial policies aim to enhance firm productivity, it seems natural that firms would cooperate with the State to align public and private objectives. However, evidence indicates that firms may resist the imposition of industrial policies (Schneider, 2015). Such policies can affect firms' natural strategies for diversification and market negotiation due to the standards imposed within the framework of these policies (Schneider, 2015).

Beyond mere interests, firms also have specific views on the state's role in the economy and the extent to which state intervention in markets is acceptable. These views can significantly influence whether firms support or oppose a public policy. For instance, in Chile, business leaders have historically aligned with economic orthodoxy (Silva, 2002) and have opposed state intervention in the economy at varied times (Bril-Mascarenhas & Madariaga, 2019), employing various strategies across different sectors (Fairfield, 2015). Thus, it is crucial to explore how firms' positions on policy influence its implementation, including whether they support or resist it.

Nevertheless, political dynamics in industrial policies—particularly the relationship between the State and businesses—have been notably underexplored (Schneider, 2015). While institutional perspectives are often overlooked in the industrial policy literature, the new transformative processes in productive structures, such as those involving lithium, necessitate reintroducing the political dimension into the discussion. This dynamic is crucial for explaining both success and failure. Consequently, the main challenge I aim to address in this book is the need to understand the specific conditions under which different policy outcomes are more likely, as highlighted by Schneider (2015). Unlike the reforms of the twentieth century, the new dynamics associated with lithium involve novel political and economic goals, new imaginaries, and different dynamics of global market integration and value addition, alongside local conflicts. This context compels a reevaluation of political-institutional relationships within public policy and their outcomes, contributing new evidence toward theoretical refinement.

Finally, it is important to note the emerging research agenda on state–business relations across various social science fields within the Latin American context. For instance, Schorr (2018) has examined the relationship between the State and businesses, focusing on its impact on mining conflicts. Schorr's study reveals that the State provides preferential treatment to public enterprises, offering protection when they generate significant fiscal revenues, as exemplified by CODELCO in Chile. Similarly, Damonte (2021) has documented how different types of entrepreneurs, such as informal miners and agro-exporters in Peru, have resisted central state institutional agendas by imposing their own informal practices in sectoral governance. Other studies have explored how state–business relations influence economic development (Sen & Te Velde, 2009). My research contributes to this body of literature by examining a less explored case, that of lithium.

State–Business Relations for a New Green Development Model

A central question within the framework of new developmentalism is identifying which institutional contexts are most conducive to the development of effective industrial policies (Burr & Whitfield, 2013). In this regard, the interactions between the State and businesses—both formal and informal (Abdel-Latif & Schmitz, 2009)—are key elements of the institutional context that help explain the diverse outcomes of industrial policies (Balchin et al., 2019). While the roles of businesses and the State are well-established in discussions of industrial policy, their interactions in the emerging arenas of energy transition and green development present a novel area of inquiry. The simultaneous economic, productive, and environmental transformations occurring globally pose new challenges for political economy to understand the various pathways that can be pursued (Newell, 2021).

In the domains of industrialization and green development, political, bureaucratic, and business actors no longer operate within the same context as in the twentieth century. Their strategies, interests, and dynamics have evolved and become more complex, necessitating a more systemic approach to understanding industrial policies through the interaction of these actors with social, technological, and environmental factors (Leach et al., 2010) that were not prominent decades ago. New narratives have emerged to justify productive transformation and energy transition processes, while simultaneously marginalizing alternative decision-making pathways (Newell, 2021), reflecting the power dynamics among key actors.

Recent research highlights the importance of state intervention in developing new industries and technologies in advanced industrial economies (Block, 2008; Mazzucato, 2011). Studies have also explored state–business relations in other contexts of green industrial policy, such as technological advancements in the automotive industry for electric vehicle development (Meckling & Nahm, 2018). However, the case of lithium requires examining a less explored area: the processes of value addition starting from the extraction of raw materials and producing more complex products at the extraction site itself.

Therefore, this discussion shifts focus from, for example, the production of a final technological product like an electric vehicle, to value addition processes that begin with a raw material and take place at the extraction site. This introduces a spatial dimension that is crucial for understanding these dynamics, as inherent tensions arise in developing products aimed at greater green development. Such processes complicate the productive matrix of the country while simultaneously imposing various environmental and community-related challenges (Dorador et al., 2018, 2020).

Another significant factor in this context is the promotion of innovation and technology development. Ambec (2017) suggests that governments can incentivize companies to invest in R&D by offering financial rewards. Additionally, governments can facilitate technology transfers through licensing agreements or by enhancing intellectual property protections for new patents. Investing in education, technological training, and knowledge dissemination is also crucial (Ambec, 2017).

However, the literature generally indicates that contemporary developmental states in Latin America are relatively weaker compared to business interests (Schrank, 2013). Decision-makers face more constraints, so the preferences of businesses play a crucial role in shaping the limits, opportunities, and collaboration within industrial policy frameworks (Schneider, 2015).

In Chile, despite some targeted efforts to advance industrial policies, these have often faced resistance from powerful actors such as businesses (Bril-Mascarenhas & Madariaga, 2019). Consequently, state-led industrialization efforts are rare in Chile, yet the case of lithium has become pivotal in public discussions about the development model for the mineral (Barandiarán, 2019). Lithium has become a crucial component for electromobility due to its central role in manufacturing batteries that can potentially replace fossil fuels and help combat climate change (Fornillo, 2018). The future prospects of lithium have prompted countries to politically scrutinize its role in their development models, leading to discussions about the roles of the State and private companies, and the types of policies, industrial or liberal, that will be adopted as a result.

Industrial Policy in Context: Lithium Extraction and Socio-Environmental Conflicts

The central theoretical argument of this book pertains to the relational dynamics between the State and businesses and how these dynamics shape industrial policies. Although this argument is grounded in a substantial body of literature from political economy, a complex causal logic suggests that other relevant factors also explain the outcomes of interest. In the case under study, lithium extraction generates various dynamics and socio-environmental conflicts at the local level. Indeed, a significant portion of the social sciences literature on lithium addresses the socio-environmental impacts of its extraction. While this phenomenon is not the book's primary focus, it serves as a contextual element that influences the dynamics between the State and businesses. This section discusses the socio-environmental dimensions of extractivist dynamics in Latin America more broadly and specifically examines the dynamics surrounding lithium extraction.

Extractivism, Socio-Environmental Conflicts, and Green Industrial Policy

In recent decades, Latin America has seen a significant rise in conflicts classified as socio-environmental (Arsel et al., 2016; Rodríguez et al., 2019). This increase is largely attributed to the growing prevalence and intensity of extractive projects. Extractivism, as extensively critiqued by Latin American scholars, is generally understood as a mode of accumulation based on the large-scale appropriation, exploitation, and export of natural resources with minimal processing (Svampa, 2013). This framework has given rise to the concept of neoextractivism, an analytical category developed in Latin America that combines explanatory power with a denunciatory and mobilizing function (Svampa, 2019). Neoextractivism illustrates how left-leaning governments in the region embraced an extractive development model in the early twenty-first century, justifying it with the promise that the revenues would be directed toward social policies (Gudynas, 2009; Arsel et al., 2016). Svampa (2019) argues that the involvement of progressive governments in promoting the illusion that extractive revenues would lead to development and well-being complicates socio-environmental mobilization in the region.

Historically, Latin America has relied on a growth model based on the export of natural resources. However, this model intensified with the commodities boom of the early 2000s, leading to an increase in social mobilizations (Svampa, 2013; 2019). Alongside this boom, Cisneros (2020) notes a shift toward free-market policies that greatly diminished the State's ability to regulate the extractive industries, especially mining. Cisneros highlights that regional governance and regulation failed to properly distribute the benefits and externalities generated by these activities.

Comparative studies have made significant contributions by explaining the processes through which conflicts develop and the interactions among the actors involved (Haslam & Tanimoune, 2016). Key explanatory factors include levels of poverty and governance issues, whether related to the community's desire for inclusion in project planning or concerns about the distribution of benefits. Another crucial factor is the nature and variety of actors involved in and around the project and subsequent conflict. This distinction includes actors who "belong" to the territory versus those who "are" in the territory, such as nearby communities, local government characteristics, existing environmental institutions, non-governmental organizations, and the company responsible for the project (Delamaza et al., 2017).

In this context, Akchurin (2020) suggests that opposition to certain extractive industries can be explained by several elements: poverty levels in the nearby population; the presence of agricultural land or communities linked to agriculture; the presence of indigenous communities; the existence of various organizations within the community; the scale and origin of the investment; and whether the project's evaluation occurred during a left-leaning administration. More systematically, Haslam and Tanimoune (2016) categorize conflict determinants for testing based on type. They first consider project attributes that may lead to conflict, such as exploitation techniques, the scale of activity, the size of the company involved, the project's capital origin, and the mineral extracted. They then address the socioeconomic characteristics of the nearby population, arguing that concerns about the project's distributional effects can increase the likelihood of mobilization. Finally, they consider socio-environmental factors and lifestyle, such as the presence of forms of life and activities incompatible with the extractive activity [e.g., agricultural practices].

Socio-Environmental Impacts of Lithium Extraction in Latin America

The extraction of lithium has surged due to the demand for a low-carbon energy transition (Ciftci & Lemaire, 2023). However, like other extractive activities, it presents a range of issues concerning income distribution, water availability, and access to decision-making processes (Jerez et al., 2021; Díaz Paz et al., 2023). Among the various methods of lithium extraction—whether from sedimentary rocks, pegmatites, or brines—the latter, used in the lithium triangle, is the most water-intensive (Godoy, 2022). Specifically, the location of salt flats often coincides with crucial water sources, posing significant risks to water conservation and local biodiversity. For instance, the evaporation technique currently requires two million liters of water per ton of lithium, which cannot be reused or recovered (Fundación Terram, 2019, as cited in Godoy, 2022).

Thus, lithium extraction in salt flats threatens the region by overexploiting the area's water resources. Both companies and the State have shown limited attention to the hydrological complexities of these salt flats, and the exclusion of local communities from water use planning continues to persist and worsen (Jerez et al., 2021). These factors contribute to the obscuring of the injustices associated with lithium extraction (Jerez et al., 2021). Although such issues are not new in extractive industries, they are now situated within a context that increasingly demands "green" extraction practices.

Despite numerous technical studies, validated by various institutions, confirming the environmental damage caused by lithium extraction in salt flats, wetlands, and glaciers, there remains a notable weakness in institutional regulation and oversight (Godoy, 2022). This has led to tensions in extraction zones, which are often protected areas, Ramsar sites, or indigenous territories. Concerning the latter, while there are consultation and participation mechanisms for communities, these processes are frequently criticized for being co-opted due to institutional weaknesses or business interests.

Díaz Paz et al. (2023) indicate that local actors, governments, and mining companies often have differing views on the advantages and disadvantages of lithium extraction. While the scientific community and media address a wide range of issues, governments and companies tend to focus on "social and economic" aspects. Companies engage with communities to address concerns about water use but often fail to account for water contamination—reporting only on water availability rather than the pollution they cause.

Lunde Seefeldt (2022) characterizes disputes over water resources involving indigenous communities and lithium companies as "fraught with confusion and uncertainty," mainly due to the legal and bureaucratic systems responsible for managing information and dialogue. Lunde Seefeldt observes that communities lack clear access to crucial project information, leading to significant mistrust toward mining companies and calls for stricter water use restrictions.

Despite the presence of socio-environmental conflicts that escalate to national and/or international levels (Paredes, 2018), much resistance occurs at the local level, with the community residing in the affected area being the principal actor. Conde and Le Billon (2017) explain that not all communities oppose mining activities, including those related to lithium, and when they do, their objectives may vary. Communities may oppose a project to either cancel it or enhance their bargaining power, for example. Resistance involves two fundamental elements that can be sporadic or sustained: opposition to existing power relations and verbal, cognitive, or physical actions (Conde & Le Billon, 2017). Conde and Le

Billon categorize various conflict elements based on their impact on resistance, whether they hinder, promote, or have a mixed effect. Additionally, it is important to consider whether participatory processes are driven by communities, companies, or governments.

Finally, given lithium's connection to the energy transition, Ciftci and Lemaire (2023) examine conflicts related to lithium extraction compared to those involving resources not required for the transition [non-transition related resources or NTR] in Chile and Argentina. Their analysis reveals distinct features of conflicts associated with lithium since 2010. While all conflicts involved mobilization and protests, human rights violations were less common in lithium industry cases. Instead, there was a greater use of mass mobilizations and legal actions as forms of resistance. However, the increasing involvement of States in promoting the lithium sector has complicated negotiations and led to breaches of certain guarantees for indigenous communities (Ciftci & Lemaire, 2023). Conflict in the lithium industry, as with other extractive industries, remains a persistent issue in Latin American countries.

CHAPTER 3

Operationalizing State–Business Relations for the Study of Green Industrial Policy

Introduction

As established in the previous chapter, the relationships between the state and business actors are central to understanding the development of industrial policies, particularly concerning lithium. This mineral presents significant challenges for developing countries striving to balance economic expansion with the achievement of environmentally relevant goals. Effective coordination between the public and private sectors is crucial for advancing these objectives through various public policies. This chapter presents the operationalization of this dynamic by providing specific guidelines regarding state capacities, power resources and preferences of business actors. It outlines how these dimensions function separately and then presents an original argument regarding the types of relationships between state and business actors.

The chapter is structured as follows. First, it examines the concept of state capacity, defining it and establising its primary constitutive dimensions, along with observable implications that will later be analyzed empirically in the text. Second, it presents the concept of state capacity from a relational perspective, noting that the state's ability to achieve public policy objectives depends on its interaction with other relevant social actors, who may support or oppose the measures. In this context, the third section addresses the power resources available to business actors and how they employ these resources in public policies. The final part

S. Carrasco, *From (De)regulation to Industrialization?*, Latin American Political Economy, https://doi.org/10.1007/978-3-031-77130-9_3

discusses business preferences in the public arena, arguing the implications these preferences have for the deployment of their power resources and the dynamics that arise in the relationship between businesses and the state regarding specific policies.

State Capacity

Operationalizing State Capacity for Industrial Policy

State capacity can generally be understood as the ability of the state to effectively exercise authority and implement policies across its territory (Mann, 1984). In recent decades, a substantial body of literature has demonstrated the utility of this concept in explaining various outcomes, such as economic growth (Evans & Rauch, 1999), levels of violence (Huntington, 1996), industrial transformations (Evans, 1996), and innovation (Weiss, 1998), among others (for a more detailed discussion, see Cingolani, 2013).

The concept of state capacity has evolved significantly from macro-analytical perspectives, such as neomarxist views on state autonomy in relation to dominant classes (Poulantzas, 1974), to more micro-analytical approaches, like those presented by Evans et al. (1985), which focus on the specific mechanisms that enable state institutions to achieve their objectives. This research adopts the latter, a more detailed focus, allowing for an examination of state capacity through various dimensions. Defining the relevant elements for understanding state capacity in its different roles is not straightforward, given that it is a multidimensional concept (Cingolani, 2013). Synthesizing the literature, state capacity encompasses key dimensions including coercive, fiscal, administrative, legal, political, and territorial capacities (Cingolani, 2013). The following sections describe each of these dimensions.

Firstly, coercive capacity refers to the state's ability to maintain a monopoly on power, primarily through territorial control, both internally and in the face of external threats. Coercive capacity is a fundamental element in state-building processes; its absence can lead to the establishment of a failed state (Centeno, 2015; Fortin, 2010). Fiscal capacity, on the other hand, pertains to the state's ability to mobilize resources from society, which is a primary activity in the development of modern states (Rosanvallon, 2012).

A central, cross-cutting element in definitions of state capacity is administrative capacity, which refers to the existence of a professional bureaucracy with a high degree of specialization and training among public officials. This dimension enables the implementation of policies as well as the functioning of institutions and political decisions (Weber, 2016; Geddes, 1994). Other dimensions include the legal capacity, which relates to the presence of clear norms that allow the state to operate, and the territorial capacity, which concerns the state's ability to extend its policies, goods, and services to various regions within its territory (North, 1990). Decades ago, authors such as O'Donnell (1993) observed that Latin American countries exhibit various "brown areas" where the state fails to provide services across different parts of the territory. Addressing such subnational inequalities in relation to state policies indicates high state capacity in this dimension (Snyder, 2001).

In addition to the dimensions previously described, Cingolani (2013) identifies another dimension of state capacity: industrial capacity, which enables the state to intervene in productive systems and shape the economy. However, I do not consider this dimension as intrinsic to the concept of state capacity but rather as a potential outcome of it. The degree of intervention in a productive system depends on the state's ability to implement policies in that area, as discussed in the sections on developmental states (see Evans, 1996). Essentially, the nature of public policy is a reflection of the state's strength, but it is not a necessary condition for the existence of state capacity.

To streamline the analysis, I have chosen to consolidate the dimensions of state capacity into three broad analytical categories: political, legal–institutional, and administrative. I argue that these three elements constitute the core of state capacity and will be utilized for empirical analysis in the subsequent chapters of this book. Table 3.1 summarizes the aggregation of these dimensions.

Research has shown that insufficient state capacity can lead to significant problems in the institutionalization and implementation of public policies. Specifically, the robustness of state institutions can affect how effectively reforms are applied; low levels of institutional capacity may result in policies failing to be enforced (Amengual & Dargent, 2020). State actors might contribute to non-compliance either by choosing not to enforce rules or by lacking the ability to do so (Brinks et al., 2020). As a result, new political institutions might be created that, in practice, have little to no impact (Holland, 2016).

Table 3.1 Dimensions of state capacity

Concept	*Dimensions*	*Indicators*
State capacity	Political	Coercion Political will
	Institutional	Legal
	Administrative	Fiscal Administrative Territorial

Source: Own elaboration

In situations of low state capacity, actors may either disregard established norms or reinterpret them to align with new interests (Brinks et al., 2020). For instance, Alisha Holland (2016) employs the concept of forbearance to explain the divergence between written rules and institutional practice, attributing it to deliberate decisions by political actors to maximize their electoral gains and rents. Considering this institutional dimension is crucial for understanding varying degrees of enforcement at the subnational level and the potential failure of public policies (Holland, 2017; Amengual, 2016).

The study of state capacity has proven highly effective in explaining institutional outcomes in Latin American countries, where there are significant variations in state strength (Levitsky & Murillo, 2010). Due to its significance, state capacity is a key independent variable in my analysis. However, a narrow focus on the state's role in policy formulation can obscure the relational nature of institutional dynamics. Evaluating the strength or weakness of an institution alone is insufficient to explain the nature of policy changes and the applicability of norms and regulations, particularly regarding lithium in Latin America. Institutions do not operate in isolation, and their effectiveness can be influenced by other factors, such as the role of informal actors (Schorr & Damonte, 2021b, Subirats et al., 2008; Stein & Tommasi, 2006).

A recent discussion in the literature has criticized the excessive emphasis that research has placed on the role of state actors in shaping and constructing institutions (Mayka, 2019). Instead, various scholars have highlighted the significant role that other informal actors play in institutional processes, particularly social actors. For instance, Amengual and Dargent (2020) have demonstrated how citizens' willingness to adhere to norms is crucial for the effective functioning of institutions. Indeed, a

Table 3.2 Operationalization of state capacity

Concept	*Dimensions*	*Observable implications*
State capacity	Política l	Relevant authorities and political actors present practices and discourses in favor of industrialization
	Institucional - Legal	There are clear rules regulating economic activity related to lithium
		There are specific institutions and structures responsible for implementing the policy
	Administrative	The public sector possesses expert knowledge (technical competence) to implement industrialization policies
		The available budget is sufficient to carry out the policies

Source: Own elaboration

committed citizenry can ensure that norms and regulations function even in contexts with low state capacity (Amengual, 2016). As noted earlier, this research argues that, in the context of industrial policies, it is not organized civil society that is the primary informal actor influencing institutional configuration. Rather, it is businesses and entrepreneurs. The following section operationalizes the role of entrepreneurs within the framework of developing green industrial policies (Table 3.2).

State Capacity from a Relational Perspective

A crucial element in the perspective presented in this book is understanding state capacity from a relational perspective. Beyond technological costs, the design and speed of industrial policy—particularly for the energy transition—are influenced by state power, political interests, and elite investment patterns (Bentley et al., 2021). Therefore, rather than merely responding to market failures, states strategically address problems within a complex global environment. In this regard, the literature reveals various dimensions of state capacity depending on the role assigned to the state. Christoff (2005) identifies several activities that a state, specifically a Green State, should be capable of performing. These include forming consensus, establishing long-term strategic planning that integrates social, environmental, and economic dimensions, coordinating public policies considering the diverse actors involved, and effectively implementing established policies. These elements are detailed in Table 3.3.

Table 3.3 Areas of State Capacity According to Christoff (2005)

Area	*Definition*
Consensus Building	The state involves civil society in institutions and processes aimed at deliberating programs that entail economic and social changes within ecological limits
Strategic Planning	The state provides the capacity for formulating long-term social and economic planning that considers ecological sustainability beyond available horizons
Policy Coordination and Integration	Strategic planning should be conducted by the state and across all sectors of economic activity and civil society. An ecological dimension must be incorporated into every decision-making process to build effective ecological governance
Implementation	The state ensures the availability of resources for tasks effectively, including regulation, monitoring, allocation, and productivity

Source: Own elaboration based on Christoff (2005, p. 44)

It is imperative to clarify the substantial difference between the body of literature addressing advanced economies and that which focuses on emerging economies. In the Latin American context, state capacity is particularly relevant as "the ability of the state to implement official goals, especially over the actual or potential opposition of powerful social groups" (Skocpol, 1985, as cited in Meckling & Nahm, 2018b). This approach has led to various conceptualizations emphasizing different aspects for measuring state capacity and the contexts in which it can be applied, as discussed in the previous section. Consequently, greater importance is often placed on identifying specific attributes within the state's bureaucracy to explain the level of state capacity.

In this vein, Meckling and Nahm (2022) seek to deepen the understanding of state capacity by proposing a strategic capacity that does not necessarily stem from the characteristics of state institutions per se but rather from their interactions with other interest groups, shaping the relationship between the state and various actors. Generally, strategic state capacity can be understood as "the ability of the state—the executive and/or the legislature—to mobilize or demobilize interest groups in pursuit of official policy goals" (Meckling & Nahm, 2022, p. 6). Given that the interests of actors in public policy debates are not homogeneous, and the reasons for opposing government initiatives are diverse, there is an opportunity to exploit these differences to enhance support and neutralize opposition. Therefore, focusing on capacity in relation to other actors, through the mobilization and demobilization of interests, the formation of winning coalitions—through positive feedback—enables the establishment of more comprehensive strategies and policies, requiring substantial political support to be built (Meckling et al., 2015).

The authors clarify that their work constructs ideal types of strategies that the state can deploy to address opposition, but in practice, these strategies are not mutually exclusive, with the cost of implementation being a significant factor. They present two dimensions of these strategies: first, mobilizing/demobilizing, which involves mobilizing those with shared objectives with the state and demobilizing those who oppose it. Within this dimension, the strategy of recruiting allies involves mobilizing allies to create a favorable balance of power, while the strategy limiting access restricts availability to negotiation and/or decision-making forums for interest groups whose opposing positions are unlikely to change. On the other hand, the state can alter the level of influence and preferences of interest groups. The strategy of quieting interest aims to silence opposition groups through tools such as compensation, whereas the strategy of aligning interest seeks to change these groups' preferences (Meckling & Nahm, 2022).

In contexts of high state capacity related to public policy implementation—such as in industrialized countries—Meckling and Nahm (2018b) suggest shifting the focus of analysis to policy formulation, addressing capacity as the ability to overcome opposition from interest groups during the formulation stage. In this regard, they highlight the importance of considering the vulnerability of both legislators and bureaucrats to capture by interest groups. If legislators have strong incentives to negotiate with interest groups for electoral reasons, and that bureaucrats are more likely to base their decisions on the mandates of their institutions, it is reasonable to assume that the latter are at lower risk of capture than the former—though a lower risk does not imply complete absence (Meckling & Nahm, 2018b).

As a result, the policy design phase is considered the most susceptible to capture, given that it defines the instrument and, consequently, the distribution of costs and benefits of a regulation. Based on these premises, Meckling and Nahm (2018b) propose that a division of tasks between the legislative branch and the bureaucracy during the public policy process is a source of state capacity, distinguishing between different types. First, in bureaucratic policy design, the legislature sets broad policy objectives while delegating the detailed design to bureaucrats, who, with greater autonomy, can formulate comprehensive policies and manage distributive effects. Second, in legislative policy design, bureaucrats define the policy objectives, while the legislature drafts the content. It is noted that this latter design type is subject to greater negotiation, often resulting in fragmented and/or sectoral policies.

Focusing on the dynamics between interest groups and the state, the study considers institutional elements and patterns in the relationships between these actors, particularly in the energy industry and within the context of decarbonization efforts agreed upon in the Paris Agreement. Broadly speaking, two systems of representation and interaction between the state and interest groups are identified: corporatism, which prioritizes coordination and consensus among key actors, and pluralism, which favors competition among relevant actors (Meckling & Nahm, 2022). These distinctions have allowed for a more nuanced analysis, leading to the construction of sub-typologies and the identification of national and sectoral interaction patterns (Meckling & Nahm, 2022).

In the case of the automobile industry, state efforts to intervene in favor of technology development for electric vehicle manufacturing have yielded varied outcomes regarding the transformative impact of the implemented policies. Specifically, Meckling and Nahm (2018a) suggest two dimensions to consider: horizontal coordination among firms, referring to the organizational level at which companies within the same industry represent their sector's interests, and vertical coordination between state agencies and firms, which considers the centralization and stability of the relationship between these actors. The authors argue that political coordination enables the industry and government to reach agreements on technological transformations through negotiation, although this coordination tends to prioritize the interests of the involved firms, thus benefiting the existing technological regime. Conversely, political competition among interest groups allows policymakers to organize coalitions in favor of technological change. In this scenario, policymakers may bypass the interests of established industries and negotiate with individual companies rather than by sector. However, this latter approach may encounter difficulties in coordinating long-term industrial processes.

Likewise, although countries may share similar goals regarding the development of industrial capacity, they will implement different policies due to the institutional differences that shape the state–business relationship (Hochstetler & Kostka, 2015). That is to say, the system of interest representation and the balance of interests within a particular sector, such as non-conventional renewable energy (NCRE), is crucial for understanding the configuration and outcomes of industrial policy. The literature highlights corporatism—previously mentioned—as significant because it fosters trust through repeated interactions between the state and businesses. This trust enhances information quality and access, as well as problem-solving capabilities, in comparison to pluralism. In their work, Hochstetler and Kostka (2015) describe, on the one hand, the corporatist/neo-corporatist State–business relationship, characterized by state interventions that align government interests with those of market actors; this is coordinated with state banks to finance and invest in state-owned or other key companies. On the other hand, they characterize public–private partnerships, where competition is encouraged, strict financial rules are formulated, and tools such as subsidies or local production protections are employed to promote the development of renewable energies (Hochstetler & Kostka, 2015).

In comparison, institutions and dynamics with strong coordination elements lead to better [environmental] outcomes, enable collective action problems to be addressed, foster greater trust (Hochstetler & Kostka, 2015), and establish the capacity to manage long-term industrial development processes (Meckling & Nahm, 2018a). However, this can also hinder incorporation of new technologies into the industry (Meckling & Nahm, 2018a). On the contrary, configurations that prioritize competition among various industry actors allow more space for the emergence and incorporation of new technological sectors but lack the necessary capacity to direct them over time. Indeed, Meckling and Nahm (2018a) reveal that there is a trade-off between stability and change in the public policy process.

Furthermore, the authoritarian regimes in Latin America left a legacy of institutional weakness related to the capacity to provide services efficiently, manage public enterprises, and enforce the law adequately (Abers & Keck, 2009). Thus, literature on Latin America first identifies the institutional weaknesses of the region's states, and then explores various ways to generate and/or enhance state capacity. In this context, civil society and bureaucracy gain relevance, being identified as actors capable of closing institutional gaps or acting strategically by seizing opportunities within the policy formulation and implementation process.

Orihuela and Paredes (2017) agree in diagnosing that when a country has a high level of formal institutional development and introduces new norms, these will be quickly institutionalized through already developed capacities. However, in cases of state weakness, the authors note that institutional changes will be incremental and often characterized by discontinuous progress over time. Besides incorporating legal norms, it is necessary to establish the required capacities within the state apparatus for these norms to truly become institutions. In this sense, the concept of bureaucratic autonomy is key, wherein institutional entrepreneurs are those who translate policy and organizational models from the international stage to the national context, thereby transforming state actions (Orihuela & Paredes, 2017). Additionally, Orihuela et al. (2021) indicate that this type of autonomy requires three conditions: political differentiation of actors seeking to control state formation; unique organizational capacities; and political legitimacy or organizational reputation embedded in an independent power base. In countries with a strong extractive industry, bureaucratic autonomy is crucial for understanding how rules and institutions—in this case, environmental ones—that are not applied or fulfilling their function can begin to become effective (Orihuela et al., 2021).

Finally, it is crucial to acknowledge that green industrial policy might encounter opposition from within the state apparatus that promotes it, due to its ties with polluting or competing industries (Nahm & Urpelainen, 2021). This issue is connected to the nature of state–business relations, which can manifest formally through official agreements and coordination meetings, or informally through less structured interactions (te Velde, 2013). In fact, te Velde points out that strong formal ties often develop because of these informal connections, and that the formation of powerful coalitions would be unlikely without them. Moreover, larger, more established companies typically have greater access to the State through informal channels, whereas smaller or emerging firms generally engage only in formal settings (Gardini, 2006).

Business Actors

Business Strategies in Green Industrial Policy

Political economy literature generally portrays Latin America as dominated by a hierarchical capitalist system, where a few large, diversified business groups maintain a hierarchical relationship with other economic actors (Schneider, 2009). Politically, these groups have succeeded in limiting the State's power to impose its preferences. In Chile, for instance, the prevalence of a neoliberal system has constrained the roles the State can play in the economy (Maillet, 2015b), with business actors being key defenders of this economic model's status quo (Madariaga, 2020). However, my aim is to move beyond macro-structural perspectives on the relationship between the business sector and the State. Instead, I seek to explore the specific dynamics that unfold in contested political arenas, such as lithium policies, where new imaginaries, discourses, and interests diverge from traditional economic processes.

The promises of lithium as a foundation for new development models prompt questions about how business actors operate, their motivations, and their strategies concerning lithium. Therefore, the preferences of business actors do not automatically translate into strategies; these strategies are mediated by the institutional contexts in which they operate. This makes it essential to specifically study business strategies within the context of lithium policies in Latin America.

In his study of business strategies in environmental policy contexts, Jonas Meckling (2015) proposes a typology where the strategies employed by businesses at any given time are conditioned by regulatory pressures and the distributive effects of environmental policies. For instance, Meckling (2015) explains that when environmental policies exert low regulatory pressure and when costs outweigh benefits, businesses tend to oppose the policy. The logic applied in this research is like that proposed by Meckling, but with different scope and context. We consider it crucial to establish whether business actors support or oppose policies, recognizing that their impact will be mediated by the levels of state capacity (i.e., the strength or weakness of state institutions and the role of public actors). Thus, in relation to industrial policies, the directly involved business actors can play two roles: support the policy or oppose it. The specific dimensions of each role are analyzed in the following paragraphs.

Regarding business opposition to public policies, the debate has focused on the various strategies businesses use to impose their preferences on public policies. Since the 2000s, there has been a resurgence of approaches to business power in comparative political economy (Hacker & Pierson, 2002), leading to various empirical studies aimed at better understanding the political role of business groups in capitalist societies. Broadly speaking, the main branch of literature identifies two types of power resources that business actors use to influence public policies: instrumental power and structural power (Fairfield, 2015). Recently, the literature has advanced in recognizing new sources of power, such as discursive power (Falkner, 2008). These three sources of power have proven useful in analyzing business dynamics in Chile (Madariaga et al., 2021).

First, structural power refers to the credible threat of reduced private investment as a consequence of state actions, such as the imposition of stricter environmental regulations (Fairfield, 2015). Beckert (2016) highlights that a central, yet underexplored, dimension of capitalism is the role of fictional expectations about the future of the economy, as these expectations influence present-day institutions and actors. The temporal order of capitalism is thus crucial (Sewell, 2008), with future imaginaries and the formation of expectations shaping the dynamics of capitalism itself (Beckert, 2016).[1] In this context, I argue that the core aspect of structural power lies in its ability to shape these fictional expectations in favor of the business sector, thereby constraining the state. The state's public policy decisions are compelled to operate within a future scenario that is strategically influenced by business interests.

Traditionally, structural power is associated with the financial sector, where capital mobility allows financiers to move investments, impacting markets. Research has analyzed this phenomenon, particularly in the context of tax reforms; for example, when policies alter tax burdens, the financial sector often responds with capital movement (Hart, 2009). There is, therefore, an opportunity to analyze these dynamics and their specificities within the context of industrialization processes.

Despite significant theoretical reflection on how structural power shapes decision-making through expectations, a major challenge remains in operationalizing this concept for policy analysis (Culpepper, 2015).

[1] According to Beckert (2016), capitalism is a system in which different actors direct their activities based on imagined futures of the economy that differ from the present.

Fairfield (2015) proposes a concrete approach to applying the concept of structural power to specific cases. According to Fairfield, the degree of influence exerted by structural power depends not only on the threat of disinvestment by business actors but also on the credibility of that threat to policymakers (Fairfield, 2015). Certain sectors, such as finance, tend to present more credible threats (Bell & Hindmoor, 2015). Furthermore, the extent of structural power is also contingent on how strategically important the sector is to the national economy.

A critical dimension to consider in the exercise of structural power is the temporal one. The temporal factor allows us to differentiate between the long-term processes of business power accumulation and the short-term processes in which this power is deployed to influence decision-making (Bril-Mascarenhas & Maillet, 2019). Business actors build their power over extended periods, shaping their preferences, defining the political landscape, and setting the agenda in alignment with their interests (Adolph, 2013; Bril-Mascarenhas & Maillet, 2019). Therefore, it is expected that firms with longer operational histories will have accumulated more power resources than their counterparts. In line with Fairfield's (2015) argument, structural power can vary in strength, ranging from strong to weak, depending on additional factors such as those described here.

Instrumental power, on the other hand, refers to the deliberate actions taken by business groups to influence public policy (Fairfield, 2015). Typically, lobbying is one of the primary tools through which businesses exert influence. However, the concept of instrumental power offers a broader perspective by incorporating other resources, such as ties to political parties, institutionalized consultation, the recruitment of businesspeople into public office, business cohesion, technical expertise, access to media, and the use of financial resources (Fairfield, 2015). In recent years, various instances have surfaced in Chile where instrumental power has been strongly exercised to influence political decisions, with the most significant cases involving irregular political financing (Maillet et al., 2019; Matamala, 2017). One of the companies involved in these cases is SQM, which is also one of the leading firms engaged in lithium extraction in Chile.

Finally, discursive power refers to the ability to shape the framings of public discussions (Madariaga et al., 2021). Business actors continually seek to legitimize their corporate interests by influencing the ideational foundations of society and the economy while simultaneously legitimizing themselves as economic producers and political actors (Falkner, 2008). Leveraging their economic power, businesses can create narratives that permeate public discourse, particularly concerning economic growth and employment—areas where businesses hold significant credibility (Falkner, 2008; Madariaga et al., 2021). In the case of lithium, discursive dynamics are crucial for legitimizing extraction activities, given the mineral's role in addressing climate change (Agusdinata et al., 2018). Therefore, discursive power is a central dimension that must be considered in the implementation of lithium policy in Chile.

Recent literature on business power has highlighted the significant success of business actors in Latin America in opposing public policy changes that conflict with their interests. Business groups have played a major role in resisting reforms related to taxation, labor, the environment, pensions, and other public policies (Bril-Mascarenhas & Maillet, 2019; Madariaga et al., 2021; Fairfield, 2010, 2015; Etchemendy, 2011). Much of the existing research focuses on contexts where the business sector's opposition is evident, such as advocating for lower taxes or minimizing labor costs and responsibilities. However, there is a gap in understanding how business power operates in areas like industrial policy, where business interests may shift depending on the strategic context (Bril-Mascarenhas & Madariaga, 2019). Given that businesses are often significant beneficiaries of such policies, this gap warrants further investigation.

This study aims to challenge the conventional view in the literature by arguing that business power resources—instrumental, structural, and discursive—are not solely used to oppose public policies. In the realm of green industrialization, for instance, businesses may strategically deploy their power to support state objectives when these align with their own interests. For example, businesses might use lobbying to influence political actors who oppose favorable policies or leverage media access and technical reports to advocate for industrialization initiatives. Additionally, businesses may employ structural strategies, such as tying their investment decisions to state support for industrialization. Such cooperative dynamics have been documented in other industrialization contexts (Meckling, 2011, 2015).

These strategies illustrate the diverse ways in which business actors can shape public policies, whether by supporting or opposing them. This book aims to deepen our understanding of these dynamics specifically within the context of industrial policies. Table 3.4 operationalizes the concept to be empirically tested.

As empirical literature indicates, these various strategies can function together, reinforcing and enhancing their effectiveness in shaping policies (Fairfield, 2015). Additionally, the development of these strategies can vary depending on the level of spatialization—whether local, national, or global (Madariaga et al., 2021). My primary focus is on understanding the strategies employed by business actors at the national level, where they directly engage with the State in the formulation and implementation of public policies. While local and global contexts involve their own distinct dynamics—such as the interactions between lithium extraction activities and local communities, which lead companies to adopt specific strategies as shown in other research on local business tactics (Leiva, 2019)—this study is concentrated on the national level. Consequently, the main analytical challenge of this research is to examine how different types of state–business relationships influence the outcomes of lithium policies in Latin America.

Table 3.4 Operationalization of business power

Concept	*Dimensions*	*Implicancias observables*
Business power	Instrumental	- Collaboration between companies in support of or aligned with decisions made by authorities - Production of technical analyses by companies to endorse (or oppose) policy proposals - Exchange of information, networks, and officials between companies and the State - Irregular financing of political activities and campaigns
	Structural	- Threats to withdraw from economic activities - Threats to withhold development of committed R&D projects - Impossibility of removing incumbent companies
	Discursive	- Consolidation of a positive public image of companies and the benefits of their activities - Use of various media to highlight the benefits/problems of policies and/or economic activities

Source: Own elaboration

Business Preferences in Green Industrial Policy

A central issue in analyzing the role of business actors in industrial policy is their public policy preferences. The previous section outlined the theoretical power resources that business actors may possess and exercise. However, it is important to consider that the exercise of these resources depends on their preferences regarding public policies. In the realm of industrial policies, business preferences are not always clear-cut and depend on their position within the productive structure as well as the incentives to achieve their objectives (Bril-Mascarenhas & Madariaga, 2017). Similarly, the interests of economic actors vary depending on the geographical scale (local, national, international) in which they operate (Carrasco et al., 2023). The following discussion examines the significance of business preferences in public policy and the relational dynamics with the State based on these choices.

Generally, the path of green economic transformations reflects geopolitical factors and industrial opportunities (Hochstetler, 2020). Lebdioui (2024) notes a high degree of interdependence between the state, businesses, and public opinion. The author elaborates that public opinion can pressure companies to shift their agendas, while businesses can influence or distort public perceptions of sustainability. Thus, the decisions a country makes regarding the industrial policies it formulates and implements are the result of interactions among state actors, businesses, and civil society, each advocating for specific interests. Consequently, countries must tailor the policies they design to their economic, political, and social contexts, considering that the interests of each group are distinct and evolve over time and space (Lebdioui, 2024).

In contrast to previous industrial policies that relied on state control measures, new industrial policies emphasize collaboration and co-production between the state and businesses (Fuentes & Pipkin, 2015). On the one hand, an "autodiscovery" approach seeks to improve information access and reduce risks through public–private coordination efforts, while on the other, a "political economy of capabilities" approach aims to invest in national innovation systems, produce public goods that reduce coordination costs, and create incentives for businesses to invest more in their organizational capacities. Nevertheless, Fuentes and Pipkin (2015) argue that assuming businesses are pre-disposed to engage in these exploratory and discovery processes is insufficient for ensuring policy success. Indeed, Lebdioui (2024) explains that many successful development policies involve the state aligning its goals with business interests and building coalitions to promote them. In other words, if industrial policy does not garner business interests willing to support the proposed policy, it is unlikely to be coherently formulated and successfully implemented (Fuentes & Pipkin, 2015).

It is also important to note that identifying interests alone does not fully explain the link between material interest and the strategies deployed during the political process (Meckling, 2015), as businesses often have short-term survival imperatives that constrain their support for industrial policy (Whitfield & Therkildsen, 2011). Consistent with the "winner takes most" model, Denney, Southin, and Wolfe (2023) provide evidence that a small number of firms control a large market share and are characterized by significant size, greater market power, and higher productivity and innovation capacity. In the case of Canada and the digital sector, the authors conclude that inadequate incentive structures, weak governmental support, and misalignment of support with expansion goals hinder business performance. Therefore, it is necessary to recognize policy instruments as products of the subjective vision of policymakers, which may oppose the vision of recipients (business actors). Thus, the selection of a policy mix should aim to incorporate both perspectives.

In contrast, Meckling (2015) approaches business behavior by describing a process through which companies shape their interests and preferences based on experiences, interactions with other actors, and institutional contexts. According to this perspective, perceptions of pressure and distributive effects shape business preferences. In line with this, preferences and the strategies to be implemented depend on the perceived costs/benefits (distributive effects) and the level of pressure for regulation. In a context of political and economic pressure that is subject to constant change, Grumbach (2015) analyzes business preferences as strategic. He suggests that true preferences of actors are not directly revealed in the political arena. There is a central priority to maintain the status quo, but businesses will also support other initiatives to have a backup option that aligns with their preferences. Thus, businesses may (i) exaggerate their support for politically feasible outcomes and (ii) shape the feedback effects of policies (Grumbach, 2015). This perspective can be complemented by Kim et al. (2019), who argue that, in addition to observing a company's position on a policy, its preferences should be evaluated across multiple dimensions of the issue. The heterogeneity of interests allows for diverse reasons to oppose or support a policy, with a company's stance also depending on the availability and consequences of other alternative options. However, certain dimensions of the policy may carry greater significance.

Similarly, challenging the traditional assumption that businesses are omniscient optimizers, Li and Csaszar (2019) suggest analyzing business behavior regarding industrial policy through a more micro lens that can capture nuances. They propose an approach from strategy and organization literature, suggesting that business behavior is not the result of optimization but of a rational and adaptive search process that is significantly influenced by the complexity of the business environment. They study the effect of industrial policy on business performance under three main contingencies: (i) government capacity, i.e., the likelihood that the government identifies and implements the optimal policy; (ii) policy stability, i.e., the frequency with which the government changes its policy; and (iii) environmental complexity, i.e., how interdependent business decisions are. It is noted that the first two contingencies have been the most studied in the literature as fundamental conditions for successful industrial intervention, while complexity, the contingency related to businesses, has received less attention.

Additionally, Fuentes and Pipkin (2015) investigate the conditions under which businesses begin to seek new long-term business models. They indicate that in Latin America, businesses possess a basic aspiration that, once achieved, leads to satisfaction and a "suspension of the search for change." In this scenario, competition does not always drive actors toward long-term maximization. In inertial contexts, various sources of pressure that hinder the achievement of established aspirations force businesses to seek new goals and means to attain them. These pressures have an accumulative effect and include: (i) supply shocks, when a production process becomes unsustainable due to intra-industrial competition or sudden changes in input prices; (ii) demand shocks, when consumer market demand shifts due to consumer preferences, government norms, trade regulations, or contraction of the internal market; and (iii) civil society conflict, when social groups exert pressure on businesses, typically in the form of conflicts between capital and labor (Fuentes & Pipkin, 2015). Without these disturbances, businesses would not seek market information to guide state assistance in industrial policy strategies.

Moreover, Genovese and Tvinnereim (2018) seek to explain why businesses may oppose gradual environmental policies. Generally, "to the extent that a policy imposes a burden due to progressively high adjustment costs, a company may be more inclined to either exploit it or oppose it." Thus, a company's stance on a policy depends on whether it perceives the policy as protective or competitive. This internalization depends both on the individual characteristics of the company and on the sector to which it belongs, as these positions may or may not be aligned. Individually, a company may oppose a policy based on its comparative advantages; however, the sector it belongs to may constrain this opposition due to structural and/or political reasons.

Rangel-Padilla (2021) starts with the premise that interactions between the state and businesses, shaped by bureaucratic quality and business cohesion, generate different patterns in policy formulation processes, influencing whether, or not, actors with veto power can be convinced. In this context, sectoral business cohesion is understood as the degree to which companies within the same sector coordinate their policy demands and actions. When the sector acts collectively, there is also a reduced search for rents. In this regard, a meritocratic bureaucracy and a cohesive business sector can foster a synergistic policy formulation process characterized by: (i) professionalized evaluation of information; (ii) formal collaboration; and (iii) joint lobbying to overcome the resistance of veto actors in Congress (in this case, referring to Congress).

To understand why the State may prefer certain industrial policies, Whitfield and Therkildsen (2011) define "ruling elites" as the political leaders in power and "ruling coalition" as the groups behind the rise of these elites. The incentive structure that explains the behavior of both groups depends on: (i) the degree of vulnerability of the ruling elite; (ii) the degree of fragmentation within the ruling coalition; and (iii) the size and type of financing available to the ruling elites (p. 19). Consistent with these premises, Buur and Whitfield (2013) identify three conditions for a successful industrial policy: mutual interest, "pockets of efficiency," and productivity learning. When the ruling elite can control the various demands within their coalition and bureaucrats have the confidence of the elites and technical expertise, a "pocket of efficiency" exists. Additionally, productivity learning helps condition the elite to increase productivity and engage in processes of updating when they are inclined to seek rents. Under this perspective, the pursuit of rents is not necessarily negative if it leads to greater productivity.

State–Business Dynamics in the Context of Global Value Chains (GVCs)

In the literature on business preferences, Global Value Chains (GVCs) are integrated as a crucial analytical component. Kim et al. (2019) contend that business preferences concerning trade policy exhibit substantial variation based on their involvement in GVCs, as a firm's position within the value chain dictates the specific risks and uncertainties it encounters. For firms embedded in GVCs, policies that safeguard their investments are particularly significant. Conversely, firms outside these networks tend to favor mechanisms for dispute resolution. Kim et al. (2019) further elucidate that companies participating in GVCs are engaged in interrelated contractual relationships, which distribute the risks associated with temporal inconsistencies. Firms involved in trade independently must depend on alternative mechanisms, such as robust dispute resolution systems, to ensure that their international trade activities remain uninterrupted.

Similarly, Eckhardt and Lee (2018) investigate the linkage between preferential trade agreements (PTAs), GVC integration, and business preferences. The authors suggest that integration into GVCs can influence firms' preferences regarding PTAs and their strategic approaches to promote these preferences. While larger and more productive firms generally support PTAs, there are notable variations in their preferences for specific provisions within the agreements, contingent upon the organization of their value chains during negotiations. They argue that policy preferences are not merely unidimensional—whether in favor of or against trade liberalization—and that achieving a common sectoral stance is challenging.

Meckling and Hughes (2017) apply this analysis to the photovoltaic solar industry, arguing that support for open trade has extended beyond multinational corporations to include vertically specialized firms due to their role in the GVC. These firms include upstream suppliers that provide inputs to a global supply chain; global manufacturers outsourcing production to firms in countries with protectionist demands; and downstream users purchasing inputs. The authors conclude that trade policy preferences are influenced by the stage of the GVC in which firms participate and their level of integration with Chinese production, asserting that this dynamic can be generalized to other sectors.

Additionally, the specific configurations of State–market relations in Latin America warrant attention. In the region, the business sector comprises concentrated groups that control a substantial portion of the Gross Domestic Product (GDP) and significantly contribute to taxes and political campaigns (Rettberg, 2001). Although it is often perceived that the Latin American states have been captured by business interests, Rettberg (2001) argues that the relationship between economic groups and the State is one of mutual constraint. For instance, in Colombia, while the State did not play a pivotal role in the formation of economic groups, these groups have relied on state credit, contracts, and regulation to expand their operations, particularly during the privatization of state enterprises in the 1990s. The study highlights the importance of understanding these dynamics within presidential systems. Although business sector support is not unconditional, there is a contextual framework explaining why businesses supported the government during difficult times, anticipating long-term benefits. While rent-seeking influences behavior, it alone does not fully explain it. Rettberg's work is notable for suggesting that this dynamic may be extrapolated to other Latin American countries where state financing of economic sectors is prevalent. Specifically, it notes that in Chile, development financing provided by the Corporación de Fomento (CORFO) was instrumental in enabling various economic groups to acquire state-owned enterprises.

In the context of constructing international organizations, Gardini (2006) examines the relationship between governments and businesses, focusing on their interaction in the formation of MERCOSUR. In this case, businesses engaged in the integration process under the premise of democratic legitimacy but were excluded from key decision-making processes, which remained under governmental control. Gardini states that governments did not intend to grant direct participation to businesses in the integration process. However, deficiencies within business organizations also contributed to this exclusion, including issues such as fragmentation, lack of coordination, and limited access to decision-makers. Consequently, businesses were perceived as unreliable partners and lacked access to high levels of government for dialogue. The author identifies the degree of political access as a crucial factor in determining the role and attitude of the business sector toward the formulation of trade and economic policies. Thus, the informal nature of interactions between government and businesses benefited the more powerful segments of the business community.

Toward a Typology for Studying State–Business Relations

Building on the theoretical discussions presented earlier, this section introduces a proposed typology of state–business relations and their role in shaping lithium policies in Latin America. Specifically, the analysis of the relationship between the State and businesses is framed through two key variables: the degree of state capacity and the degree of business support/opposition to public policy. This approach involves examining the deployment of various resources by political, bureaucratic, and business actors. The interaction of these two variables results in different types of state–business relationships, which, according to the established typology, may influence the likelihood of specific industrial policies. The proposed typology will be empirically tested through an analysis of Chile and, complementarily, the cases of Bolivia and Argentina (Table 3.5).

The industrial policies discussed vary in scope and depth and can therefore be understood within a framework of levels, ranging from policies that generate minimal value addition to those that create more substantial value. In this context, we can conceive of a "ladder of industrialization," similar to the "ladder of citizen participation" used to describe other policy types (see Arnstein, 1969).

Firstly, I argue that a low level of state capacity combined with business opposition to state-imposed value addition processes would inhibit the establishment of industrial policies. Even with political support, the lack of state capacity and business resistance would prevent progress in scaling the lithium value chain. Such a dynamic theoretically results in state capture by the private sector, perpetuating traditional extractive activities with low levels of value addition. In this scenario, the lithium industry would resemble other mining industries prevalent in the Global South. From

Table 3.5 Typology of State–Business Relations and Types of Industrial Policy

State capacity	*Business role*	
	Business support	Business opposition
High state capacity	Frontier Industrial Policy	Selective Industrial Policy
Low state capacity	Stagnant Industrial Policy	Non – Industrial Policy

Source: Own elaboration

the perspective of business interests, firms are unlikely to seek to scale up in the value chain due to the associated uncertainties and increased risks (Kim et al., 2019).

Given the existing low capacities, the State would be unable to drive industrialization processes independently. Without business support, a cooperative dynamic between the State and enterprises would be unfeasible, making it challenging to establish liberal policies aimed at promoting competition and regulating markets. For the lithium sector, this would mean encouraging increased exploitation of lithium while establishing norms to promote competition and regulate the market. Thus, the extractivist logic characteristic of mining activities in the Global South would persist.

Secondly, even within a context of low state capacity, industrial policies may take on a different character if supported by business actors in the lithium sector. Specifically, a context of low state capacity, coupled with business support, may lead to the implementation of stagnant policies. This implies that the State might advance ambitious industrial strategies aimed at scaling up the value chain, but these would not result in significant aggregate economic changes. Instead, the main instruments remain in pilot phases without generating substantial economic impacts, although other types of policy instruments could be developed. For example, strategic information transfer, infrastructure development, and specialized advisory services could foster value addition in the lithium value chain. Thus, while the State lacks the tools for decisive industrialization, the cooperative dynamic with businesses enables for the provision of specific instruments that marginally advance value addition within the production process.

An entirely different scenario arises when there is high state capacity. In this context, I argue that high state capacity, combined with business support for industrialization, could lead to the implementation of frontier industrial policies. This implies that robust strategies could be employed to promote specific companies and sectors. These policies would involve substantial government investment in certain industries and protectionist measures aimed at upgrading extractive activities to achieve greater value addition in production processes.

Finally, high state capacity for industrial promotion can also enable the development of more selective industrial policies, even in the face of business opposition. With adequate capacity, the State can craft industrial policies centered on value creation by establishing research and development centers and setting up funds to invest in green technologies. In conclusion, the complex interplay between state actors, businesses, and societal forces highlights the multifaceted nature of industrial policy design and implementation. Business preferences, shaped by factors such as their position in the productive structure, geographic scale of operations, and perceived costs and benefits, play a critical role in influencing policy outcomes. The heterogeneity of these preferences underscores the need for tailored approaches that align state and business interests while addressing sectoral and institutional dynamics. Furthermore, the evolution of industrial policy from state-centered control to collaborative co-production reflects a growing recognition of the importance of shared goals and adaptive strategies. Ultimately, the success of industrial policy hinges on the capacity of policymakers to integrate diverse perspectives, foster coordination, and respond to both structural challenges and changing economic conditions.

CHAPTER 4

Contextual Analysis of Lithium Policies in the Latin American Context

Introduction

This chapter outlines the contextual foundations related to lithium extraction, with a particular focus on Chile while providing relevant background for understanding the phenomenon at both the Latin American and global levels. Addressing the current climate crisis necessitates revamping the global energy supply system while simultaneously reducing greenhouse gas emissions (Bolin, 2007). Lithium plays a critical role in this transition due to its use in electromobility and its potential to replace fossil fuel sources—primary contributors to greenhouse gases—with lower-carbon energy sources (World Bank Group, 2017).

Thus, any medium- or long-term strategy to combat climate change must consider lithium: its extraction, the industries involved, and the production chains linked to global markets. This has led to a sustained increase in lithium demand in recent years, with expectations for exponential growth in the future, particularly driven by demand from China (La Nación, 2019). Currently, South Korea, China, and Japan are the leading global importers of lithium, with the European Union trailing significantly behind. Consequently, demand is concentrated in countries with advanced technological industries where lithium plays a central role (Sager, 2014).

Lithium is significant for social science research in at least three ways. First, in the context of climate change, lithium is a key component in

S. Carrasco, *From (De)regulation to Industrialization?*, Latin American Political Economy, https://doi.org/10.1007/978-3-031-77130-9_4

batteries that enable: (a) energy storage in the renewable energy sector and (b) the replacement of fossil fuels with electric power in motorized transportation. On a large scale, this could facilitate an energy transition to mitigate the effects of the climate crisis (Hochstetler, 2020). Second, this mineral is an important economic resource for exporting countries, as the exponential growth in lithium demand has significantly boosted their revenues. For some countries, lithium presents an opportunity to overcome underdevelopment by producing complex products, advancing toward sustainable energy sovereignty, and transforming their energy matrix and local transportation systems (Kazimierski, 2018). However, a third key issues is that lithium extraction has detrimental effects on communities and ecosystems near lithium mining sites. These various factors create a complex social, political, and economic framework that must be thoroughly understood to analyze lithium public policies within the South American context.

This chapter explores in detail the political economy of lithium, structuring the discussion across three key areas: 1) The environmental and energy significance of lithium, including its role in local energy sovereignty and its contribution to mitigating climate change; 2) The dynamics of lithium markets at both the Latin American and global levels; and 3) The context of lithium policies in Latin America, with a particular focus on socio-environmental conflicts.

The integration of these areas sheds light on the empirical challenges involved in crafting a lithium industrial policy in developing countries. On the one hand, there is a growing global demand for the mineral, driven by its importance in producing technological products that support the energy transition (by replacing fossil fuels) and combating climate change (by reducing pollution). On the other hand, the market has historically been dominated by private companies with high-level specialized knowledge of lithium and minimal state regulation, accompanied by varying degrees of socio-environmental conflict. Therefore, the foundational analysis provided in this chapter is crucial for a comprehensive understanding of how public policies, businesses, and state actors interact within the context of lithium extraction.

Climate Change, Energy Transition, and Lithium Extraction

Given its critical role in energy storage, lithium holds substantial implications for electromobility, the energy transition, and consequently, climate change (Fornillo, 2018). In recent decades, climate change has emerged as a global public challenge, necessitating coordinated efforts across all sectors of society to mitigate its effects. Strategies to address the climate crisis vary widely, ranging from enhancing corporate management through regulatory measures—viewing environmental issues as resource management challenges—to overhauling development models—seeing environmental problems as outcomes of capitalist dynamics (McEachern & Doyle, 2008). As such, climate change policy, like other public policies, involves diverse perspectives on how to address the issue, making the political and policy dimensions central to its formulation (Dente & Subirats, 2014).

The global climate crisis is intrinsically linked to the accumulation of greenhouse gases in the atmosphere. In this context, energy supply and transportation are the primary sectors contributing to greenhouse gas emissions worldwide, accounting for over 50% of global totals (Carter, 2018). International organizations, including the OECD, have emphasized that addressing many environmental challenges requires advancements in technology to ensure cleaner production processes (Braconier et al., 2014). There is broad consensus that environmental policy strategies aimed at combating the climate crisis must include the modernization of the energy supply system and the exploration of alternatives to fossil fuel-dependent mobility (Bolin, 2007). Recent years have witnessed significant industry shifts: many regions have transitioned from fossil fuel-based energy generation (e.g., thermal power plants) to renewable sources (e.g., solar and hydroelectric power), which produce minimal or zero carbon emissions (Carter, 2018). Chile serves as a prominent example, having achieved a notable transformation in its energy matrix, with renewable energy comprising approximately 20% of its total energy mix within a few years (Allain & Madariaga, 2020).

In contrast, the transportation sector has shown greater resistance to reducing greenhouse gas emissions (Carter, 2018). The global automotive fleet has expanded progressively, with increased demand aligning with a surge in supply. The rise of new automotive industries in Asia—particularly in China—has stimulated the market, providing consumers with more affordable options compared to traditional industries (Song et al., 2020). This expansion of fossil fuel-based mobility has had a considerable impact on pollution levels.

Although the automotive sector has not experienced a profound transformation, the advancement of electric vehicles presents a significant opportunity for transitioning to electromobility in the near future. Some European and Asian nations, such as Norway and China, have made substantial progress in reconfiguring their transportation systems to operate on electric energy. In Latin America, the decarbonization of transportation through the promotion of electric mobility has increasingly become a priority for both governmental bodies and civil society organizations.

In response, various public policy measures have been implemented, including tax incentives for the acquisition of electric vehicles, differentiated electricity tariffs, the establishment of charging infrastructure, and the formulation of national electric mobility strategies (UNEP, 2020). In this regard, Chile, and particularly its capital Santiago, stands out as a leader in Latin America in terms of electromobility advancements, exemplified by the integration of electric buses into the city's public transportation system (RED; formerly Transantiago) (UNEP, 2020). However, electric vehicles have not yet been widely adopted among the population due to their higher cost compared to traditional vehicles.

Lithium is identified as a pivotal element in the global energy transition (Kazimierski, 2018). Effectively managing this transition requires understanding of the sources, processes, and potential changes in energy production and consumption (Newell, 2021). From a political economy perspective, it is crucial to investigate how the interplay between political institutions and market forces will either sustain the reliance on fossil fuels or facilitate the transition to renewable energy sources (Newell, 2021).

While these initiatives are recognized as significant steps toward environmental protection, they underscore an inherent paradox in lithium-related activities. The push for electric transportation and renewable energy relies heavily on lithium for energy storage. Consequently, while these efforts contribute to global environmental goals, they also perpetuate and expand the lithium extraction industry, which adversely impacts the regions where extraction occurs.

Socioeconomic Dynamics of the Lithium Industry

Global Economic Dynamics in Lithium Extraction

The increasing demand for lithium necessitates specialized technical knowledge, both in terms of extraction (mining) and technological development (applications and usage), as well as market dynamics (supply and demand) (Martin et al., 2017). This underscores the strategic value of information about lithium for companies and other interested stakeholders. Consequently, the most detailed studies on lithium are often disseminated through high-value commercial reports, which are generally inaccessible to the public (Martin et al., 2017). Thus, a comprehensive characterization of the dynamics surrounding lithium becomes an essential empirical analysis for contextualization.

Lithium is a mineral utilized across a wide array of industries in the production of complex and specialized products. Specifically, lithium is used as a deoxidizer and plays a crucial role in the manufacture of glass, construction activities, industrial refrigeration systems, industrial soap production, the polymer industry and has significant applications in the nuclear industry. However, the exponential growth in lithium demand over the past two decades is primarily attributed to its pivotal role in the production of batteries for energy storage. Lithium carbonate endows these batteries with significant comparative advantages over those that do not contain this mineral. Key characteristics of lithium batteries include their high-power output, substantial storage capacity, and low weight (Martin et al., 2017). These types of batteries are commonly used in computers, mobile phones, and other technological devices. More recently, and increasingly, the use of lithium has expanded into the automotive market to produce batteries used in electric vehicles, thereby making it a crucial component in advancing electromobility (Agusdinata et al., 2018).

Over 35% of the globally extracted lithium is used in battery production, and since 2000, the global production of lithium for battery applications has grown at an annual rate of approximately 20% (Martin et al., 2017). In most of its technological applications, lithium lacks viable substitutes, making it likely that its demand will continue to grow exponentially in the coming years, especially due to its crucial role in energy storage (Martin et al., 2017). Additionally, the supply of lithium is concentrated in a few countries that possess the necessary reserves for its industrial exploitation. As of 2024, global lithium resources are estimated at 105,000 million tons—nearly ten times the estimated 14,000 million tons in 2004. Currently, half of these resources are in Latin America, specifically within the so-called 'Lithium Triangle,' a contiguous region spanning the border areas of Chile, Argentina, and Bolivia (See 4). It is important to note that "resource" refers to the results of exploration and the estimation of quantities based on geoscientific models, which have economic potential for future extraction (Fig. 4.1).

Within the total estimated global lithium resources, a subset known as Lithium Reserves refers to those resources located within a productive framework that enables their utilization. The extraction of lithium occurs in specific ecosystems, particularly salt flats, where brine containing the mineral is extracted. Globally, an estimated 23 million tons of lithium are considered extractable, with the 'Lithium Triangle'—dominated by Argentina and Chile—accounting for approximately 52% of this total (See Fig. 4.2).

Lithium extraction yields various derivatives, with lithium carbonate being the most critical for battery production. Figure 4.3 presents the evolution of lithium carbonate exports from Argentina, Chile, and Bolivia between 1990 and 2020. Significant disparities are evident in the export volumes among these Latin American countries. Chile, as the world's leading exporter of lithium, commenced its extractive operations in salt flats as early as the 1990s. A modest increase in exports is observed up

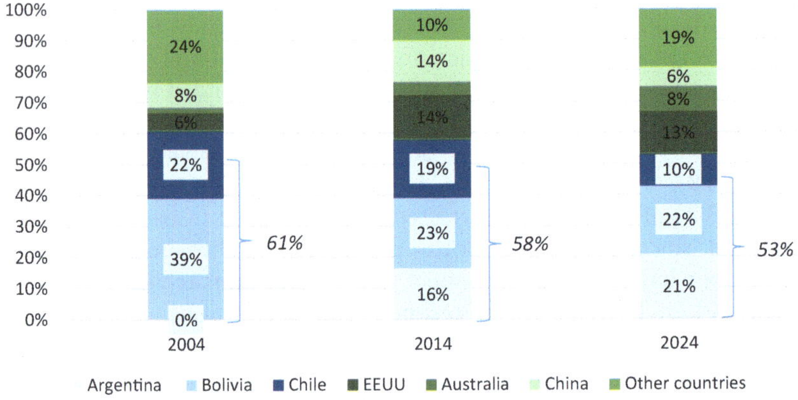

Fig. 4.1 Major lithium resources in the world. Source: Own elaboration based on U.S. Geological Survey, Mineral Commodity Summaries 2004–14-24

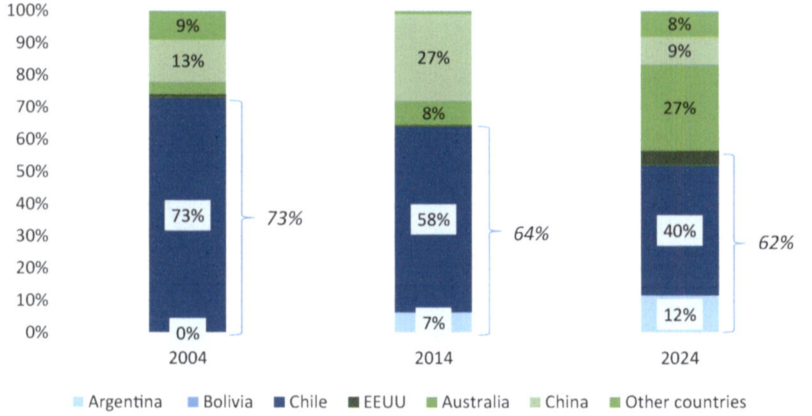

Fig. 4.2 Major Lithium Reserves in the World. Source: Own elaboration based on U.S. Geological Survey, Mineral Commodity Summaries 2004–14-24

until the 2000s, corresponding with the rising demand for this mineral in the technological industry. However, it was not until 2010 that a substantial surge in export volumes occurred, although a slight decline was noted in 2020 due to the global health and economic crises. In the mid-1990s, Chile's annual lithium carbonate exports were valued at approximately $2.7 million, whereas preliminary data for 2023 indicates production has reached 44 million tons (see Fig. 4.3). Over nearly three decades, Chile's lithium production has expanded more than 15-fold, underscoring its high global demand and strategic significance. Meanwhile, Australia has emerged as the world's largest producer, with an estimated production of 86 million tons in 2023.

In summary, Chile's lithium economic activity primarily revolves around exporting the mineral as a raw material, integrating it into global value chains where lithium is processed and used in batteries for technological products and automobiles. The battery manufacturing value chain can be broken down into five distinct stages (Jones et al., 2021): extraction/chemical refineries (which includes lithium extraction), precursor production, cathode manufacturing, battery cell production, and battery pack assembly. Figure 4.4 presents a simplified analytical model of the battery value chain, illustrating the interrelation of its various stages. Lithium is particularly critical in the production of cathodes. The most

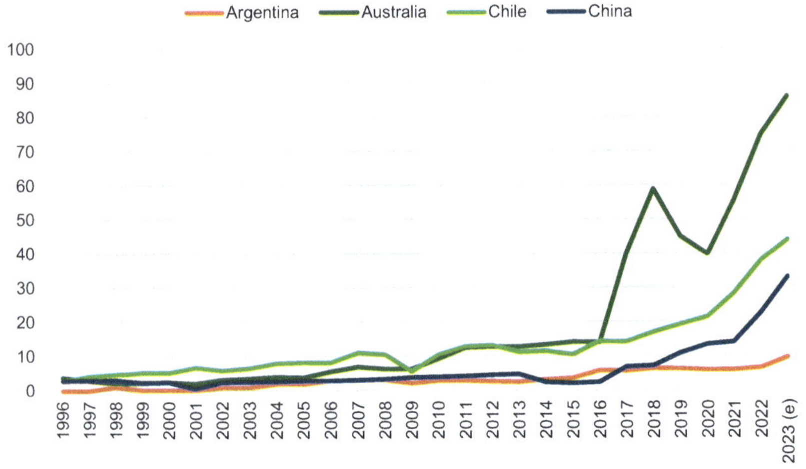

Fig. 4.3 Million Tons of Lithium Carbonate Exported by Leading Exporters Worldwide. Source: Own elaboration based on data from the U.S. Geological Survey, Mineral Commodity Summaries

specialized stage in the value chain is battery pack assembly, with packs typically customized according to the end-use device. The current trend is for end-product manufacturers, particularly in the automotive industry, to build their own battery packs.

The industry is moving toward vertical integration, as battery manufacturers aim to reduce costs and add value to their product lines. Moreover, the industry is dominated by a relatively small number of key players. Over the past 20 years, Australia, Chile, and China have emerged as the leading

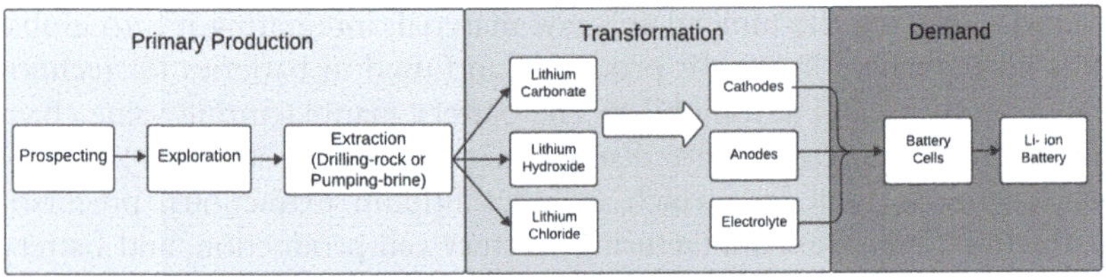

Fig. 4.4 Value Chain of Lithium-Ion Batteries. Source: Own elaboration based on Irarrazaval and Carrasco (2023)

global exporters of lithium resources (see Fig. 4.5), together accounting for approximately 80% of the world's lithium exports.

As illustrated in Fig. 4.6, the world's leading lithium-importing countries are predominantly Asian (South Korea, China, and Japan), which aligns with global economic dynamics and Asia's dominant position in the manufacturing and export of technological products (Goldin, 2016). Notably, China is the global leader in cell production, accounting for 76% of global capacity as of 2020 (Jones et al., 2021). Consequently, lithium extraction in South America is a key component of a much broader global value chain, primarily involving Asian and other Global North countries.

Moreover, it is important to highlight that the projected growth in demand is closely linked to the electromobility plans and targets of various countries. For instance, European Union countries, through the European Green Deal, have committed to reducing greenhouse gas emissions from transport by 90% by 2050, using 1990 as the baseline (European Court of Auditors, 2021). Similarly, during COP24 (2018 in Poland), the Declaration on Electromobility was signed by over 40 countries to promote the development of technologies related to electromobility. Specifically, the demand for lithium for electric vehicles is expected to

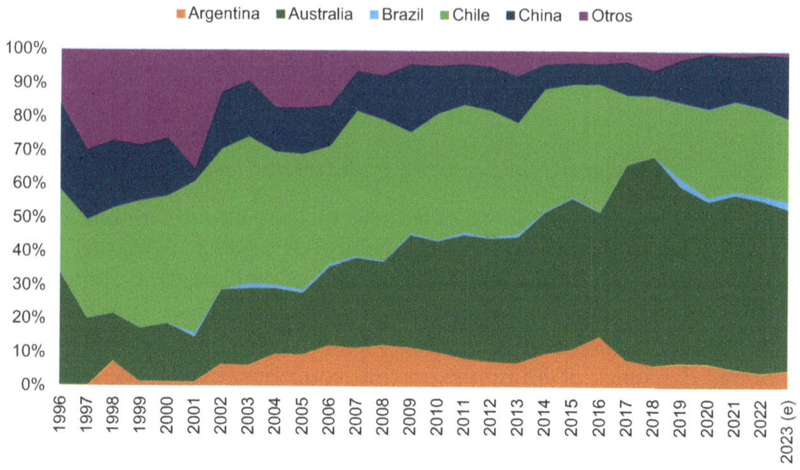

Fig. 4.5 Market share of lithium carbonate exports by major global exporters. Source: Own elaboration based on data from the U.S. Geological Survey, Mineral Commodity Summaries

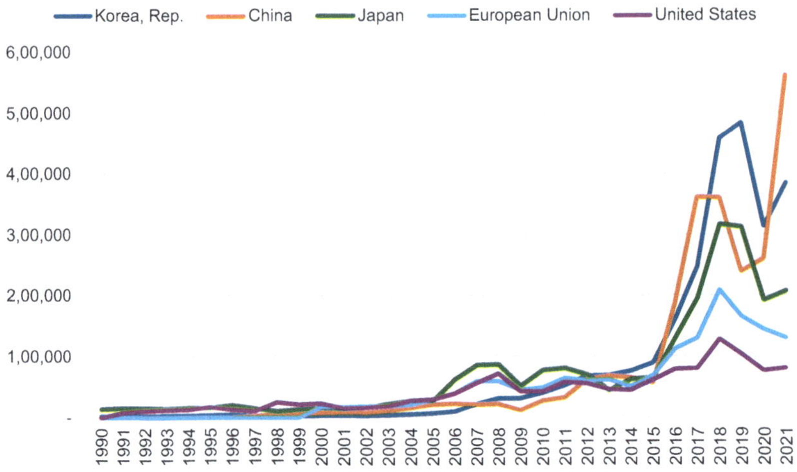

Fig. 4.6 Leading Lithium-Importing Countries in 2021 (import values in thousands of USD). Source: Own elaboration based on data from WITS

increase by 38 times between 2016 and 2030. By 2030, according to COCHILCO (2020), demand from electric vehicles could account for 79% of global lithium consumption. Even the Chilean government has set ambitious electromobility targets, aiming for 100% of vehicles sold in Chile to be electric by 2035 (San Juan, 2021).

Economic Challenges of the Lithium Industry

The development of extractive activities, such as lithium mining, often causes significant—sometimes irreversible—damage to people, livelihoods, and the environment, posing a major challenge for contemporary societies (Goldin, 2016). In fact, empirical evidence suggests that economies specializing in the export of primary goods, as seen in the economic dynamics of lithium-exporting countries, experience hindered long-term growth (Dowrick, 2004).

Another economic challenge arising from lithium exploitation pertains to the labor market. The globalizing context of extractive economies has introduced new commercial dynamics that impact the labor market, such as unemployment, job precarization, and informality (Hay, 2018). Employment is a central issue for governments, companies, and citizens, with it being a major concern in Latin America (Pagés et al., 2009). The incorporation of new technologies has displaced some traditional trades and jeopardized others, generally marginalizing less skilled workers and exacerbating inequality (Acemoglu, 2002). In development economics, there is a consensus that in a globalized world, technological scaling and the development of advanced human capital are crucial for creating high-value niches distinct from basic commodity markets (Pérez, 2010). However, in the case of lithium, mineral exploitation is heavily dependent on international prices.

In extractive activities, a common discursive justification for such economies is the significant role they play in the local labor market. It is often claimed that companies provide employment opportunities to local workers, thereby stimulating the economic activity in the areas adjacent to mining operations. Nonetheless, this is not occurring in the case of lithium. Empirical evidence indicates that, particularly in the lithium industry, local labor has been declining in recent years (Liu & Agusdinata, 2020). Despite being an extractive activity, lithium extraction requires a certain level of technical expertise often unavailable in the local area. Consequently, companies attract foreign workers who possess the necessary skills and knowledge for this sector.

This section has developed two arguments regarding the economic dynamics of lithium. First, there is a growing demand for the mineral to produce batteries used in technological products and the electromobility industry. Among Latin American countries, Chile has consistently increased resource exploitation in line with this demand, integrating with global value chains, primarily with Asian and European markets. Conversely, there are implications for the local labor market, as the benefits of employment are questioned since many lithium workers come from regions other than the extraction site. Therefore, economic implications can be observed at both micro and macro levels, where the global boom in lithium provides a context for better understanding the actions of companies involved in mineral extraction. This topic will be revisited in the forthcoming chapters of the book.

Institutional Context of the Latin American Lithium Policies

Lithium policies are feasible within specific institutional contexts that support the activities undertaken. In this regard, understanding the general characteristics and capacities of Latin American countries is crucial for contextualizing the specific dynamics surrounding lithium.

The Latin American state is not inherently weak; rather, its strength varies depending on the country and historical period analyzed. For instance, Chile demonstrates significant institutional strength, particularly concerning the professionalization of public management (Osorio, 2019; González-Bustamante et al., 2016; Arámbula, 2015; Soifer, 2012) and the scope of its public policies. These aspects align with comparative empirical evidence, such as data collected by the World Bank, which indicates that Chile exhibits higher levels of government effectiveness compared to Argentina and Bolivia, as illustrated in the Fig. 4.7. Although Chile has seen a decline in this index in recent years, it remains at levels significantly higher than those of Argentina and Bolivia, with Bolivia exhibiting the lowest levels of effectiveness among the three countries.

A similar trend is observed when examining other indices that reflect state capacity at an aggregate level. For example, according to V-Dem data, Chile exhibits the lowest levels of public sector corruption, even considering recent corruption cases uncovered in the country (Schorr, 2021). Despite this, more nuanced differences emerge in subnational

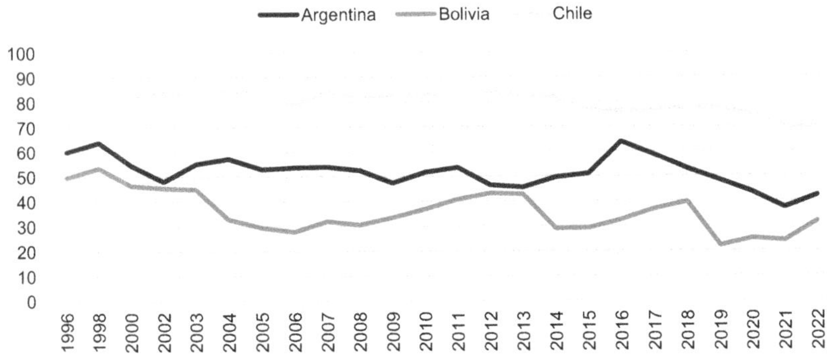

Fig. 4.7 Government Effectiveness Index in Lithium Triangle Countries. Source: Own elaboration based on World Bank data

indicators; for instance, access to public services in rural areas of Chile is comparable to that of Argentina. While historical levels of state capacity provide context for understanding state functions in the Lithium Triangle countries, they do not necessarily dictate the feasibility of lithium-related initiatives. High levels of state capacity do not automatically translate into the capability to advance value-added processes in a productive sector. Countries with lower state capacity can still develop specific capacities to advance the industrialization of certain sectors.

The argument, following the relational perspective of state capacity outlined in previous chapters, is that a state's capacity varies depending on the sector being analyzed and its relationship with other key actors. This approach moves beyond a purely national-level analysis of the State. While general state capacity indicators provide an overarching view, in the context of green industrial policy, the development of sector-specific capacity becomes particularly crucial—especially as this is a relatively new challenge for countries in the Global South. Thus, state capacity in this domain cannot be understood in absolute terms alone.

Regarding companies, several factors must be considered, particularly the context in which they operate and their interests, as these may vary between types of companies and sources of capital. In the current economic context, lithium is commonly referred to as "white gold," with Chile, Argentina, and Bolivia being likened to the "Saudi Arabia of lithium" (Fornillo & Zicarí, 2019). However, it is currently not feasible to achieve 100% domestic production of lithium batteries. Even China must import components (Fornillo & Zicarí, 2019). Consequently, most companies (whether European, Asian, or American) have primarily chosen to partner with various mining companies—typically transnational corporations—to finance their projects, exploration, and exploitation efforts, aiming to secure access to the resource for extended periods ranging from 20 to 50 years. No company is likely to undertake a multimillion-dollar, long-term technological conversion plan without confidence in the consistent provision of necessary inputs (Muscatelli, 2010).

This situation implies that strategies for adding value to lithium require the collaboration of both national and transnational companies. Another important contextual factor is the existing conditions in countries for integrating companies into the value chain. In this regard, the World Bank's Ease of Doing Business Index summarizes a range of indicators related to contract enforcement, credit acquisition, tax payments, investor protection, and the reliability of contracts with the government.

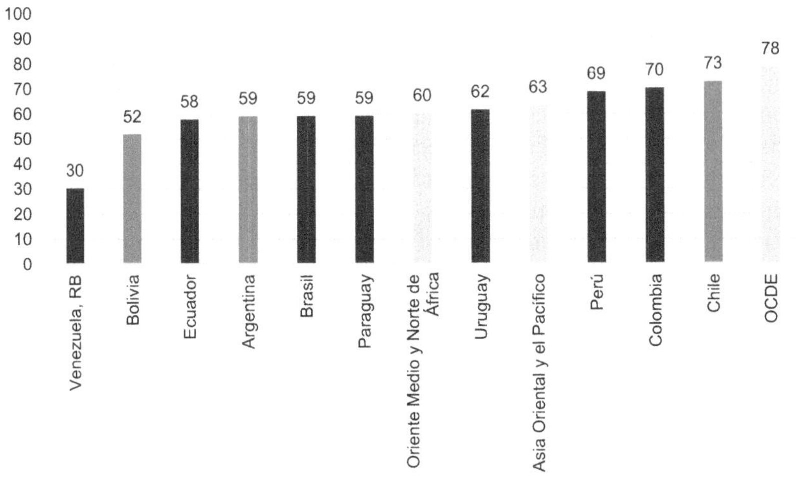

Fig. 4.8 Ease of Doing Business Index in Latin America, Lithium Triangle, and Major Global Regions (2020). Source: Own elaboration based on data from the Ease of Doing Business Index

Using this index, Fig. 4.8 illustrates the ease of doing business across various Latin American countries. The index ranges from 0 to 100, with higher scores indicating greater ease of conducting business in a country. As shown, the lowest scores are around 30 points for Venezuela, while the highest is Chile, with a score of 72.6. Among the Lithium Triangle countries, Chile is followed by Argentina, which has an index of 59 points, and Bolivia, with a score of 51.7. Although the index itself does not have direct implications for lithium policies, it reflects the broader economic-institutional contexts in which these policies are developed.

Socio-Environmental Dynamics of the Lithium Industry

In recent years, environmental issues have increasingly occupied the political agendas of Latin American governments. Since the 2000s, the rise in commodity prices has spurred economic growth in Latin America. Concurrently, the intensification of extractive activities has led to increased environmental degradation and heightened socio-environmental conflict (Amengual & Dargent, 2020). In response, many countries in the region have implemented institutional changes, establishing agencies dedicated to environmental protection (Orihuela & Paredes, 2017). However, some critics argue that these changes have merely served as a facade, demonstrating governmental concern for environmental damage while maintaining the status quo in resource exploitation (Fernández & Garay, 2020).

A similar situation pertains to the institutional framework and environmental issues associated with lithium. Over a decade ago, Chile undertook a significant transformation of its environmental institutions aimed at enhancing environmental protection (Madariaga, 2019). This led to the creation of a complex institutional framework, including a Ministry of Environment, an Environmental Superintendence, an Environmental Impact Assessment Service, and Environmental Courts. Nevertheless, these institutions have not adequately addressed certain socio-environmental issues surrounding the Atacama Salt Flat.

Lithium extraction generates various socio-environmental impacts at the local level. One of the most significant issues highlighted by the literature is the depletion of available water resources, which are crucial for the communities and ecosystems of the salt flats (Agusdinata et al., 2018). Lithium extraction and associated refining processes require substantial amounts of water, already scarce in extraction areas due to the prevailing desert climate (Lunde, 2020). Estimates suggest that obtaining 300–400 kilograms of lithium requires between 20,000 and 30,000 liters of fresh water, with a water reuse rate of between 30 and 40% (Fornillo, 2018). However, estimates of water consumption in lithium activities are not yet fully resolved, with different experts providing varying calculations (Calvo, 2017; Romeo, 2019).

The issue of water extraction has been identified in all three countries, as they use similar techniques involving the pumping of brines from within the salt flats followed by evaporation in large pools (Romeo, 2019). Additionally, lithium mining is often referred to as "water mining" due to the high-water consumption associated with this activity (Garcés, 2018). The following analysis examines the main conflictual dynamics surrounding lithium extraction in Chile, Argentina, and Bolivia, highlighting the socio-environmental tensions and providing context for the political and economic dimensions central to this book. After all, the interaction between political and economic actors does not occur in a vacuum; rather, in activities related to natural resource extraction, socio-environmental contexts are crucial for understanding the interactions within public policy arenas and across various spatial levels (Carrasco et al., 2023). To better contextualize the conflicts in the Lithium Triangle countries, Fig. 4.9 presents a map identifying the number of lithium mining projects, with data for 2023–2024 for Chile, Argentina, and Bolivia.

Socio-Environmental Conflict in Chile

In Chile, various conflicts and tensions related to water use in lithium mining have emerged. These issues are frequently compared to copper mining, given its economic significance and geographical proximity. For instance, the Peina community is simultaneously impacted by both lithium and copper projects (Blair et al., 2022). The most prominent case in lithium mining involves the Atacama Salt Flat (Romeo, 2019). According to a report from the General Water Directorate (DGA), the Atacama Salt Flat is overexploited due to industrial usage, as the same water sources are utilized for both copper and lithium mining (Romeo, 2019).

The Atacameño people, indigenous to the area around the Atacama Salt Flat, face significant water supply issues due to the water stress caused by mining activities and excessive water rights in the basin (Jerez, 2018). These communities have expressed concerns that both state and company-provided information inadequately represents the scale of water resource exploitation. For example, companies report the volumes of brine pumped, leading to a conflict of interest as the information is produced by entities with a financial stake in the resource (Romeo, 2019). Additionally, it has been suggested that the Chilean State lacks sufficient independent data on the salt flats' hydrology (Morales, 2021), revealing an information asymmetry between the public and private sectors. The public policy implications of this issue are explored in more detail in Chapter 4.

Socio-environmental conflict in Chile has also taken on legal and institutional dimensions. For example, the Environmental Superintendence filed charges against SQM for exceeding their authorized extraction volumes between 2013 and 2015 (Romeo, 2019). Moreover, companies create competition for natural resources with local communities due to the establishment of mining camps near freshwater sources. The Toconao Community in northern Chile illustrates this problem (Jerez, 2018), having to rely on alternative water sources such as the Vilaco River and the Peana and Silapeti springs to supplement their water supply (Romeo,

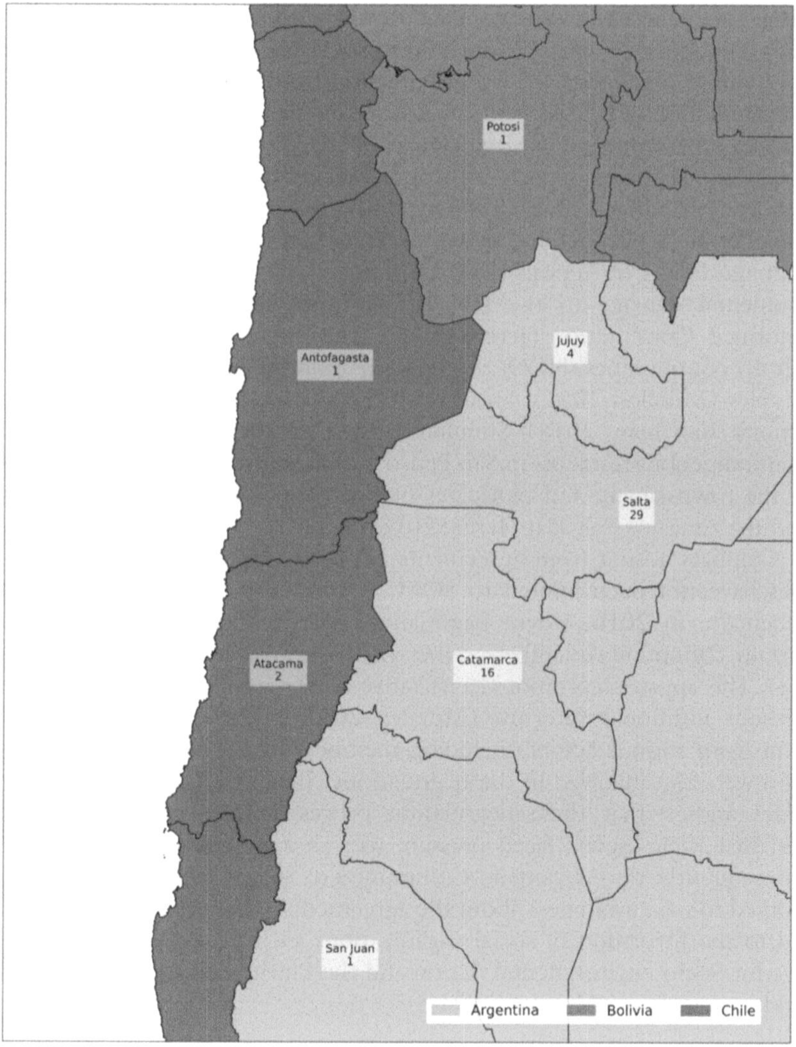

Fig. 4.9 Lithium Projects by Region in the Lithium Triangle. Source: Own elaboration based on the Ministry of Mining of Chile, the Secretariat of Mining of Argentina, and YLB data

2019). Conflicts between companies and communities are not a new phenomenon. For example, in 2007, SQM clashed with the Toconao community over increased water extraction from unauthorized wells and contamination of the salt flat from sewage discharged from mining camps, causing environmental damage (Jerez, 2018).

Different aspects of socio-environmental conflict are evident in Chile. For instance, after the 2018 agreement between CORFO and SQM to triple lithium production, two protection actions were filed with the Santiago Court of Appeals (FIMA, 2018). These actions addressed environmental damage to the salt flat and the lack of Free, Prior, and Informed Consultation (Jerez, 2018). They were initiated by Atacama salt flat communities, NGOs, foundations, and the Council of Atacameño Peoples (Morales, 2021). However, the courts ultimately rejected these actions (San Juan, 2018). Simultaneously, Atacameño communities and non-indigenous residents in San Pedro mobilized, staging demonstrations in the town square and blockades on roads between SQM's operations and the Atacama Salt Flat (Jerez, 2018).

Conflicts arising from agreements between communities and companies have not been limited to SQM. A similar situation occurred with Albemarle in 2016, where negotiations were conducted directly with certain community members rather than through indigenous consultation. This approach promoted a narrative of increasing lithium production without additional water use (Morales, 2021). The situation faced criticism from various actors, including members of the same communities who were not involved in the negotiations (Blair et al., 2022). Communities argued that these negotiation processes were poorly informed and that their leaders faced pressure to sign agreements (Jerez, 2018). Consequently, the Atacameño Community of Solcor, along with activists, worked to raise awareness about the agreements. These circumstances also led to the formation of social organizations such as the Chañar Collective for Socio-environmental Action and the Plurinational Observatory of Andean Salt Flats (Morales, 2021).

Socio-Environmental Conflict in Argentina

In Argentina, various conflicts related to mining have emerged, particularly in the northeastern region, with recent years witnessing notable disputes concerning lithium mining. Historically, these areas have voiced opposition to mining activities, primarily due to water usage concerns.

Slogans such as "water is worth more than gold" echo throughout the provinces, where communities express their resistance to the mining industry (Gómez, 2022). Regarding lithium, Wagner and Walter (2020) identified four conflicts associated with lithium mining using the Environmental Justice Atlas as a tool. They also note an increase in conflict related to lithium mining in recent years.

From the perspective of indigenous communities, lithium is not viewed as an opportunity in the face of climate change. Instead, it is perceived as a threat to the already arid and low-precipitation areas they inhabit (Sticco et al., 2019). These communities, guided by their worldview, regard the salt flats and land as common goods (Argento & Zicari, 2017), establishing a spiritual connection that respects ecological cycles (Jerez, 2018). This sentiment is articulated in the "Manifesto of the Table of Original Communities of the Salinas Grandes and Laguna de Guayatayoc Basin," which states:

> "They say that with this mineral, they will be able to manufacture electric cars that supposedly do not pollute the planet. But what no one mentions is that extracting lithium consumes enormous amounts of freshwater from the Puna's underground. (...) The price of lithium is the death of our territory and our people" (Indigenous Communities of the Salinas Grandes and Laguna de Guayatayoc Basin, and Jujuy, Argentina, 2023).

On the other hand, Argentina's federal political-administrative structure places the management of natural resources in the hands of provincial governments (Gómez, 2022; Blair et al., 2022). This institutional arrangement exacerbates conflicts over permits issued by subnational units and the diffuse responsibilities assumed by these entities. One of the most problematic issues, similar to Chile, is water consumption. In Argentina, there is a lack of clarity regarding water consumption data, as such data are provided by the companies without effective state oversight (Gómez, 2021). Consequently, state capacity regarding water usage information has been limited. For instance, when the province of Catamarca sought to invoice FMC Lithium for groundwater usage, it had to request the information from the company itself, as it lacked the means to obtain it independently (Gómez, 2022). Issues of reporting have also been questioned, as, in various cases such as with the mining company

Orocobre, only the water consumption per ton of lithium carbonate has been reported, not the water used for maintenance tasks (Gómez, 2022).[1]

In Argentina, water conflicts have been significantly influenced by interactions with indigenous communities, who have opposed extraction activities in various regions due to concerns about irrational water use. In some instances, these communities have hired independent professionals to measure water levels separately from company activities (Villa María Vivo, 2014). The conflict is particularly evident in the provinces of Salta and Jujuy. In Jujuy, the Australian company Orocobre has conducted exploration activities in the Salinas Grandes region, while French companies Bolloré and Eramet have shown interest in the Salta sector of the basin. The presence of mining machinery, vehicles, sample collection activities, social aid programs, and failed attempts to establish agreements with local communities have heightened concerns (Jerez, 2018).

Mining operations by Orocobre, Bolloré, and Eramet have resulted in significant environmental damage to the Salinas Grandes basin. This has led to contamination of the salt flats, with freshwater aquifers becoming mixed with saline water, thereby disrupting the basin's hydrological cycles (Jerez, 2018). These adverse effects have prompted community resistance to exploration and extraction activities and led to the formation of the "Mesa de las 33 Comunidades de la Cuenca de las Salinas Grandes y la Laguna Guayatayoc" (Argento & Zicari, 2018), which represents 6,600 Kolla and Atacameño families. This conflict has been recognized as one of the most "intense" in Argentina (Gómez, 2022). The Mesa's initiatives include providing legal support, assistance, and research within the Salinas Grandes and Laguna Guayatayoc basin (Argento & Zicari, 2018). Furthermore, communities have organized vigils in the basin to prevent mining companies from extracting mineral samples (Jerez, 2018).

In the Olaroz salt flat, residents of Cranzulí and Susques reported in 2018 that Orocobre was using specialized missiles to disperse clouds with water to prevent rain from affecting the lithium brine drying process. This intervention was due to climatic conditions impacting evaporation rates, which had reached their lowest values in a decade (Jerez, 2018).

In Catamarca, notable incidents have occurred. Environmental organizations accused Minera del Altiplano of depleting the Trapiche

[1] "Se referiría al agua usada para mantener caminos de acceso y otras infraestructuras, apoyar las actividades del campamento minero y proveer condiciones de vida adecuadas a los trabajadores" (Gómez, 2021).

River aquifer (Gómez, 2022). Additionally, the Catamarca government approved the Livent project (El Ancasti, 2020), which led to resistance from the "Atacameños del Altiplano" community. They requested that the Ministry of Mining suspend the construction of an aqueduct by Livent to extract water from the Los Patos River. Authorities in Catamarca responded by asserting that the river had sufficient water and that the local population did not rely on that basin. In 2020, the same region faced conflict with Canadian company Galaxy Resources, which conducted drilling in the river and extracted water to assess the feasibility of the Sal de Vida project located in the Salar del Hombre Muerto (Gómez, 2022).

This section has outlined and exemplified some of the most significant conflicts in Argentina. Although other conflicts may exist, the focus here has been on illustrating their occurrence and discussing these emblematic cases.

Socio-Environmental Conflict in Bolivia

The situation in Bolivia may be less contentious compared to its neighboring countries, yet it is not devoid of issues. The country currently lacks the necessary infrastructure for large-scale industrial production, with only one project in Uyuni managed by Yacimientos de Litio Bolivianos (YLB) under state control (Romeo, 2019). Nonetheless, once production scales up, impacts on indigenous communal lands are anticipated, particularly as the planned mining area is already occupied by an existing mining venture (Campanini, 2013). Estimates based on the pilot plant suggest that annual water consumption could range from 225,000,000 to 612,500,000 liters, depending on the efficiency of water use (Romeo, 2019). Furthermore, other researchers argue that Environmental Impact Assessments remain inadequate and could endanger both the ecological stability of the salt flats and the communities and rural settlements that depend on livestock and agriculture (Campanini, 2021). Conflicts have also emerged concerning partnerships with other stakeholders, such as the German firm ACI Systems GmbH. The Comité Cívico Potosino has raised objections and mobilized against the establishment of this company, citing concerns about its technical expertise, financial stability, and experience in lithium mining (Campanini, 2022).

Empirical evidence indicates that lithium extraction adversely impacts biodiversity in the salt flats. The water in these ecosystems contains crucial microorganisms for sustaining larger organisms. For instance, flamingos that inhabit these areas rely on these microorganisms for food, and disruptions in the ecosystem force them to migrate, among other detrimental effects (Dorador et al., 2020). Salt flats are closed evaporitic basins that host significant biodiversity and endemism, in addition to serving as water reserves (Fornillo, 2018; Dorador et al., 2020). This highlights their considerable ecological importance.

Additionally, lithium extraction impacts the culture and livelihoods of local communities in at least two significant ways. First, mining activities disrupt hydrological cycles that are integral to certain community rituals. Second, water scarcity resulting from mining threatens traditional practices, such as pastoralism, in the highlands (Kalazich et al., 2019). Consequently, water shortages undermine livestock farming, affecting local economic development, and reduce water availability for human consumption.

These different factors offer a clearer understanding of the specific dynamics and challenges associated with lithium extraction. There are significant expectations surrounding the development of renewable energy and electromobility technologies as potential solutions to the major economic and environmental risks facing the world today (Sager, 2014). However, this also introduces a range of local socio-ecological issues that are often overlooked. In conclusion, the socio-environmental conflict of the Lithium Triangle countries highlights the difficulty of reconciling economic growth expectations with environmental considerations. At the same time, it poses significant challenges for public policies to address a central issue in new strategic sectors linked to energy transition, such as lithium. On the one hand, economic activity promises of future improvements in material and environmental conditions due to its utility in the electric mobility industry; however, it simultaneously generates socio-environmental problems at the local level.

PART II

The Configuration of Lithium Policies in the South American Context

CHAPTER 5

State Capacity in Chile's Lithium Policy

Introduction

The section explores the state–business relationships within the lithium industrial policies of Chile, Argentina, and Bolivia. In the Chilean context, I argue that, while there have been advancements in administrative, political, and institutional capacities to enhance the value-added processes of lithium, these developments often face resistance from companies regarding various policy provisions. This dynamic has led to the emergence of a selective industrial policy, as discussed in Chapter 3.

Chapter 5 specifically examines the state capacity that has been developed concerning lithium and their connection to public policy. This chapter is organized into three sections. First, it outlines the legal dimension of the lithium sector in Chile, detailing the existing legislation, the operational framework of the lithium industry, and the historical context from which it emerged.

Second, it presents the process of building political capacities to formulate lithium policies. This section analyzes the evolution of public discourse on lithium in Chile, the key actors involved, and how these discourses have been contested, demonstrating the dominance of specific narratives about the lithium industrialization.

Third, I discuss how specific discourses have been channeled by influential political actors to shape industrial policies concerning lithium. I argue that administrative capacities have been developed to support

S. Carrasco, *From (De)regulation to Industrialization?*, Latin American Political Economy, https://doi.org/10.1007/978-3-031-77130-9_5

lithium policy. This includes the formation of a broad coalition of political and social actors advocating for policy change, the establishment of an expert committee for policy formulation, and the creation of an institutional framework within CORFO, designed to coordinate and implement the policy effectively. This framework includes officials trained to manage the related processes.

The Institutional–Legal Dimension of Lithium Extraction in Chile

Historical Background of Lithium Policy

Prior to its recognized use in electromobility, lithium was considered a strategic element during World War II to produce thermonuclear bombs, albeit as a minor component. Given its nuclear applications, during Augusto Pinochet's military dictatorship (1973–1990), Chile enacted a decree to regulate lithium as a strategic resource. Decree Law No. 2886 of 1979 established lithium as a mineral with a unique legal status, distinct from other minerals governed by the Mining Code. This regulation prohibited the granting of mining rights for lithium to private entities and instead placed it under the jurisdiction of the Chilean Nuclear Energy Commission (CCHEN) for any extraction activities (Lagos, 2012; Poveda, 2020).[1] Subsequently, the Organic Law on Mining Concessions of 1982 reaffirmed that no mining concessions could be granted for lithium. The Mining Code of 1983 further solidified the legal framework, affirming the non-concessible nature of lithium.[2]

[1] Article 5 of the decree states: "Due to national interest, from the effective date of this decree-law, lithium is reserved for the State. The only exception to the previous provision is: a) Lithium found in mining rights established on lithium or any of the substances listed in the first paragraph of Article 3 of the Mining Code, which, at the time of publication of this decree-law in the Official Gazette, have their survey act registered, are in force, and whose claim has been registered before January 1, 1979.".

[2] Article 6 of the decree-law stated: "Due to national interest, natural atomic materials and lithium, as well as their extracted and concentrated forms, and their derivatives and compounds, shall not be subject to any legal transactions unless executed or concluded by the Chilean Nuclear Energy Commission, with or under its prior authorization. If the Commission deems it appropriate to grant authorization, it will also determine the conditions under which it is granted. Except for reasons specified in the grant of authorization, such authorization may not be modified or revoked by the Commission, nor waived by the interested party.".

However, this regulation did not extend to mining titles established prior to the promulgation of Decree No. 2886 of 1979. Existing mining claims as of that year were organized as follows: the Corporación de Fomento de la Producción [Corporation of Production Promotion] (CORFO) held more than 50% of the Atacama Salt Flat, the principal global source of lithium extraction. Additionally, the state-owned company CODELCO owned the entire Pedernales Salt Flat, and a portion of the Maricunga Salt Flat was held by private entities (Poveda, 2020).

It is worth noting that the mining legislation grants the president the authority to establish exploitation conditions in three ways: through the State or its enterprises, via administrative concessions, or through special operations contracts with private entities (Poveda, 2020). In the context of lithium, these mechanisms can be employed based on the configuration of lithium mining claims established before 1979. Given that CORFO holds most of these, it remains a key player in the future of lithium and its associated policies. Table 5.1 illustrates this configuration.

Finally, a central paradox emerges within the legal framework established around lithium. On one hand, the institutional structure creates a distinct regulatory regime for lithium, separate from traditional mining, to protect it from exploitation by private actors. However, during the same dictatorship, legal mechanisms were established to permit exploitation, initially on an exceptional basis. Over time, this exception has increasingly become the rule, as CORFO gradually incorporated various private actors into the exploitation of lithium resources from the salt flats. The next section examines CORFO's specific role in shaping the current governance of lithium.

Table 5.1 Lithium mining holdings by type of actor

Type of actor	*Salar*	*Percentage of Salt Flat Ownership*
CORFO	Salar de Atacama	55%
CODELCO	Salar de Pedernales	100%
	Salar de Maricunga	18%
ENAMI	Salar de Aguilar	4%
Other private groups	Salar de Maricunga	25%

Source: Own elaboration based on Poveda 2020

Institutional Framework for Lithium Exploitation in Chile

The Corporación de Fomento de la Producción (CORFO) has been the primary public institution involved in developing lithium policies in Chile. As the owner of the largest lithium reserves in northern Chile—comprising half of the world's known reserves—CORFO has played a pivotal role in shaping public policy, particularly during President Michelle Bachelet's second term (2014–2018). To fully understand the development of lithium exploitation in Chile, it is essential to examine CORFO's historical context.

Established in 1939 in response to a devastating earthquake that struck central-southern Chile, particularly Chillán, CORFO was created to address the widespread destruction caused by one of the most catastrophic earthquakes in Chile's history. This disaster acted as a critical juncture, significantly enhancing state capacity, particularly in the productive sector (Gil, 2022). Over the decades, CORFO has evolved into a central institution in Chilean state development, serving as a financier, entrepreneur, innovator, and researcher (Gil, 2022). CORFO has become a leading Latin American institution in promoting industrialization (Nazer, 2016). From its inception, this institution has been characterized by a governance structure based on a strategic alliance between the State and business groups, facilitated by technocratic government officials with a strong sense of cohesion (Silva, 2010).

Before the 1973 coup, CORFO was the most significant public organization in Chile, exemplifying state-led development in Latin America (Orihuela, 2018). During the dictatorship, however, CORFO's role, and more broadly, the state's role in national industrialization, was dismantled. The economic liberalization of this period, which included reducing the state's economic role, deregulating economic activities, and privatizing state-owned enterprises, is well-documented (E. Silva, 1996; Álvarez, 2015).

In this context, during the 1980s, CORFO initiated studies to assess the viability of exploiting potassium and lithium from its mineral holdings in the salt flats (CIPER, 2015). Reflecting the economic logic of the dictatorship, CORFO sought commercial partners—private companies—to invest in these resources. In 1980, CORFO and the American company

Foote Mineral established the Sociedad Chilena del Litio (SCL),[3] with CORFO holding a 45% stake through the transfer of lithium mining rights in the Salar de Atacama (Lagos, 2012). The contract granted SCL exclusive rights to operate in the Salar de Atacama for an eight-year period (Poveda, 2020; Gravel, 2015).

In 1983, leveraging previous initiatives, CORFO launched a bidding process to involve private companies in the extraction of lithium, along with other minerals found in the salt flats, such as boron and potassium. As a result, in 1986, CORFO entered into a new agreement with the American firm Amax Exploration Inc. and the Chilean company Molymet. Together, these companies formed the Sociedad Minera Salar de Atacama (Minsal), which was tasked with managing operations in the Salar de Atacama. Amax Inc. held the largest share in the partnership, as illustrated in Table 5.2.

A lease agreement was established, allowing CORFO to rent its mining rights to both companies until 2030. In return, the lease contract stipulated a royalty of 6.8% (canon) that Minsal was required to pay CORFO (Poveda, 2020). However, this joint venture never proceeded with mineral extraction due to the dominant role SQM began to assume, a topic that will be discussed in the subsequent section. It is noteworthy that, unlike the agreement with SCL, the contract with Minsal was a lease arrangement and did not involve the transfer of mineral ownership. Feasibility studies conducted in 1989 estimated that an investment of $360

Table 5.2 Formation of SQM and Albemarle from the 1980s privatization process

Society	*Institutions*	*Percentage of participation*
Minera Salar de Atacama (Minsal)—today SQM	Amax Inc	63,75%
	CORFO	25%
	Molymet	11,25%
Sociedad Chilena del Litio (SCL)—today Albemarle	Foote Mineral	55%
	CORFO	45%

Source: Own elaboration based on Lagos (2012)

[3] Subsequently, the Chilean Lithium Company would become Albemarle, which, together with SQM, is responsible for lithium exploitation in Chile until now.

million would be required to extract up to 180,000 tons of metallic lithium (Lagos, 2012).

Among the primary private entities involved in lithium extraction today are Albemarle and SQM, whose origins trace back to the privatization processes and contracts arranged by CORFO during the 1980s and 1990s. Albemarle's involvement began when CORFO sold its 45% stake in SCL to its partner Foote Mineral at the end of the 1980s, thereby completing the privatization process initiated earlier (Poveda, 2020). SCL continued as a private entity until it was renamed Rockwood Lithium in 2012. In 2015, the American company Albemarle Corporation acquired the holding, establishing itself as one of the two companies currently engaged in lithium extraction.

SQM, on the other hand, is the leading company responsible for lithium extraction in Chile. Originally a state-owned enterprise established during President Frei Montalva's administration in the late 1960s (Cofré, 2019), SQM was privatized during the Pinochet dictatorship. Julio Ponce Lerou, Pinochet's son-in-law and a high-ranking official during this period, acquired significant control of SQM through the so-called "cascade companies"[4]—Pampa Calichera, Oro Blanco, and Norte Grande (Hernández, 2018). This led him to serve as president for 28 years, until 2015, when he was forced to step down amid political corruption scandals (Matamala, 2015). With the return to democracy in the early 1990s, the government opted not to reverse the privatizations carried out during the dictatorship (Cofré, 2019). Instead, to support economic growth and avoid political conflicts, many of the policies from the dictatorship era were continued (E. Silva, 1996). Consequently, SQM remained a private company and began investing in lithium.

For feasibility reasons, Minsal—the company established during the dictatorship—began lithium production in 1996, four years later than originally projected. Amax, the primary partner in the joint venture, was unwilling to absorb these additional costs. At this juncture, SQM intervened, acquiring 75% of Minsal's shares in 1993, with prior authorization

[4] SQM divided its ownership into various investment entities traded on the stock exchange, all of which included Ponce Lerou. These entities were referred to as "cascade companies" because their ownership controlled SQM "upstream" (Hernández, 2018). Years later, the Superintendency of Securities and Insurance (SVS) found that Ponce Lerou, along with other executives, devised a scheme to benefit certain shareholders at the expense of others, who incurred significant financial losses (Hernández, 2018). This scheme was orchestrated through the cascade companies.

from CORFO, as the mining rights still belonged to this entity. Thus, although CORFO retained a 25% stake in the company, SQM emerged as the principal actor responsible for lithium extraction within Minsal.

In 1994, Minsal, now comprised of SQM and CORFO, was restructured into a public limited company. Under the new legal framework, the partners increased their capital, effectively reducing CORFO's stake to 18% (Poveda, 2020). In 1995, CORFO held a public offering of its shares, which were fully acquired by SQM, making it the sole owner of Minsal. The company was subsequently renamed SQM Salar S.A., securing control over a significant portion of the Salar de Atacama's mining rights.

This development must be understood within the broader context of the privatization process during President Frei's administration (1994–2000), when CORFO sold its shares in various companies, including those of Minsal. While privatization and deindustrialization are often associated with the dictatorship, it was under Frei's government that the final blow was dealt, as noted by one interviewee:

> "Basically, it relates to the fact that the Chilean State decided to proceed this way. There is much discussion about how SQM was handed over to Ponce Lerou at the end of the 80s, before the 1988 plebiscite and before Aylwin assumed the presidency. However, later, Frei's government made a very drastic handover of lithium to companies. I mean, a contract that, if you look at it, is a contract without any restrictions—like handing over everything" (Interview 1—National Lithium Commission).

Therefore, the contracts established during Frei's administration conferred a central role to private companies with minimal state control, setting the institutional trajectory for state–market relations in the subsequent years. It is argued that the benefits granted to private companies align with the Frei government's emphasis on private investment projects (Carruthers & Rodríguez, 2009), alongside the relatively minor role of lithium exploitation during the 1990s. At that time, it was difficult to foresee lithium's future significance as a strategic sector for energy transition processes, as recalled by a deputy minister of that era:

> "To be fully transparent, during the 1990s, when the Sociedad Minera del Litio was established, and the second company with SQM was formed, the future significance of lithium in technological development for the mid-21st century was not anticipated. At that time, there was no indication that

lithium would become a highly strategic sector—not only for Chile but for humanity as a whole. This is important to mention and understand to explain the limited development of public policies in this sector, as lithium was relatively minor in the 1990s. In terms of products, it was not seen as highly strategic. The military considered it strategic in the 1970s due to its potential military applications, which is why it was declared a strategic resource. It was removed from the Mining Code because, in the early years of the dictatorship, there was an assumption that lithium could be an important material" (Interview 9—Ministry of Mining).

This perspective will be crucial in the following chapters to understand the business dynamics in relation to state actors' strategies. Initially, the state's role in lithium extraction was subordinated to corporate control due to state actors' decisions who did not foresee the strategic potential of lithium or its future uses. This reflects a decision-making process highly influenced by the prevailing technocratic mindset, which aimed to reduce the state's role in favor of economic development driven by private actors (P. Silva, 2010). Consequently, the relationship between CORFO and various companies positioned the private sector advantageously, replicating the neoliberal economic logic of the military regime, which was based on market liberalization and expansion to achieve development (Ffrench-Davis, 2001). This contrasts with the potential for enhancing lithium extraction through public enterprises that also held mining rights during that period.

Finally, the legal framework developed here outlines the structure that has governed lithium extraction dynamics. With this institutional framework, by the twenty-first century, lithium began to attract greater interest from the State and its policies. Its new economic and environmental implications, alongside technological advancement, became significant factors in discussions about lithium, framing it as a "resource of the future" with potential benefits for countries—and the world—that had not been previously considered. The following sections will delve into the economic and environmental foundations of lithium, complementing the legal elements just explained, to provide a comprehensive context for analyzing lithium policies in detail. Generally, the model established during this dictatorial period remained largely unchanged until the public policy discussions initiated during Sebastián Piñera's first presidency (2010–2014), which are analyzed in the subsequent sections. Figure 5.1 shows a brief timeline

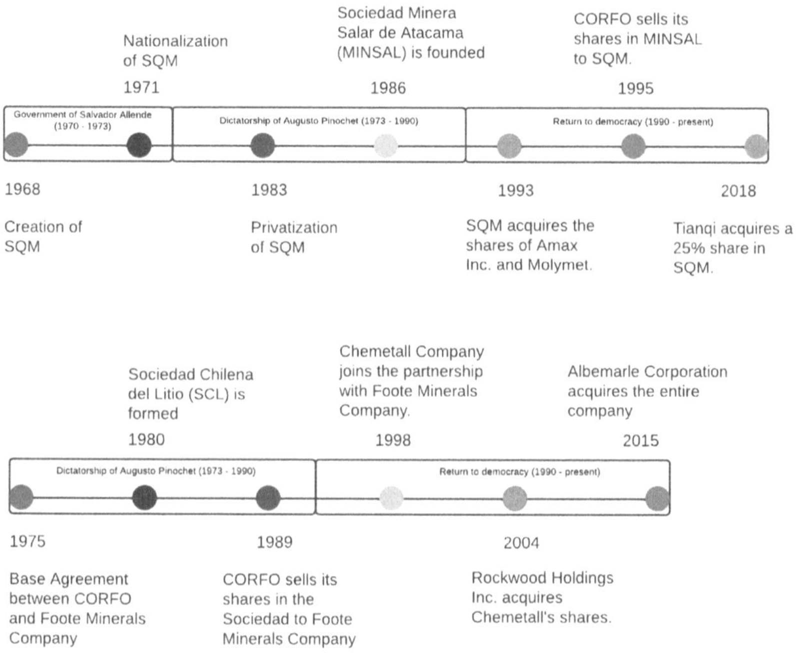

Fig. 5.1 Timeline of the history of SQM and Albemarle. Source: Own elaboration

of the history of the incumbent companies in the lithium industry, SQM and Albemarle.

Renewed Interest in Lithium in the New Century

Economically, lithium was considered a minor market for many years. By 2010, lithium sales in Chile were approximately USD 1 billion.[5] However, this decade saw the emergence of projections forecasting substantial growth in global demand for lithium, driven by its applications in the technology sector, with an anticipated annual growth rate of 7% (Pérez-Cueto, 2012). This shift in market dynamics elevated lithium

[5] For example, this figure is well below the billions of US dollars that copper has historically produced annually.

to a significant topic in political discourse. During the early years of President Sebastián Piñera's administration (2010–2014), there was a growing recognition of the need to enhance lithium extraction. Reflecting the center-right government's liberal economic stance, the political strategy focused on market expansion.

Chile's substantial lithium reserves,[6] low extraction costs, the experience of mining companies, and potential revenue for the national treasury were central arguments used by the government to advocate for increased lithium extraction through competitive bidding processes, known as CEOLs (La Tercera, 2012a). The Ministry of Mining initiated a bidding process that awarded the contract to SQM for expanding its extraction quotas. However, as will be discussed later, this process was marred by irregularities involving high-ranking government officials and SQM, resulting in the annulment of the entire procedure.

In response to the failed expansion efforts, President Michelle Bachelet's administration (2014–2018) introduced a new policy known as the Lithium Policy and Governance of the Salares. The primary goal of this policy was to enhance the value-added potential of lithium. This new policy encompassed a range of interconnected elements, which not only involved revising existing tools but also implementing new administrative, contractual, and institutional measures.

Firstly, the policy reaffirmed the non-concessionable status of lithium, meaning that the State retained ownership and rights over the mineral, while continuing to allow for the granting of mining concessions to private companies, as had been customary. Secondly, the policy designated CORFO as the central coordinating body for lithium governance. A new institutional framework was established within CORFO through the creation of a Non-Metallic Mining Committee, tasked with coordinating and ensuring consistency among public agencies for integrated and sustainable governance of the salt flats. Additionally, the policy aimed to advance the development of complex lithium-based products within the national industrial landscape through two main strategies: eliminating industry malpractices and coordinating companies to extract and process lithium for domestic production of complex products. Finally, the policy also emphasized the need for improved community relations and enhanced environmental protection.

[6] At that time, Chile already held 43% of the global market and was also one of the countries with the largest reserves in the world (La Tercera, 2012a).

To implement these objectives, the policy mandated a review of existing contracts with private companies (Peña, 2014). Various compliance issues were identified, necessitating updates to contracts to secure better terms in terms of fiscal, environmental, social, and economic conditions. These updated contracts aimed to increase state revenue and establish more effective control mechanisms.

The contracts also played a crucial role in advancing other policy goals related to communities and R&D. Specifically, they negotiated royalties to be paid to the communities living in the Atacama salt flats and secured funding for research and development related to lithium. As a result, these contracts established significant financial compensation for the local communities, marking the largest economic contribution from a private company to civil society in Chile. Furthermore, they outlined funding for research centers through a combination of public and private investment. Under CORFO's coordination, but financed by the companies, the policy mandated the creation of the country's largest applied lithium research center, later known as the Institute of Clean Technologies (ITL). This center represented a major step forward in fostering collaboration among universities, businesses, and public agencies to innovate and enhance the value of lithium production in Chile. Figure 5.2 highlights the key elements of the new lithium policy.

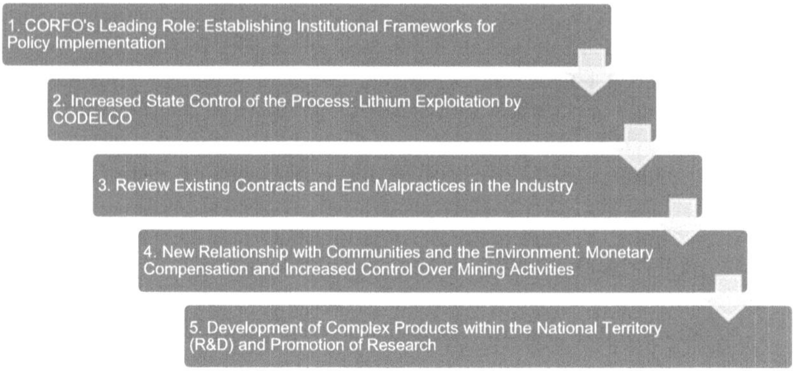

Fig. 5.2 Key Components of the Lithium Policy and Governance of the Salt Flats. Source: Own elaboration based on empirical evidence collected

Consequently, a range of short- and medium-term measures were implemented to address long-standing issues within the industry. These reforms encompassed a variety of areas, including tax regulations, production practices, environmental concerns, and community relations. Despite these efforts, the policy has encountered several challenges in both its formulation and execution. The forthcoming sections and chapters of this research will provide a detailed analysis of these issues.

The Political Dimension of State Capacity in Chile's Lithium Policy

Piñera Administration (2010–2014)

Based on the empirical evidence gathered, I argue that a shift can be observed in the public discourse regarding the governance of lithium and associated policies in recent years. The expectations and discourses surrounding lithium are crucial for analyzing the political dimension of state capacity, as they form the basis for generating broad support among political actors for the development of a lithium industrial policy, promoting a type of third-order change—using Hall's (1993) terminology—in policy.

My argument is that initially, there was no hegemonic discourse surrounding lithium. Instead, the discourses were divided into two main positions: some focused on the economic benefits of the mineral, while others emphasized its significance for technological development. Subsequently, after the failed tender during Piñera's administration (2010–2014), the idea of lithium industrialization gained traction in public discourse, especially given its role as a "fuel of the future" (Riofrancos, 2021), incorporating socio-environmental considerations into the discussion. This discursive shift redirected the debate, placing industrialization at its core. Thus, I argue that the predominance of certain discourses shaped concrete practices that supported specific policies, serving as a key component in the establishment of state capacities.

In Chile, lithium did not become a public discussion topic until Sebastián Piñera's first term (2010–2014). The involvement of private companies in the mineral's exploitation emerged from the state's passive role during the 1990s, even though CORFO was the principal owner of the mineral rights. The process of "publicization" (Subirats et al.,

2008)—i.e., the transition from a specific issue to a public problem—occurred with the global increase in demand for the mineral (World Bank, 2019), driven by new uses in the technology industry, such as batteries for computers, cell phones, and electric vehicles, which are crucial for electromobility and energy transition strategies (for a more detailed discussion, see Chapter 4). The beginning of public discourse about the future of lithium also entailed a discussion about the role of the State, in a context where Chile was the world's leading exporter, as recalled by an interviewee:

> "I believe that until the early 2000s, lithium wasn't much talked about. But when electromobility began to develop more strongly and the need for lithium became more discussed, I think that's when everyone started talking much more about lithium. By that time, there were already projections of demand growth. So, what would be Chile's role? What would its participation be? Because Chile was the world's top lithium producer" (Interview 14—CORFO).

The government's focus on the economic dimension alone faced criticism from various actors: politicians, union representatives, and even academics argued for the need to develop a public policy that centers on industrial and environmental considerations (La Tercera, 2012a). During this second phase, these actors emphasized lithium's use in advanced technological products related to energy storage, aligning with academic literature linking lithium to energy transition processes and addressing global climate change (Fornillo, 2018). Ultimately, public opinion began to build a consensus around the need to advance battery manufacturing—or its components—to move toward a new development model and transition away from fossil fuels (Pérez-Cueto, 2012). The empirical analysis of media reports reveals that discourses advocating for a greater role of the State converge on the importance of lithium for sustainable development, highlighting its role in electromobility and emphasizing the "green" aspects of this activity.

Therefore, economic expectations are interwoven with energy and environmental perspectives regarding the mineral. Economically, opposition politicians, particularly from the Socialist Party (PS), the Party for Democracy (PPD), and the Christian Democracy (DC), criticized the limited role of the State in the lithium exploitation processes and the fact that the industry's expansion did not involve the country's primary public enterprise, CODELCO.[7] Additionally, concerns were raised that the bidding process would lead to the privatization and sale of the resource as a raw material, without adding value through the development of clean technologies (UPI, 2012).[8] This critique marks the beginning of a public discussion on the need for a green industrial policy that transcends the traditional extractive dynamics established within the Chilean economic system.

Discursively, arguments favoring strong state control over lithium emphasize that the mineral contributes to a "better future," focusing on its role in energy transition and electromobility. This discourse is articulated by various political and social actors, including academics, center-left legislators, trade unions and workers' federations (from mining companies), and representatives of subnational governments, among others.

Table 5.3 presents some of the primary discourses in the public debate about lithium during this period. Although the list is not exhaustive, it highlights some of the most active participants in the public discussion and provides a broad overview of the key issues raised during this time. In terms of actor participation, social organizations and NGOs did not become prominent until a later stage (Poveda, 2020).[9]

Overall, it is evident that the position of Sebastián Piñera's government was to increase exploitation to meet global demand. This stance was supported by coalition legislators who argued that failing to seize this opportunity would result in Chile losing its global competitiveness in the sector.

Opposition lawmakers—primarily from the Socialist Party (PS) and the Christian Democratic Party (DC)—are the main critics of private

[7] Chilean center-left political actors criticized the potential expansion of the lithium market under private control, while the country's primary public enterprise, CODELCO, owns mining concessions in salars that could be exploited for lithium extraction.

[8] Similarly, the Socialist Party's parliamentary caucus introduced a bill proposing that CODELCO take on the responsibility for the extraction and production of lithium in Chile. This initiative represents one of the first significant efforts to increase state control over lithium exploitation processes. The bill argues that "it is a sovereign imperative for the State of Chile to lead the extraction of this mineral and develop policies that enable the creation of an industry associated with this exploitation" (LT 19/6/2012).

[9] The most prominent organizations, such as the Plurinational Observatory of Andean Salt Flats, were only established in 2019, several years after the period under discussion. In contrast, groups like the Council of Atacameño Peoples and local organizations gained prominence in the public policy of the Bachelet administration (2014–2018).

Table 5.3 Members of the National Lithium Commission

Member	*Profession*	*Position*
Aurora Williams	Economist	Minister of Mining
Ignacio Moreno	Economist and MBA	Undersecretary of Mining
Luis Felipe Céspedes	PhD in Economics, New York University	Minister of Economy
Ana Lya Uriarte	Lawyer	Former Minister of Environment
Manuel Riesco	Doctor in Political Economy	Vice President, National Center for Alternative Development Studies
Juan Carlos Zuleta	Bolivian Economist	Lithium Market Expert, International Guest
Carlos Chávez	PhD in Natural Resource Economics	Director, Master's Program in Natural and Economic Resources, UdeC
Cristián Quinzio	Lawyer	Legal Advisor, CODELCO
Pedro Pavlovic	Chemical Engineer	Lithium Expert
Manlio Coviello	PhD in Geophysics and Seismology	Specialist in Sustainable Development, CEPAL
John Tilton	PhD in Economics, Yale University	Professor of Economics and Business, Colorado School of Mines and PUC, International Guest
Aníbal Gajardo	Geologist	Researcher, Non-Metallic Mining
Rodrigo Azocar	Industrial Civil Engineer	Corporate Manager, CORFO
Marcelo Zambra	Physicist, PhD	Head of Nuclear Application Department, Chilean Nuclear Energy Commission
Raúl O'Ryan	Economist	Specialist in Natural Resource Economics
María Daniela Desormeaux	Economist, PUC	General Manager and Founder, SigmunBOX Market Intelligence
Francisco Zuñiga	Lawyer	Professor of Constitutional Law, University of Chile
Samuel Lira	Lawyer	Mining Law Expert, Minister of Mining during the 1980s

(continued)

Table 5.3 (continued)

Member	*Profession*	*Position*
Annie Dufey	Economist and MA in Environmental Policy and Development	Head of the Prospective and Energy Policy Division, Ministry of Energy
Valentina Durán	Lawyer and Master in Environmental Law	Specialist in Environmental Law, Academic at University of Chile
Vicente Pérez	Chemical Engineer	COCHILCO
Rolando Humire	Biochemist	Representative of the Atacameño Peoples
Gonzalo Gutiérrez	–	Union Representative

Source: Own elaboration

exploitation of lithium, advocating instead for state-run enterprises to manage its extraction. Some lawmakers who chair key committees—such as the Environment and Future Committees—emphasize the importance of advancing toward more complex products that add value to this crucial mineral for the future. These perspectives are strongly supported by civil society and academia. Mining workers emphasize the necessity of having the mineral extracted by public enterprises, while academic voices stress the importance of developing more sophisticated lithium-related products.

Even within the conservative segments of the center-left, there were calls to reform the existing policies on lithium. The Christian Democratic Party, led by its president Ignacio Walker, urged the government to establish a national lithium policy. This would require establishing a medium- to long-term strategy for the mineral, with clearly defined roles for both the public and private sectors in its management. Additionally, there was a call to incorporate sustainability into resource extraction and to diversify the productive structure through industrial policy instruments. A critique was also directed at the inadequacy of the government's resignation, as indicated by Undersecretary Wagner, suggesting that President Piñera's administration was not addressing the underlying issues.

From other center-left parties, numerous deputies and senators criticized the issue in which the bidding process was conducted, with some labeling it an international embarrassment due to the perceived inexperience and poor management by government officials. Senator Lagos

Weber (PPD) noted that the process encountered problems from the outset.

> "—This tender, or covert concession, was criticized by various stakeholders. We urged the government to undertake a different process through legislation, as many of us believe is necessary for a strategic mineral as defined by the constitution. However, the government was determined to proceed in its own way, and it did so, but poorly" (La Tercera, 2012e).

Thus, the call for a central role of the state in lithium exploitation was not limited to leftist parties but extended into the political center.

Figure 5.3 illustrates the key issues discussed during this period concerning lithium. Based on an analysis of media coverage, several prominent themes emerge in the public discourse: environmental, economic, and productive considerations. The discussions highlight Chile's global competitiveness due to its low exploitation costs and substantial lithium reserves. Environmentally, the emphasis is placed on lithium's role as a future fuel, particularly its use in electromobility. Finally, there is a strong call for lithium exploitation to be managed by a public enterprise, notably CODELCO.

During President Piñera's first term, increased lithium exploitation triggered a public debate regarding the mineral and its extraction methods. Broadly, two major competing discourses emerged during this period. The first, represented by the government and right-leaning political sectors, advocated for expanded mineral exploitation through private companies to maintain international competitiveness. The second discourse focused on the need for lithium industrialization and greater state control over production processes.

However, there was a noticeable shift toward the second perspective. This shift is evident both qualitatively, in the broader range of arguments presented, and quantitatively, in the greater number of stakeholders supporting industrialization. This perspective not only tilted the public debate in favor of state involvement but also called for a fundamental change in the development model associated with lithium.

Bachelet Administration (2014–2018)

During President Bachelet's second term (2014–2018), the lithium sector received renewed attention, translating into several significant actions: the

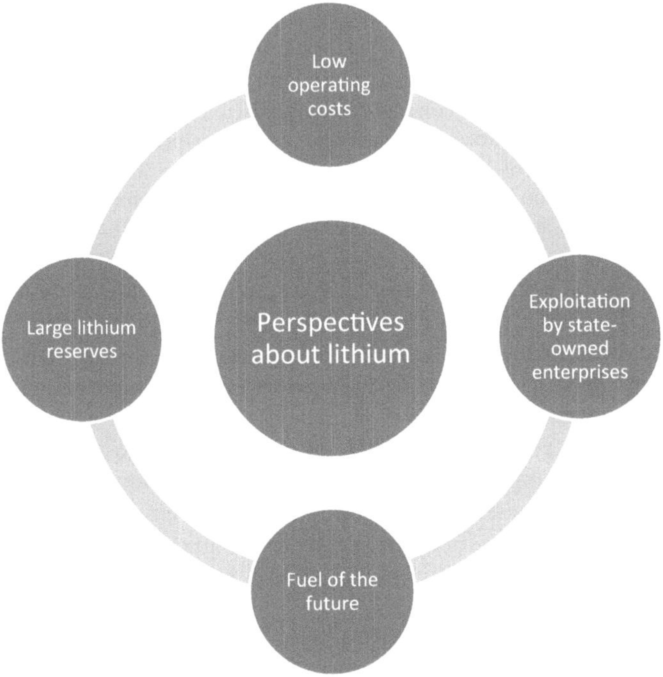

Fig. 5.3 Main topics in the public discussion on Lithium. Source: Own elaboration based on press analysis

incorporation of lithium into the government's program, the establishment of a presidential advisory commission on lithium, and the formulation of a comprehensive lithium policy and governance framework. This section argues how political capacities were developed to promote an industrial policy for lithium in Chile, focusing on Bachelet's commitment, favorable international conditions, and support from various political actors.

First, the favorable international context was shaped by Chile's participation in the Paris Agreement, which emphasized electromobility and energy transition as central challenges for countries worldwide. Within this framework, Chile positioned itself as a strategic global player capable of contributing through lithium exploitation. As a high-ranking public official noted:

> "There was a conviction that Chile needed to better utilize these resources. It was clear from the beginning of this administration that lithium would play a key role in the development of global electromobility. After the Paris Agreement, it was evident that electromobility would be crucial" (Interview 3—Corfo).

This strategic vision regarding lithium is consistently reflected in interviews, showing alignment between internal perspectives and international viewpoints. As one interviewee articulated:

> "The motivation was to address this challenge, this window of opportunity provided by lithium, in relation to energy. Lithium has the potential to contribute significantly to electromobility, carbon neutrality, and climate change mitigation. It allowed us to position ourselves as a country rich in this strategic resource, akin to the entire lithium triangle" (Interview 5—National Lithium Commission).

Thus, the drive toward value-added processes is framed by an international political context that facilitated the formation of domestic political support.

Secondly, President Bachelet's commitment to advancing value-added processes in lithium was evident. Lithium was a prominent theme in her campaign, and her government program recognized its potential environmental benefits and economic implications. Upon winning the election, Bachelet prioritized lithium as one of the key issues for her initial 100 days in office. In early March 2014, shortly after assuming power, she announced the creation of a commission to determine the optimal approach for lithium exploration and exploitation, aiming to address considerations beyond purely economic factors (Pérez-Cueto, 2014). An actor from that period recalled the public positioning of the issue as follows:

> "The rationale for convening the commission was tied to the bidding process under the previous Sebastián Piñera administration, during which SQM was improperly awarded the concession. This issue later uncovered political financing concerns, leading to the annulment of the tender. Consequently, the topic of lithium became a significant focus during the campaign and pre-campaign discussions, and once the new administration took office, addressing this issue became a priority, culminating in

the establishment of the commission" (Interview 1—National Lithium Commission).

This perspective is further supported by other stakeholders who highlight the absence of regulation and an inadequate institutional framework for structuring the lithium industry. Historically, the development of this industry since the 1990s had been driven by private enterprises, with a largely absent state. These issues are explored in greater depth in Chapter 6.

"There is an institutional fragmentation and a lack of regulation, primarily related to the misconduct of SQM. The commission's objective was to conduct a diagnostic assessment, focusing on governance and institutional issues concerning lithium" (Interview 4—Civil Society).

The following figure summarizes the main dimensions of the political capacity developed by the state related to lithium policy (Fig. 5.4). These elements form the foundation for the development of administrative capacities, which are established in the next section.

Administrative Dimension of the State Capacity in Lithium Policy

The Role of Experts: Presidential Lithium Advisory Commission

Alongside political capacities, the Bachelet administration also focused on building administrative capacities to advance lithium industrialization processes. In June 2014, President Bachelet issued a decree to establish the National Lithium Commission, comprised of various specialists and stakeholders related to lithium. In Chile, Presidential Advisory Commissions (hereafter CAPs) are ad hoc organizations created by the president for a specific period and to address a defined issue. Formally, these commissions typically have a president and a technical secretariat to support administrative tasks, with their work centered on producing a report that serves as the foundation for public policy development (Cisternas & Vásquez, 2018). Since the return to democracy, CAPs have been employed by various administrations across different policy areas (Aguilera, 2009), and in some cases, they have been used to address political crises by delegating proposals to experts (Maillet et al., 2019).

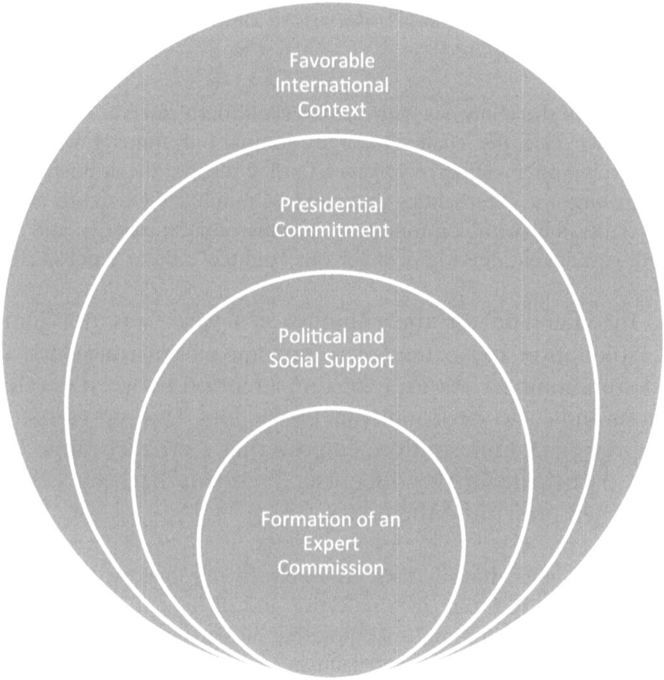

Fig. 5.4 Constitutive elements of political capacity in Chile's lithium policy. Source; Own Elaboration

For the lithium commission, the stated objective was to develop a public policy proposal for lithium, aimed at beginning implementation in 2015. At the commission's launch, President Bachelet underscored the significance of lithium for Chile, noting that the country possesses one of the largest reserves of this mineral globally (Pérez-Cueto, 2014).[10] Beyond its strategic importance, the authorities recognized the challenge of balancing mineral exploitation with socio-environmental

[10] In 2014, President Bachelet stated: "We are embarking on the task of collaboratively considering a crucial aspect of our development: what is the best way for Chile to utilize and exploit its lithium reserves, which are a strategic resource for both the country and the world. We cannot afford to miss this opportunity.".

dynamics associated with such activities. As then-Minister of Mining Aurora Williams articulated:

> "We are one of the countries with the largest lithium reserves in the world, and thus, we face the challenge of exploiting our mineral with added value, developing productive linkages, and boosting the industry, while also addressing the externalities generated by mining. We need to establish a new relationship with communities, the environment, energy, and water, ensuring sustainable development for our country" (Pérez-Cueto, 2014).

Thus, the mandate for the commission's work was not limited to mineral exploitation but extended to encompass environmental dimensions and community relations, reflecting a tension between development expectations and socio-environmental protection. This represented a shift from the previous administration, empowering a broader range of stakeholders to participate in the discourse. President Bachelet echoed this sentiment when presenting the policy:

> "With lithium and the salt flats, as rarely in our history, we have the chance to build the future in a reflective and dialogued manner, considering the common good and incorporating all perspectives of society. We have experiences of successes and failures in our history of opportunities and development, and now we can make that experience translate into well-executed work" (Cooperativa, 2016).

An actor holding a senior position within the Ministry of Mining during the analyzed period recalls these considerations in the political mandate of the commission:

Here is an improved English translation of the passage, incorporating an analytical tone:

> "The first issue identified by the Commission was that the salt flats are an extremely fragile and sensitive ecosystem. It is crucial to understand this because brine is essentially water with mineral salts, and the Atacama Salt Flat has several communities that have lived around it for centuries, since pre-Hispanic times, and have traditionally thrived in relation to the salt flats. Therefore, any intervention in the salt flat can have a negative environmental impact, particularly for the communities residing around the salt flat" (Interview 9—Ministry of Mining).

In designing the new lithium policy, the commission included a range of stakeholders beyond just the mining sector. The lithium commission was comprised of 20 members (see Table 5.3). A brief descriptive analysis reveals several significant aspects regarding the composition of the commission. Primarily, the commission consisted of professionals from the fields of law and economics, with fewer members from the scientific disciplines related to mining. Many of these members held postgraduate degrees and even doctorates. This professional composition, characterized by its level of specialization, is not particularly novel within the Chilean political system. In fact, this type of expert aligns with the general profile of technocratic actors who have increasingly influenced the State apparatus over the past decades (P. Silva, 2011), and specifically with the type of composition seen in presidential advisory commissions in Chile since the return to democracy in 1990 (Aguilera & Fuentes, 2011).

Another significant aspect of the lithium commission's composition pertains to the professional backgrounds of its members. As illustrated in the previous table, the majority of the commission's members are experts in their respective fields, primarily drawn from higher education institutions, and a minority are government officials. This mirrors the logic observed in other presidential advisory commissions during President Bachelet's first term, which were constituted by an "expert elite," thereby delegating public policy deliberation to a group of specialists (Aguilera & Fuentes, 2011).

Furthermore, it is noteworthy that this commission formally excluded business actors involved in lithium exploitation. Instead, only a union representative from the lithium companies (Gonzalo Gutiérrez) was invited, reflecting a deliberate exclusion of the business sector from the policy formulation process. Generally, presidential advisory commissions in Chile have been composed of experts in the relevant fields, emphasizing their technical nature (Aguilera & Fuentes, 2011). However, these instances also aim to ensure the representation of stakeholders and interest groups directly related to the issue at hand, which typically constitute about a quarter of the participants (Aguilera, 2009).

Despite the exclusion of business representatives from the commission, empirical evidence does not indicate any public discontent or attempts by business actors to join this body. My hypothesis is that the corruption cases involving SQM effectively marginalized this actor from the public discourse on the future of lithium. This is significant because, traditionally, business actors in Chile have been very proactive in defending their interests during public policy changes, utilizing various forms of power (Madariaga et al., 2021; Madariaga, 2020; Bril & Maillet, 2019; Fairfield, 2015). Even among state actors, this situation is viewed as an anomaly, as noted by an interviewee:

> "As a result, this commission of experts was formed, composed of individuals with certain industry knowledge, but without participation from the lithium industry itself. There were no representatives from the industries. Thus, those with the most knowledge might have had some level of involvement" (Interview 14—CORFO).

As indicated in the above quote, the process lacked representation of expert knowledge related to the industrial organization of the lithium sector. Analytically, two major types of expertise are evident in the lithium discussion. One is associated with academic knowledge, particularly concerning the economic, legal, and environmental impacts of lithium exploitation. This is the expertise represented by the commission members and is clearly reflected in the lithium policy formulation. On the other hand, there is expertise related to the operational aspects of the industry itself, including the production processes for mineral extraction, which was absent from the commission. Given that lithium is a non-metallic mineral, the industrial processes involved differ from traditional mining and require highly specialized knowledge that was not incorporated into the lithium policy formulation process.

A New Institutional Framework for Lithium Policy Management in Chile

The work of the National Lithium Commission culminated in the production of a report, which largely served as the foundation for the development of the Lithium Policy and the Governance of Salars, presented by President Bachelet in 2015. The commission's report is considered a valuable resource, as it does not focus solely on the technical aspects of mining but also addresses environmental, social, and economic dimensions. An interviewee summarizes this perspective as follows:

> "I believe that report is highly valuable because, fundamentally, it is the first time that natural resources are discussed in terms of governance. Governance seeks to understand the issues from all perspectives, not just the

technical, economic, or social viewpoints. It aims to integrate all stakeholders involved in industry development so that together they can find solutions and address problems that the state or market has been unable to resolve" (Interview 2—CORFO).

As indicated at the beginning of this chapter, the policy aims to reposition the role of the State in the lithium industry by granting greater authority, control, and direction over the process. Some actors view this strategy as an ambitious industrialization plan designed to address various issues that had been developing in the management of the mineral. A key actor of the time observed it as follows:

"In 2015, the Bachelet government convened the National Lithium Commission, which proposed a series of short- and medium-term reforms that I believe were quite ambitious. However, the general aim of these proposals was to address various weaknesses. One issue was revenue, where the State was missing out on potential gains. Without benefits for the companies, the State could not capture revenue. The proposals also addressed productive linkages, community relations, and environmental concerns related to comprehensive management of the salars" (Interview 25—Academic).

To achieve its new industrialization objectives, the actors involved recognized the need for specialized institutional mechanisms. The new policy required the State to play a more active role in coordinating, regulating, and enforcing the rules and new development perspectives. Consequently, two primary elements were developed in the short term to strengthen the state's administrative capacities. First, there was an effort to reorganize existing structures, specifically to enhance the state's regulatory role by enforcing contracts and renegotiating terms with companies to meet policy objectives. Interviewees agree that this short-term measure was quickly implemented and improved the state's position relative to companies in managing the production process, as reflected in the following quote:

"The immediate response to that commission was the signing of contract renegotiations, first with Albemarle and then with SQM. What the new contracts ultimately achieved was an improvement in the state's ability to capture revenue, as new systems for progressive royalties were established" (Interview 25—Academic).

In addition to regulatory measures, another significant administrative step was the establishment of an institutional framework within CORFO: the Non-Metallic Mining Committee. Formed in 2016, this committee was tasked with overseeing lithium contracts, ensuring sustainable development of the Salar de Atacama, and fostering value addition in the industry. Consequently, the committee became the primary body responsible for implementing the policy and ensuring the sustainable exploitation of lithium. Interviewees have noted that the decision to integrate the policy into CORFO's institutional framework was influenced by the institution's flexibility and its statutory authority to create specialized working committees. Furthermore, CORFO owns the mineral rights to the salars where private companies conduct mining operations. As a result, the committee could operate without the constraints of traditional bureaucratic structures and possessed the authority to negotiate directly with companies regarding contract terms, modifications, and even terminations. An interviewee involved with the Non-Metallic Mining Committee provided the following explanation:

> "Why was the CORFO model (the Non-Metallic Mining Committee) chosen? Because CORFO, as a private law corporation, has greater operational flexibility than a state institution. Under the powers granted by law, it is allowed to create working committees for specific issues. CORFO effectively transforms state policies into a set of committees with defined objectives and budgets. The Non-Metallic Mining Committee was essentially a rapid response mechanism to establish a structure for implementing state policy, providing agility to the state" (Interview 2—Non-Metallic Mining Committee).

Interviews also highlight that the Non-Metallic Mining Committee brought together various state actors on its governing board, offering an intersectoral perspective that extended beyond mere economic considerations to address lithium policy comprehensively. The key ministries involved in the committee included Mining, Environment, Energy, and Finance, along with civil society representatives, to ensure broader participation beyond formal institutional bounds. This inclusive approach is emphasized by a committee member:

> "If you look at what happened over those four years, for the first time there was a comprehensive perspective. For the first time, the various institutions with competencies in this area were seated around the table,

bringing different viewpoints... The governing board of the Non-Metallic Mining Committee was composed of the Undersecretaries of Mining, Economy, Environment, Energy, and Finance, as well as representatives from CORFO, Sernageomin, the CCHEN, Cochilco, and the DGA. All the necessary institutions were represented. Additionally, there were two civil society members who were required to be distinguished professionals or academics in non-metallic mining" (Interview 7—National Lithium Commission).

Despite this inclusive structure, the absence of companies from these formal decision-making bodies was notable. While companies were not members of the committee, they also did not present their concerns or participate in the various sessions held, even though they were the primary target of the industrial policy (Bulfone, 2022). One actor from that period remarked on the absence of companies from the formal decision-making processes related to the lithium industry:

"(…) the governance committee that emerged from the Salar and Non-Metallic Mining table, as far as I remember, companies did not even come to present. I must have attended 80% of the meetings that were held. I do not recall that SQM or Albemarle came to present or sit in" (Interview 31—COCHILCO).

Another component of administrative capacity that emerged from the policy is the creation of technical information about lithium. For years, technical knowledge about lithium and its extraction had been monopolized by the companies, with the State playing a marginal role in regulating the activity. However, as evidenced by the empirical data collected, one of the initial decisions in implementing the policy was to conduct studies to acquire specialized information about lithium and salars more broadly. This included the development of hydrogeological studies to understand the characteristics of the salars and the effects of extractive activities. Additionally, technical and economic analyses were conducted on the levels of lithium exploitation and exportation, and their alignment with contractual agreements. An interviewee directly involved in many of these studies describes this process as follows:

"Basically, the goal… the initial objective in that… in that CORFO committee was to try to understand what we have. The first step was to conduct hydrogeological studies of the Salar de Atacama, followed by

> a sequence of studies: first, the hydrogeological study of Maricunga, then a hydrogeological study of Pedernales. This was based on an economic prioritization of the salars using information available at the time (…) And these were fundamental data for establishing this prioritization" (Interview 31—COCHILCO).

Therefore, considering all these elements, it can be stated that efforts to establish administrative capacities in the lithium policy in Chile focused on three major areas: the recruitment of experts to formulate policy strategies (technocratic dimension), the design of new institutions for administrative coordination of the policy (bureaucratic dimension), and the conduct of studies to develop comprehensive knowledge about how the industry operates in its various aspects (information-building dimension). These different elements reflect the administrative capacities developed for the implementation of the lithium policy.

Conclusions

This chapter has outlined the process of building state capacities within Chile's lithium industrial policy. Analytically, based on the presented empirical information, three interrelated dynamics explaining the policy configuration can be observed. First, a public discourse on lithium and related public policies was developed. A thorough media analysis revealed that political actors predominantly dominated the public debate, although academics, experts, officials, and civil society actors were also present. Despite the fact there was no unanimous perspective among these actors on the future of lithium, the majority favored a more active role for the State, advocating for industrialization processes and applied research concerning the mineral.

The second dynamic pertains to the marginal role of lithium-related companies in shaping these issues on the public agenda and in the subsequent policy formulation process. This situation emerged following the discovery of political corruption cases involving SQM, which had illegally financed political campaigns across the political spectrum to influence them. Given this context, companies did not appear in the media or participate in more formal settings, with SQM itself focusing on an internal organizational restructuring as a result of this process. There was even a noticeable conflict among different businesspeople, further delegitimizing their actions due to the aforementioned corruption cases.

This situation impeded the sector's engagement with the lithium issue and its formal involvement in the public policy decision-making process. During the same period, other public policy reform attempts were undermined by opposition from business actors. For instance, Bachelet's tax reform proposal was significantly altered due to the use of various power resources by the business elite (Fairfield, 2018).

The third dynamic observed is the development of state capacities to manage regulatory and industrial processes related to lithium. The establishment of these capacities is evident in the political, legal, and administrative spheres, which together constitute some of the main dimensions of state capacity (Cingolani, 2013). Politically, there was an explicit mandate from the president to implement the policy, mobilizing various resources to support institutional change. Technically, the policy was initially executed by a commission of experts whose knowledge is highly regarded by various actors. Administratively, an institutional framework was created within CORFO, with various powers and trained personnel assigned to achieve its objectives. Additionally, the policy was closely overseen by CORFO's vice president at the time, Eduardo Bitrán, who prioritized advancing lithium industrialization. Table 5.4 summarizes the analysis of state capacity concerning lithium, breaking down the different dimensions of the concept and their observable implications.

Table 5.4 Empirical findings on state capacity in lithium policy in Chile

Dimensions	*Empirical observations*	*Analytical description*
Political Capacity	The explicit mandate from President Bachelet to implement lithium policy, mobilizing diverse resources for institutional change	Strong political will to advance lithium industrialization, with high-level support and strategic prioritization by the President
Administrative/Technical Capacity	Formation of a specialized commission of experts to develop policy recommendations, reflecting extensive knowledge and positive reception by stakeholders	The commission's expertise in various fields related to lithium, including environmental and socio-economic dimensions, was highly valued and instrumental in shaping the policy
Administrative Capacity	Creation of the Non-Metallic Mining Committee within CORFO, equipped with specific powers and trained personnel to oversee policy implementation	Effective administrative setup with the ability to negotiate contracts, supervise mining operations, and ensure sustainable practices. The presence of CORFO's vice president ensured strong oversight
Administrative Capacity	Development of specialized technical studies on lithium and salars, including hydrogeological assessments and technical–economic analyses	Increased state control over technical knowledge, previously monopolized by companies, leading to better-informed policy decisions and prioritization of research on salars and extraction methods
Institutional Capacity	Lithium as a strategic resource	Lithium recognized as a strategic resource under state control. Management entrusted to CORFO, which owns mining rights and oversees exploitation decisions

Source: Own elaboration

CHAPTER 6

The Role of Business in Chile's Lithium Policy

Introduction

The previous chapter examined the role of state capacity in shaping lithium policy, with a focus on the dynamics involving political and bureaucratic actors. The evidence gathered revealed a process of state capacity building, manifested through the mobilization of various resources, actors, and institutions, alongside discourses promoting the addition of value to lithium. Notably, there was limited involvement from business actors during the initial phase of policy formulation. However, I argue that this situation evolved during the implementation phase, as business actors linked to lithium exploitation began to oppose certain policy instruments.

This section seeks to characterize the role of business actors in Chile's lithium policy process. Initially sidelined in the lithium debate, later business actors activated their power resources to oppose specific measures, influencing the implementation of certain industrial policy instruments. This opposition is observed through classic strategies of instrumental power, such as the revolving door and lobbying (Fairfield, 2015), enabling business actors to preserve their preferences regarding some of the instruments developed by the State. Structural power dynamics are also observed, where the privileged position of lithium companies builds and accumulates power over the long term, making them indispensable for lithium exploitation in Chile. The chapter thus develops an argument

S. Carrasco, *From (De)regulation to Industrialization?*, Latin American Political Economy, https://doi.org/10.1007/978-3-031-77130-9_6

about the conflicting relationship between the state and businesses, and its implications for public policy outcomes.

The first section examines the mechanisms through which businesses exercise instrumental power. Specifically, it examines the contract breaches by SQM and Albemarle, and the resulting implications for incorporating new business actors into research and development (R&D) efforts. It also addresses the legal conflicts between public institutions, particularly CORFO, and corporate actors, alongside the challenges of involving new private participants in the lithium industrialization process. Additionally, the section explores the flawed bidding process for the Clean Technologies Institute (ITL), which was intended to become Chile's largest research center focused on applied lithium research, jointly funded by the State and lithium-extracting companies. The bidding process was plagued by irregularities, which can be interpreted as mechanisms of corporate influence over the proceedings.

The second part discusses the dynamics of structural power observed in the case, illustrating how these resources reinforce the instrumental power dynamics addressed in the first part. The third section examines the dynamics of public companies, focusing on the role of the state-owned enterprise CODELCO, which was charged with advancing lithium exploitation and industrialization. While CODELCO, as a public entity, did not explicitly oppose the policy, it adopted strategies that delayed the implementation of the state's mandate to integrate CODELCO as a new market participant.

In the first two cases, private companies employed more confrontational strategies against the State and the new regulatory provisions of the policy, deploying various power resources and leveraging their position within the economic system. In contrast, the third case presents a subtler form of resistance, driven by information asymmetries between the State and private entities, as well as CODELCO's own developmental priorities, which did not place lithium at the forefront.

The third section also analyzes business preferences, shedding light on how these preferences relate to power resources and the extent to which these dynamics help explain the types of relationships between the State and businesses. This section moves forward to consider the dynamics that have emerged more recently during Gabriel Boric's administration. In this regard, it identifies the challenges and opportunities that this period presents.

Finally, the last section presents the chapter's central argument. It contends that the chapter demonstrates how state–business relations evolve during the policy implementation phase. Despite the state's substantial capacity—evidenced by political will, human and financial resources, and the establishment of new institutional frameworks—it faces significant challenges in enforcing key elements of the policy. This outcome is largely attributed to the power strategies employed by companies to resist the policy, as well as the adversarial nature of state–business relations, most notably manifested in the numerous legal disputes. The chapter also highlights the differing strategies between private and public companies.

Instrumental Business Power in Chile's Lithium Policy

The Original Sin: Corruption Cases in the Lithium Sector

During Sebastián Piñera's first administration (2010–2014), the Ministry of Mining identified the expansion of lithium exploitation as a key objective. In 2012, a public bidding process was initiated to achieve this goal. However, the unique legal status of lithium in Chile prevented its exploitation by private companies through standard bidding mechanisms. As one interviewee highlighted, lithium production quotas were effectively frozen, as they were centrally defined by the Chilean Nuclear Energy Commission, which was counterproductive given the rapidly increasing global demand for lithium at the time:

> "There was a rapid growth potential in the global lithium market due to the explosion of battery use in electromobility, yet Chile had effectively frozen its production quotas, which prevented production increases. Consequently, the country was losing its share of global production. We had accounted for 50% of the world's production, with nearly 50% of proven global reserves, but we were seeing a dramatic decline because there was no possibility to increase production. Lithium was declared a strategic resource with a quota set by the Chilean Nuclear Energy Commission, preventing operating companies from increasing their production and market share" (Interview 3 – CORFO).

Despite opposition from various political parties (such as the Socialist Party, PPD, and members of the Christian Democratic Party), as well as civil society actors—primarily organized labor and academia—who advocated for expansion through a state-owned enterprise, the government proceeded with a special bidding process under the framework of Special Lithium Operation Contracts (CEOL).[1] From the outset, the Chilean company SQM expressed interest in expanding its activities by participating in this process. To ensure its expansion, SQM engaged in deliberate actions to unduly influence high-level political decisions for its benefit. Specifically, the company bribed the then-undersecretary of mining to modify the bidding process, enabling SQM to increase its lithium extraction quota without the entry of new competitors. The following paragraphs detail the narrative of this process.

Once the Ministry of Mining initiated the bidding process, three companies submitted bids for the new contracts to lease state-owned mining rights in the Atacama salt flats. Notably, the state-owned company CODELCO did not participate, despite insistence from members of parliament and labor organizations (La Tercera, 2012b). The Ministry awarded the contract to SQM, granting it the rights to exploit up to 100,000 tons of lithium over 20 years. This outcome raised significant economic and legal-political concerns. Economically, the bidding process was seen as reinforcing Chile's role in global lithium production but also as consolidating market power in the hands of a single company (La Tercera, 2012f).

Beyond SQM, the Chilean Lithium Society (SCL)—now Albemarle—was the only other company exploiting lithium, albeit on a much smaller scale. Francisco Javier Errazuriz, president of Sociedad Legal Minera NX Uno de Peine, one of the companies that participated in the bidding process, criticized the outcome:

> "This is very sad for the country because it will create an even greater oligopoly than what we have today. SQM already dominates lithium production in Chile, and it's a shame that only SQM will continue producing for the next 20 years. I hope this can be corrected" (La Tercera, 2012f).

This situation highlights the divide among business actors, marking significant differences between established companies exploiting lithium and those seeking entry into this economic sector but unable to do so.

[1] The companies could submit their bids until July 31, 2012.

On the legal-political front, concerns were raised about the legality of the bidding process. The Special Lithium Operation Contracts were to be designed and implemented by the Ministry of Mining. However, the Minister at that time, Hernán de Solminihac, recused himself from the process due to a conflict of interest—his brother was a high-ranking executive at SQM. Consequently, the responsibility fell to the undersecretary of mining, Pablo Wagner, who had previously built his career as an executive in private companies, particularly those associated with the Penta business conglomerate. After the contract was awarded, it was revealed that SQM had engaged in lobbying activities aimed at the undersecretary to secure favorable treatment in the bidding process. Although the guidelines prohibited companies with pending litigation against the State could from participating, SQM was still able to win the contract.

Under mounting pressure, the government—acting on the president's directive—convened a Special Bidding Committee within the Ministry of Mining, which ultimately declared the entire lithium bidding process null and void (La Tercera, 2012d). Companies that participated in the bidding but did not win activated various legal mechanisms against both the winning company, SQM, and the State. Minera Li Energy Spa, which accused SQM's award of being illegal, filed a reconsideration request, arguing that the bidding process's invalidation should result in the contract being awarded to the Posco consortium, of which Li Energy Spa is a member.

In parallel, the Errazuriz Group filed a perjury lawsuit against SQM. The Errazuriz Group, through Sociedad Legal Minera NX Uno de Peine, had made the third-highest bid in the auction, offering \$2.750 billion CLP (approximately \$5.79 million). Similarly, Minera Li Energy Spa, the company that requested SQM's disqualification from the lithium bidding process, pursued legal action. Cristián Quinzio, Li Energy Spa's attorney, emphasized that his client had recently submitted a document processed by CEL's office. He pointed out that they chose not to focus on the ongoing legal disputes between SQM and the DGA, instead directing their argument toward a specific claim against the State, particularly the Ministry of National Assets, regarding the imposition of mining easements. Quinzio further highlighted that the defense of this case was under the jurisdiction of the State Defense Council (CDE), underscoring the complexity and significance of the ongoing legal battle. Meanwhile, Asogemin, an association representing industrial miners, also filed a lawsuit against SQM for fraud against the State.

The Association of Mining Industrialists additionally filed a complaint in court for fraud against the State, arguing that SQM had failed to fulfill the conditions of its bid bond, which guaranteed the seriousness of their offer. They also accused SQM of falsifying public documents certifying that the company had no pending legal disputes with the State. All these events unfolded within a matter of days. In this turbulent context, on October 2, 2012, Pablo Wagner was forced to resign from his position as undersecretary, amid widespread criticism of his management and facing judicial proceedings.

Years later, in 2017, the courts found Wagner guilty of accepting payments to favor SQM in the bidding process by falsifying public documents. The judiciary confirmed that the records from the bidding process had been falsified to allow SQM's participation. As a result, the former undersecretary reached a plea deal with the Public Prosecutor's Office, which involved a fine of 1 million CLP and an 18-month ban from holding public office. Figure 6.1 presents the key milestones related to the lithium bidding process initiated during President Piñera's first administration.

It is worth noting that during this period (2010–2014) measures were implemented by the government, to increase competition and extraction quotas for lithium in response to rising international demand, continuing the extractivist approach that had characterized Chile's lithium sector. These measures were carried out through an irregular process, wherein high-ranking government officials favored SQM in the bidding process in exchange for monetary payments. Specifically, SQM leveraged instrumental power resources, such as establishing informal connections with

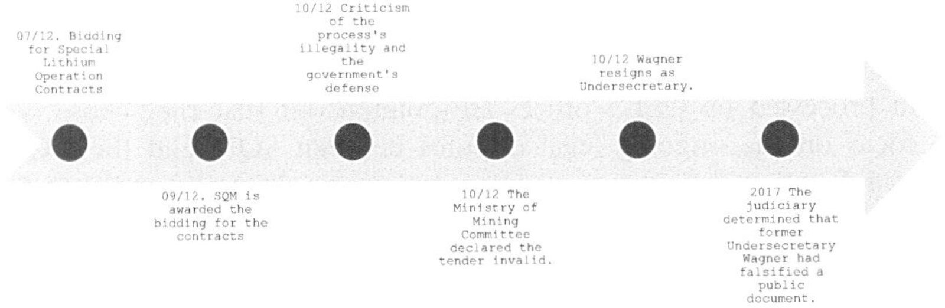

Fig. 6.1 Timeline of the lithium bidding process during Piñera I Administration. *Source* Own elaboration

politicians, positioning business figures in key roles (e.g., Undersecretary Wagner), and using financial inducements to influence the process in their favor. The use of money by business actors to gain advantages in public policy regulations is a widespread practice in Latin America, but it is particularly relevant in natural resource extraction activities, such as lithium (Fairfield, 2015; Ross, 2015). Thus, this case not only illustrates a corruption dynamic—where payments to a political actor were made to secure benefits in an administrative process—but also reveals a systematic effort to influence political decision-making processes.

Furthermore, the criticisms from other business actors regarding SQM's legitimacy to conduct lithium extraction activities generated public conflict between incumbent and challenger business actors and led to a loss of credibility in the public eye. This situation for SQM was exacerbated in subsequent years. Starting in 2013, various political scandals emerged regarding the irregular financing of political activities by large national companies. Initially, a judicial investigation was launched against Empresas Penta, which revealed a connection to SQM as a company that had been irregularly financing political campaigns across the spectrum for years.

Indeed, it was determined that SQM had issued false invoices and receipts, using "ideologically false" vouchers as a mechanism to transfer money to various political leaders, including those from the center-left coalition "Nueva Mayoría," which brought Michelle Bachelet to the presidency (2014–2018). This crisis prevented business actors linked to lithium extraction from publicly positioning themselves or employing strategies to influence lithium public policy reforms under Bachelet's administration. As one interviewee acknowledged, SQM's primary fault was corruption:

> "The great sin of SQM, as I said, is not the management; the great sin of SQM is corruption. And that is unacceptable. I believe that a country has every right to say, 'we will not accept this'" (Interview 18—CODELCO).

Thus, it is evident that incumbent companies in lithium extraction, particularly SQM, have utilized instrumental power mechanisms to influence public policy instruments. However, during this initial stage, rather than obstructing industrial policy instruments, they used their power to capitalize on liberal measures aimed at reinforcing the low-value-added extractivist approach to lithium exploitation. In this context, the private actor sought to increase its market share by securing extraction quotas aligned with projected demand growth. As will be discussed in subsequent sections, other influence strategies have continued to be employed in the following years, some of which focus on opposing industrialization measures.

Legal Conflicts, New Contracts, and Lithium Industrialization

In 1993, the Chilean government entered contracts with SQM for the extraction of lithium, which provided substantial benefits to the company, as detailed in previous chapters. However, over the years, it became evident that the mining company had repeatedly violated its exploitation contracts. In 2016, illegal political financing practices by SQM, funded by lithium profits, were uncovered (Pizarro & Ramírez, 2018).[2] With the renewed focus on lithium industrialization under President Bachelet, CORFO initiated various legal actions demanding the dissolution of SQM Salar and the return of mining assets and water rights to CORFO. The aim was to remove the company's control over lithium resources and advance toward a state-led process.

The lawsuit filed by CORFO against SQM Salar in 2014 was due to SQM's failure to pay the agreed lease rents to CORFO. Additionally, SQM failed to maintain and conserve the boundary markers of CORFO's mining rights in the salt flats (Pizarro & Ramírez, 2018). In 2016, new charges were brought against SQM Salar for registering groundwater rights on peripheral lands around the mining claims. Other allegations included improperly requesting servitudes on third-party lands, acquiring mining concessions on peripheral lands, and diverting resources from the Atacama salt flat to finance illegal political activities.

After four years of legal disputes, CORFO reached a settlement with SQM that resulted in the signing of a new contract, known as the Atacama Salar Contract. The terms of this agreement significantly improved CORFO's position compared to the 1990s contracts. However, the original goal of terminating the existing contracts, which had been

[2] During President Bachelet's second term, several cases of tax crimes came to light, involving irregular financing by SQM to political actors across the political spectrum, including members of President Bachelet's cabinet. At the time, Interior Minister Rodrigo Peñalillo (PPD) expressed concern to the Minister of Finance and the Director of the Internal Revenue Service about the ongoing investigation into SQM (Cofré, 2019).

the initial impetus for CORFO's legal actions, was not achieved. Accusations arose that Bitrán, a key figure in this process, had been subjected to various forms of pressures. Bitrán himself acknowledged receiving pressures while negotiating an agreement with SQM to remove Julio Ponce Lerou (La Tercera, 2018). He also mentioned receiving pressure from his own political sector, stating, "I received pressures from distinguished politicians precisely for these kinds of considerations" (Nuñez, 2018). However, Bitrán later revised his statement, suggesting that instead of pressures, legislators had merely offered their opinions (Pulso, 2018b). These situations, or opinions, aimed to undermine the ongoing legal process against SQM and reach a settlement.

A central figure in this process was José María Eyzaguirre,[3] one of SQM's directors and a lawyer for the Canadian company Potash (Nutrien), which owned 32% of SQM shares. Eyzaguirre frequently met with Bitrán to persuade him to halt the legal conflict. Eyzaguirre even threatened Bitrán with a parallel lawsuit from Potash, as the current lawsuit jeopardized SQM investors' interests. Jochen Tilk, the president of Potash, also met with Bitrán to urge him to reconsider his stance. At that time, Potash had merged with another company, which required it to divest its shares in SQM. The forced sale would harm the company due to the low value of SQM shares resulting from the ongoing legal conflict.

Thus, SQM engaged in a legal battle with CORFO while simultaneously holding various lobbying meetings with authorities, particularly with Bitrán, but also with other state actors who could potentially dissuade the CORFO vice president from pursuing his actions. Theoretically, this demonstrates an attempt to directly influence the authorities through lobbying, while also employing threats of further legal action. In essence, faced with direct confrontation, the company utilized a classic repertoire of instrumental power influence (Fairfield, 2018), though it notably refrained from using certain methods, such as monetary incentives. The use of financial leverage was not a viable option, as the company was concurrently under investigation for the illegal financing of political parties, particularly in the context of political campaigns (Maillet et al., 2019). This situation had significantly eroded its legitimacy in the public sphere, as highlighted by an interviewee:

[3] It is also noteworthy that Eyzaguirre served as legal counsel for Augusto Pinochet during his detention in London, related to the human rights violations committed during his dictatorship in Chile (1973–1990).

"But what really frustrated me was that we couldn't make progress. The solution was so simple. It was basically for CORFO to find a way to revoke the concessions of these companies. Albemarle didn't seem like a bad company to me, and in fact, they renegotiated a pretty good contract. There wasn't much of an issue there. But with SQM, I did have a problem, because regardless of whether, if one studies SQM, it's not that it's a poorly managed company. The issue is that it's a company that was used to corrupt Chilean politics, so it had no legitimacy" (Interview 18—CODELCO).

Ultimately, Bitrán reached an agreement with SQM that significantly improved the state's position vis-à-vis business. Among the key terms set in the Salar de Atacama Contract were the removal of Julio Ponce's control over SQM, a fine of US $17.5 million, and a substantial increase in the extraction quota, tripling the originally agreed amount (Brion, 2018a). Table 6.1 outlines the main agreements reached between CORFO and SQM.

From the state's perspective, the new contract substantially increased revenue from lease payments and stipulated that 25% of SQM's production would be sold at preferential prices to domestic producers, fostering R&D projects centered on lithium. This initiative was realized through an international tender offering lithium at preferential rates, which was awarded to Nanotec for the development of lithium super nanoparticles for the battery industry. Currently, the company has initiated value-added

Table 6.1 Main agreements reached in the negotiation between CORFO and SQM. *Source* Own elaboration based on Ciper (2018)

Agreements Reached in the SQM-CORFO Conciliation (2018)	
SQM	*CORFO*
Remains the holder of the lease agreement	Receives a payment of US$20 million
Permitted to exploit and commercialize lithium until 2030	Increase in revenues from lease payment collections
No recognition of debts by SQM to CORFO for lease payments	In 2030, will receive mining legal easements free of charge
At the end of the contract, CORFO will have a preferential option to purchase water rights	25% of production will be allocated at preferential prices to producers in Chile
Will pay between US$10 and US$19 million annually to Indigenous communities in Atacama	Corporate governance standards are introduced for SQM Salar

processes by producing nanoparticles that enhance the performance of lithium batteries. Thus, despite the conflict between SQM and CORFO, the state successfully established conditions that promote R&D policies, which now enable value-added processes, directly influencing value chains and contributing to the diversification of the lithium extractive economy.

Concurrently, in his final days as Vice President of CORFO in 2018, Eduardo Bitrán lodged a complaint with Chile's National Economic Prosecutor's Office (FNE) concerning the potential acquisition of SQM shares by Tianqi (Brion, 2018b). The Wall Street Journal reported that this acquisition could lead to SQM and Tianqi controlling 70% of the global lithium market due to the significant share of SQM acquired by the Chinese multinational (Pulso, 2018a). This move is widely interpreted as Bitrán's final effort to advance the lithium value chain in Chile.

Lithium Preferential Prices

As part of Chile's lithium policy, the renegotiation of contracts was not limited to CORFO but also extended to Albemarle. The new contracts granted Albemarle an increase in lithium production at the Salar de Atacama in exchange for fulfilling various tax obligations, community engagement commitments, and R&D processes, all aimed at promoting greater industrialization around lithium. In terms of taxation, Albemarle's royalty payments to the state increased by 60%. Regarding community relations, Albemarle was required to raise its royalty payments to the communities residing in the salar. Additionally, from 2017 and throughout the duration of the agreement, Albemarle committed to contributing up to $12 million annually to one or more non-profit research and technological development entities to develop technology focused on the use and/or application of solar energy, non-metallic and metallic mining, as well as applied research studies. Furthermore, the new contract stipulated that Albemarle must sell 25% of its production at preferential prices to companies designated by CORFO, under similar conditions to those previously established with SQM. According to Eduardo Bitrán, CORFO's Vice President at the time, the agreement was expected to significantly advance the industrialization of the mineral:

> "This agreement is expected to drive an innovation agenda to capitalize on the unique global advantages of northern Chile. The Atacama Desert, with the best solar radiation in the world—30% more than that of the Sahara

> Desert—is home to the planet's largest copper mining district and boasts the best lithium and salt resources for energy storage globally. The availability of resources for innovation allows us to pursue sustainable industrial mining development in northern Chile, positioning us as a world leader in intelligent mining with low CO2 emissions. Additionally, it will enable us to engage in the development of higher-value-added lithium products" (Eduardo Bitrán, Executive Vice President of CORFO—La Tercera, 2016).

The sale of 25% of Albemarle's production at preferential prices for the development of lithium-related R&D was one of the key measures for lithium industrialization, as it would make it attractive for companies to produce complex products based on low-cost lithium. In 2017, CORFO conducted an international tender to allocate this 25%, with offers submitted by Chinese, Russian, Korean, Canadian, and Chilean companies, reflecting the significant interest in lithium-related production. Finally, in 2018, the consortium formed by Posco-Samsung of South Korea and Molymet of Chile was selected to produce lithium cathodes, a primary component of lithium-ion batteries. Additionally, the Chinese company Sichuan Fulin won a contract to build a cathode material plant in Chile. These companies were notified of their successful bids in CORFO's tender, which aimed to foster investments for the industrialization of Chilean lithium (Orellana, 2018).

However, despite the theoretical soundness of the agreements, efforts to establish new companies to add value to the lithium supply chain faltered due to disagreements between CORFO and Albemarle over the interpretation of the preferential pricing clause. This disagreement escalated into a confrontation, leading CORFO, after failed negotiations, to announce its intent to seek arbitration at the International Court of Arbitration in Paris to address Albemarle's breach of contract and establish a formula for calculating the preferential price. Albemarle, for its part, argued that CORFO was the party disregarding the agreement. During the negotiations and attempts to reach an agreement, Albemarle proposed that CORFO compensate the company for the preferential price given to specialized producers. In simple terms, the proposal was that:

> "If the company sold to specialized producers at a price of 100, but Albemarle's real price was 160, CORFO would have to cover the difference of 60 by deducting it from the sales commission owed to CORFO" (Interview with María Elena Cruz, Legal Counsel of CORFO—Minería Chilena, 2018).

In 2019, Albemarle and CORFO reached an agreement on the preferential pricing for producers, thereby avoiding the need for CORFO to pursue arbitration (Nogales, 2019).

Empirical evidence highlights two primary challenges in implementing this public policy. First, Albemarle and CORFO had differing interpretations of how to determine the preferential price at which the mineral would be offered to companies. Second, Albemarle contended that it was not obligated to sell lithium to industrial firms but merely to "offer" it (Orellana, 2019a). Beyond the legal intricacies of the contract, Albemarle intended to circumvent the underlying purpose of the legislation. The company exploited legal ambiguities to avoid completing sales to new enterprises meant to participate in the industrialization process, leading to their eventual withdrawal. Key actors from that period saw Albemarle's actions as an excuse to evade their contractual obligations:

> "Unfortunately, when the time came to set the prices at which lithium would be sold to these companies, Albemarle sought to alter the agreement by excluding the sales it made to its parent company, Albemarle USA, from the price calculation. They were selling to their parent company at a lower price than to others. This created transfer pricing practices that benefited the parent company while harming Chile by reducing tax payments and established royalties. During my tenure at CORFO, we opposed this arbitrary interpretation that the lower export parity price should exclude related-party sales because such an exclusion was not stipulated in the contract, making it a breach of contract" (Interview 3—CORFO).

This sentiment was echoed by business leaders of the time. For instance, Mauricio Mora, Director of American Lithium and Cobalt Corp, specifically criticized the reasons behind the failure to advance the industrialization process, emphasizing that the issue was not technical feasibility but rather the conflict between the government and corporations:

> "The problem wasn't that industrialization was technically infeasible or lacked investment. The real issue was that there was no genuine intent on the government's part to pursue it. Instead, the premises of the negotiations with both Albemarle and SQM were flawed" (Orellana, 2019b).

This case illustrates how corporate opposition can manifest even when the state demonstrates substantial capacity. While the conflict between

SQM and CORFO eventually led to the establishment of new regulations that facilitated progress in adding value to lithium, Albemarle failed to honor its contractual commitments, resulting in the withdrawal of the companies that had won the tender. This dynamic supports the central argument: the State possesses the capacity to drive value-added processes in the lithium sector, even in the face of corporate resistance, particularly in areas under its direct control, such as establishing selective industrialization funds, coordinating these efforts, and promoting research and development. However, advancing to the next stage, which entails developing large-scale, structural lithium projects, is challenging without corporate cooperation. The following sections will examine additional instances of business opposition to Chile's lithium policy to further substantiate this argument.

The Controversial Progress of the Clean Technologies Institute

A critical element in the configuration of Chile's public policy on lithium revolves around research and the development of technologies related to the mineral. Specifically, the policy outlines the establishment of a research institute focused on generating advanced products associated with lithium. Under the coordination of CORFO, this initiative was formalized in the Atacama Salt Flat Contract, mentioned in the previous section. The agreement provided for the funding of a public or private, non-profit research and technological development center. The co-funding arrangement included a cap of $193,485,024 CLP,[4] sourced from the R&D contributions stipulated in the Atacama Salt Flat Contract, with at least 30% co-financing required by 2030. Private sector contributions were expected to cover at least 60% of the costs, with the remaining funds provided through non-monetary contributions.[5] This represented the largest investment ever made for a research institute in Chile.

Given the significant scale of the funding,[6] this public policy instrument aimed to achieve several objectives: creating advanced technological infrastructure, developing a portfolio of R&D projects oriented toward

[4] 1000 Chilean pesos is approximately 1 dollar.

[5] Source: Corfo. Available on: https://www.corfo.cl/sites/cpp/convocatorias/instituto_de_tecnologias_limpias_fase_rfp

[6] The investment planned is the largest ever made in the country for the financing of a research center.

industry, and, most importantly, developing materials and innovations that add value to lithium within the supply chain for electromobility and green growth.[7] The ITL was envisioned as a central entity for advancing the technological potential of lithium and as the largest institute of its kind in the country.[8]

The bidding process for the institute began in October 2019, with the initial award date set for April 2020. However, the results were only announced at the end of that year, amid widespread criticism regarding the transparency of the process. Generally, the bidding process involved consortia primarily composed of companies and higher education institutions (Álvarez, 2019). Among the proposals submitted, three stood out: one led mainly by Chilean universities; another by mining and energy companies; and a third by a consortium of American universities.

In January 2021, CORFO announced that the bid had been awarded to the American consortium Associated Universities Inc. (AUI). In response, the Council of Rectors of Chilean Universities expressed regret over CORFO's decision, criticizing both the process (the way the bidding was conducted) and the outcome (the decision not to award the contract to Chilean universities) (La Tercera, 2021). The proposal from the group of Chilean universities, the Association for the Development of Clean Technologies (ASDIT), voiced concerns about the outcome. The winning

[7] Source: CORFO. Available on: https://www.corfo.cl/sites/cpp/convocatorias/instituto_de_tecnologias_limpias_fase_rfp

[8] Sebastián Sichel, who was the Vice President of CORFO at the time, states that the establishment of the Chilean Institute of Clean Technologies was the result of collaborative efforts by an intersectoral committee consisting of the Ministries of Economy, Mining, and Energy. The vision for the institute was to create an innovative foundation that, in addition to fostering research and development (R&D), would support and promote entrepreneurial ventures. The development of the institute was part of an agreement between CORFO and SQM Salar S.A. concerning the exploitation of the Atacama salt flat, under which SQM was required to provide resources for R&D activities. Government officials of the time, particularly Sebastián Sichel, viewed the institute as a strategic initiative to enhance the production chain and address the global demand for electromobility and hydrogen economy. For the implementation of the Institute of Clean Technologies, CORFO initiated a competition from October 18, 2019, to March 21, 2020, for submissions. The requirements outlined by CORFO included supporting the creation and implementation of the technological institute through the following activities: Research and Development; Technology Transfer and Innovation; Specialized Technological and Technical Assistance; Technological Dissemination; and the Generation of Research and Information to Support Regulation and Public Policy in areas such as Solar Energy, Low-Emission Mining, Advanced Lithium Materials, and other minerals.

consortium was an international group with limited ties to Chile's mining and energy sectors, and there were also criticisms regarding the transparency of the project evaluation process (Cuevas, 2021).

Ignacio Sánchez, Rector of the Pontifical Catholic University of Chile, expressed concerns about the potential risks to the future of science in the country. He noted that "this [the bidding process] did not go through the Comptroller's Office because it is said that these are private funds derived from the lithium royalty" (Montes & Quezada, 2021). Sánchez also pointed out that while the international advisory council had given a positive evaluation of their project, they were never invited to present it. Similarly, Alejandro Jofré, who led the University of Chile's proposal, mentioned that although their proposal was selected internationally, the decision was reversed at the local level. Dr. Cecilia Hidalgo, president of the Chilean Academy of Sciences, criticized the process as lacking transparency: "the entire process was conducted in a dark, non-transparent manner, very different from the processes Chilean scientists are accustomed to" (Montes & Quezada, 2021).

The controversy escalated to the parliamentary level, where similar accusations of irregularities were raised. Senator Guido Girardi, president of the Environment Committee and the Challenges of the Future Committee, condemned the process as irregular and announced that they would pursue all necessary actions: "*We will pursue this to the fullest extent. We are evaluating and will likely file a criminal complaint in the coming days for serious irregularities, incompatible negotiations, and potential malfeasance*" (Andrews, 2021). In addition, a group of senators and deputies called for a special Senate session to address the issue and for the creation of a Chamber of Deputies investigative committee to examine the bidding process and its outcome. Senator Alejandro Guillier mentioned that during his discussions with Eduardo Bitrán, the director of CORFO during President Bachelet's administration (2014–2018), the focus was always on involving local stakeholders in the creation of the institute (Romo, 2021). On January 11, 2021, the Association of Electrical, Electronic, and Automation Industries (AIE) urged reconsideration of the award, arguing that the winning consortium had little connection to the Chilean context (Prensa PM, 2021).

Throughout this process, evidence has surfaced suggesting that corporate influence may have played a role in shaping the outcome. For instance, Pablo Terrazas, who was the vice president of CORFO at the time, had to recuse himself due to conflicts of interest. Despite this, he continued to lead CORFO, making decisions that directly benefited AUI, with whom he had conflicts of interest. Specifically, Terrazas held an extraordinary meeting of CORFO's Board of Directors on October 30, 2020, during which a clause in the original project was amended, reducing the budget by $50 million and reallocating those funds to green hydrogen projects—an adjustment that aligned perfectly with AUI's proposal. This action violated agreements made with the Senate's Energy and Mining and Challenges of the Future Committees, which required transparency measures to be implemented before finalizing the bidding process. Additionally, his successor, Felipe Commentz, led the committee that evaluated the proposals despite having direct ties to the AUI team, which ultimately won the bid. The Chamber of Deputies' investigative committee reported evidence that the bidding terms were irregularly altered during the process to favor one of the consortia (Cámara de Diputados, 2021).

In response to these developments, Chilean universities filed a legal challenge, resulting in the suspension of the bidding process until a judicial resolution was reached. This situation highlights the influence of corporate actors in redirecting the process to their advantage, thereby creating a conflict between State and private actors. Although the State remains a strong player in this process, preventing a complete capture, the policy process—specifically the bidding—has become mired in controversy. As of now, the outcome remains uncertain, leaving stakeholders unclear about the institute's future. Some view the flawed process as a "lost opportunity" for advancing research and development in the lithium industry. Even those directly involved in managing this policy are unsure of what might happen next. However, others remain optimistic, believing that since the funds are already committed, the push toward greater industrialization will continue.

Structural Business Power in Chile's Lithium Policy

Lithium-related business groups have established significant power resources over time (Bril-Mascarenhas & Maillet, 2019) by developing technical expertise and specialized knowledge, which they have leveraged during the implementation of policies. Historically, the management of lithium has been under the purview of the Ministry of Mining, although it is treated quite differently from traditional mining operations. This has led private actors to develop an industry that is unlike any other managed by public companies or state organizations. In fact, very few companies globally possess the specialized expertise required in the lithium sector.

For decades, the State did not adequately regulate these companies, remaining largely unaware of the realities surrounding lithium extraction. As a result, the specialized knowledge developed by the private sector has rendered it unlikely that any other company could effectively undertake this economic activity. From a power dynamics perspective, companies involved in lithium extraction have accumulated substantial institutional business power over the decades. This, combined with minimal regulation, has created a significant power asymmetry. Today, there is a consensus among industry stakeholders that dismantling these companies would be challenging, as it would likely lead to a decline in productivity and global competitiveness, especially compared to countries with more liberal policies, such as Argentina.

In this context, many of the dynamics observed previously are only possible by understanding the structural power of these companies, which have developed resources and a privileged position within the productive structure, allowing them to act more confrontationally. In this case, structural power does not operate through the traditional threat of investment flight (Hacker & Pierson, 2002). Instead, the threat is a less conventional one, involving the risk of service or economic provision discontinuity, which cannot be easily replaced in the short term by another company. This characterization of structural power has been applied in other studies, such as the case of public transportation in Santiago, where the threat of service disruption prevented the regulatory authority from enforcing regulations and sanctions against the companies (Maillet & Carrasco, 2019). More recently, some authors have described this exercise of structural power as a new form of power. Busemeyer and Thelen (2020) refer to this as "institutional business power," which "arises when policymakers invite or allow private actors to share in the delivery of public responsibilities, setting in motion feedback effects that over time enhance the power of private interests vis-à-vis publicly accountable government actors" (2020, pp. 448–449).

The empirical evidence collected provides several insights into how institutional business power operates, particularly concerning information control. First, lithium extraction differs from traditional mining activities, requiring specific expertise that only a few companies worldwide—those dedicated to lithium extraction—have developed. The unique ecosystems of salt flats (Dorador et al., 2020) necessitate equally specialized knowledge for their intervention. In the Chilean context, the withdrawal of CORFO from the forefront of extractive activities allowed companies to develop proprietary information, which the State does not possess. As one interviewee noted:

> "The issue of developing a lithium policy in Chile is extremely challenging. The entrenched powers are formidable, and it is very difficult to work on a government policy that is realistic without agreement with the private sector. It is nearly impossible to access complete information. The truthful information on everything is held by the two companies in Chile, which are SQM and Albemarle" (Interview 1, National Lithium Commission).

The legal provisions in the contracts required companies to provide information regarding extraction quotas and other specific matters. However, subsequent lawsuits revealed the limited and often distorted information these companies provided. Given that the extraction activities occur in one of the world's driest deserts, far from urban centers, effective monitoring and enforcement by the State become challenging, leading to an information asymmetry, as noted by another interviewee:

> "There is a significant information asymmetry between the private companies extracting lithium in the Atacama salt flat and the State. The State is essentially 'naked,' lacking the necessary information to regulate effectively and to make informed decisions about this industry" (Interview 7—National Lithium Commission).

For some, this situation can only be understood in the context of long-term periods, where the initial legal framework for lithium in the 1980s assigned a passive role to the state, failing to promote proper lithium development and leaving decisions to the discretion of private actors:

> "Albemarle, under different company names, has been producing lithium since the 1980s, and SQM since 1992, with zero regulation on one hand, and zero structure to promote the proper functioning of lithium extraction" (Interview 6—Albemarle).

In terms of exercising power in opposition to policy, these activities manifest as resistance to industry regulation and the effective enforcement of existing contracts. It is at this juncture that lithium entrepreneurs leverage their specialized knowledge to impose official figures regarding export volumes, lithium reserves, and other relevant quantities in the institutional context for decision-making. Several years ago, Weil et al. (2009) highlighted the discrepancies between existing figures on lithium, to the point where each actor had different numbers, particularly regarding resource estimates (measured, indicated, and inferred values). This has clear implications for regulation, where the state has struggled to actively control exported lithium resources. Although mechanisms have been established to better measure extraction quotas as part of policy efforts, companies still provide the final figures. One interviewee even suggests that Chile may have sold lithium for nuclear use to countries where such sales were prohibited, though this is no longer the case under new regulations introduced by the Bachelet administration:

> "—The initial contract, signed during the Frei administration by Sandoval—who is now involved in the salmon industry—went unenforced for at least 10 to 15 years. The State of Chile simply collected the taxes declared by exporters... and as you probably know, Chilean Customs has very limited capacity to verify whether the exported materials are accurate. There is not much random inspection of shipments. The State, in general, does not guarantee the protection of its natural resources. There are failures at every level. It was so bad that at one point, there was a traceability issue where SQM sold nuclear-grade lithium to a country sanctioned by the United Nations. We lack control over our natural resources—neither at the extraction site, during transport to the port, nor at the point of export or delivery to the end consumer. These issues arise from contracts and the country's inadequate enforcement systems" (Interview 1—National Lithium Commission).

The monopolization of the public function related to lithium has enabled SQM to build and consolidate power resources over time, similar to what has occurred in other public policy areas, such as pensions (Bril-Mascarenhas & Maillet, 2019). These power resources manifest in public policy discussions, granting SQM a privileged position that allows for a confrontational dynamic in which the State is constrained in implementing its strategies or enforcing regulations. For instance, it becomes exceedingly difficult to terminate contracts or impose sanctions and legal actions against these companies, as they have evolved into an oligopoly, making their replacement impractical in the short term. Moreover, considerations about the future, the role of lithium in the energy transition, and the revenue it generates for government coffers make it impossible to formulate any strategy without accounting for the incumbent private actors.

The Marginal Role of State-Owned Enterprises

Throughout the discussion on the industrialization process, CODELCO—the country's principal state-owned enterprise, primarily focused on copper extraction and export—was consistently highlighted in public debate as a key player in lithium exploitation. However, its role during the analyzed period remained relatively marginal. This section argues that the expectations for CODELCO to industrialize and exploit lithium were not realized due to two primary factors. The first relates to technical challenges, while the second pertains to the company's development priorities and strategies. In this context, CODELCO adopted an indirect strategy of opposition by not prioritizing lithium, despite the political mandate to do so. Nonetheless, this did not lead to significant repercussions from state actors. After all, as the evidence suggests, the State has historically treated CODELCO favorably, given its substantial economic significance to the country (Schorr, 2018).

Initially, when SQM was awarded the lithium contract in 2012, CODELCO announced its intention to enter the lithium market by exploiting the Maricunga salt flat, which it owned. The company indicated that it was preparing a plan for this market and would reveal it in the following days (Pizarro et al., 2012). Later that same year, Gerardo Jofré, then president of CODELCO, declared that the state-owned company would commence lithium extraction in the Maricunga salt flat, in collaboration with the Japanese firm Mitsui, a strategic partner of CODELCO in other projects (Pizarro et al., 2012). Over the years, CODELCO pursued partnerships to develop lithium extraction projects in the Maricunga and Pedernales salt flats (González, 2017). In November 2017, CODELCO's CEO, Nelson Pizarro, traveled to China to gain insights into lithium extraction. Although CODELCO possessed lithium assets and expressed intentions to exploit them, the company had not done so due to a lack of experience in lithium extraction.

During President Bachelet's second administration, CORFO's Non-Metallic Mining Committee established a Special Contract for Lithium Operation (CEOL) for CODELCO. This fulfilled the committee's mandate, granting CODELCO the legal authority to exploit the Maricunga and Pedernales salt flats. Despite CODELCO's long-standing intentions to enter the lithium market, concrete steps only began to materialize in 2019. In July of that year, the company's board of directors convened to review the progress of the so-called Lithium Project and to establish specific guidelines for the exploitation of the salt flats it owned (O'Ryan, 2019). It was decided that exploration efforts would continue, potentially leading to drilling, the recruitment of experts, and investment in exploration. However, none of these initiatives have been implemented yet.

This case analysis highlights the insufficient institutional capacity to effectively manage lithium exploitation. As argued in Chapter 4, lithium is a complex mineral, and its proper extraction is a technical process that only a few companies worldwide have mastered (Martin et al., 2017). A former undersecretary reinforces this point, stating:

> "For us miners, lithium mining in Chile is not truly mining in the traditional sense; it more closely resembles an agricultural production process. You pump brine, concentrate it in ponds, harvest the salts from the brine, and then transport it to a chemical plant for processing. Objectively speaking, there is very little actual mining involved; there is no mining technique, no mine plan, no mine development, etc. Therefore, it is a sector somewhat on the periphery of traditional mining. While it does respond to some mining variables, since we are ultimately dealing with subsoil, it is quite different from the conventional mining sector" (Interview 9—Ministry of Mining).

Despite the sustained emphasis in policies and public discourse on positioning CODELCO as a pivotal actor in the future of lithium, both as a driving force and leader in the industrialization process, the situation is more nuanced. Although CODELCO stands as Chile's largest mining enterprise, it possesses limited expertise in lithium extraction. The technical processes involved in lithium extraction are fundamentally distinct from those of copper mining, presenting significant challenges for CODELCO. Over nearly a decade, the company has expressed intentions to develop its lithium assets, yet these efforts have been impeded by technical constraints.

In addition to these technical challenges, interviews with key stakeholders within CODELCO reveal that lithium was not a primary focus in the company's strategic development. A former CODELCO executive noted that the company faced various economic and managerial issues. Consequently, CODELCO's attention remained predominantly on copper extraction, which holds far greater economic significance than lithium:

> "To be quite honest, my main concern was copper and CODELCO's inefficiency, trying to... I mean, the company was handed to me in a disastrous state. And not just because of the right-wing. To a large extent, it was our own fault through the unions. To be very frank. So, my main concern was to get the Salvador division into the black, lower production costs, and get the politicians and corruption out of the company. That was my focus. As for lithium, if I'm being very honest, it wasn't something I addressed; it wasn't my main concern" (Interview 18—CODELCO).

Some interviewees associated with CODELCO argue that there is a discrepancy between the perceived significance of lithium and its actual economic impact on the national budget. They contend that the market value of lithium transactions remains substantially lower than the revenues generated by copper, despite the rapid expansion of the lithium market in recent years. In Chile, lithium continues to contribute only a fraction compared to copper in terms of export volumes and revenue, as depicted in Fig. 6.2. From this economic standpoint, it is understandable that lithium did not emerge as a priority in the decision-making processes of the state-owned company, particularly given its simultaneous engagement with other political, labor, and social issues (Schorr, 2018).

Lithium extraction and development were not central to CODELCO's operational strategy. Despite its inexperience in the sector, the leadership demonstrated a lack of strategic foresight to pursue lithium exploitation actively. Although CODELCO secured special contracts to access its lithium reserves, it consistently failed to allocate the necessary resources to initiate comprehensive industrial processes. While there were occasional discussions with other stakeholders regarding potential strategic alliances for lithium development, these efforts remained fragmented, and no substantial projects materialized, reflecting the marginal importance placed on this sector within the company's broader objectives.

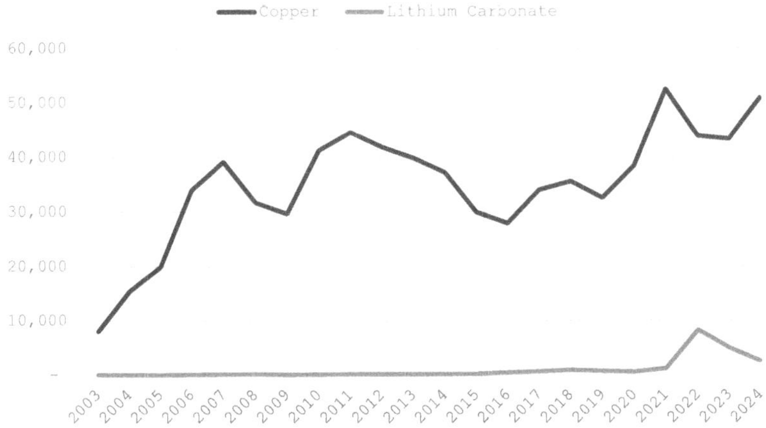

Fig. 6.2 Chilean copper and lithium exports (2010–2023) (in millions of US dollars). *Source* Own elaboration based on Central Bank of Chile database

Business Preferences

As discussed in the previous sections of the chapter, incumbent business actors since 2010 have deployed various forms of power to maintain and expand their positions in global markets. Initially, they sought to enhance their standing within the framework of liberal policies, while in a subsequent phase, they opposed strategies aimed at advancing within the value chain. The privileged position of these companies within the production structure reinforced this dynamic, allowing them to adopt a confrontational stance toward the State. In terms of preferences, it is clear that during the period under study, private companies favored expanding the extraction and marketing of raw lithium, increasing their market share. Indeed, business actors argue that Chile should leverage its competitive advantages by boosting extraction quotas to prevent losing its position in the global market (Carrasco et al., 2023). There is a prevailing view that expanding the market from an extractivist perspective is necessary, as failing to do so would mean missing an opportunity, with other countries potentially filling the global demand or rendering lithium obsolete through the development of new technologies for batteries and electromobility. Thus, the strategic importance of lithium in the market is mediated by current expansion and decision-making.

State-owned enterprises, however, have faced a dilemma that has made their preferences less defined. On the one hand, they are subject to the government's political and strategic directives, which have intermittently sought to involve them in the lithium market, particularly through CODELCO and ENAMI. Yet, as mentioned earlier, these enterprises have struggled with internal management challenges and lack the expertise needed to effectively engage in lithium-related activities. As a result, lithium has not been prioritized within their operations. This neutrality further weakens the state's position relative to private companies, perpetuating a power imbalance that has allowed private actors to influence policy decisions on multiple occasions.

At various points, foreign companies have attempted to leverage opportunities for industrialization in Chile by participating in bidding processes to contribute to domestic lithium value addition, while also negotiating with political and bureaucratic actors to establish new lithium industries. In some cases, these efforts have succeeded, and Chile is currently involved in value-adding processes linked to lithium, particularly in products from the second stage of the value chain. For instance, lithium carbonate is utilized in the production of other goods, although these transformations remain in their early stages. In this setting, corporate collaboration has played a significant role, yet it has not been enough to counterbalance the influence of established private firms. Traditional private companies, with their substantial power resources, continue to dominate the political landscape, making it difficult to align the expectations of diverse stakeholders.

Advancing the Lithium Agenda? Gabriel Boric's Strategic Shift

It is crucial to understand that the relationship between businesses and the State regarding lithium policy is a dynamic and evolving process, with much still to be developed. The current government under Gabriel Boric (2022–2026) exemplifies how interactions between the State and the business sector are continually reconfigured, even as the outcomes remain uncertain. Undoubtedly, lithium is a sector characterized by ongoing advancements and changes, highlighting its strategic importance in the current political and economic landscape.

In April 2023, President Gabriel Boric presented Chile's new lithium policy, which aims to guide the nation toward a transformative development model. Central to this strategy is the establishment of a national lithium company, designed to manage the entire production process, foster partnerships with private sector entities, and drive technological advancements to mitigate environmental impacts while enhancing extraction efficiency. The policy also emphasizes the importance of community engagement and the development of advanced lithium-based products, marking a significant shift in how Chile plans to leverage its vast lithium resources.

While the policy draws on key elements from the Lithium Policy and Salar Governance framework developed during Michelle Bachelet's second administration (2014–2018), it introduces notable changes that reflect Boric's vision for the sector. Initially, Boric sought to establish a fully state-owned lithium company; however, recognizing the challenges of completely replacing existing players, the approach has since evolved. The current strategy maintains the involvement of pre-existing companies, acknowledging the complexities involved in replacing these established entities. Nevertheless, it also opens the door to new dynamics of collaboration aimed at advancing the lithium value chain.

One of the key components of this updated strategy is the introduction of new bidding processes and projects that invite both national and international companies to contribute to Chile's lithium sector. In a significant announcement during the InvestChile Forum in 2024, President Boric revealed plans for a second call, led by CORFO, to select specialized lithium producers who can drive value-added initiatives within Chile. This follows the first successful bidding process where BYD, a major Chinese firm, was selected to develop a lithium cathode plant, and the subsequent award to Tshingshan, another key player. The upcoming third call will involve the full quota previously managed by Albemarle, offering 9,500 tons of lithium carbonate equivalent (LCE) per year until 2043.

Additionally, the Empresa Nacional de Minería (Enami) has initiated a call for both local and foreign investors to partner with the state company in developing, operating, and financing the "Salares Alto Andinos" lithium project. This strategy aims to build productive linkages, deepening the complexity of Chile's development in the lithium sector.

In this way, the Boric administration has advanced in strengthening the State's capacities by incorporating strategic alliances with private companies. It appears that there is a more decisive push toward an industrial policy, although the specific outcomes remain to be seen by the end of his presidential term. Analytically, it is crucial to understand how this new configuration in the state–business relationship is shaping public policies.

While these transformations have historically been sensitive to changes in government in Chile, it is expected that these capacities will be more difficult to alter as a more virtuous relationship between the State and businesses becomes institutionalized.

During Boric's administration, traditional business actors have shown signs of shifting their preferences. For instance, in 2024, CODELCO and SQM signed an agreement to form a public–private partnership aimed at expanding their operations and producing higher-quality products (Riffo, 2024). However, shortly after, the Chinese group Tianqi, which holds a 22% stake in SQM, filed a legal action to halt the agreement, citing concerns that it conflicted with their interests, among other reasons (Cofré & Aguilera, 2024). This development raises questions about the feasibility of advancing deeper green industrial policies or whether the dynamics observed in previous administrations will persist.

Conclusion: Conflictual State–Business Relations and Selective Industrial Policy in Chile

The episodes described in this chapter reveal the conflictual dynamics between businesses and the state, particularly highlighting business opposition to certain regulations and its impact on the implementation of lithium policy in Chile. Companies have resisted these regulations through various strategies, including contract breaches, litigation, the use of technical expertise, and delaying industrialization processes. However, given the state's demonstrated institutional strength, the outcome of these interactions does not indicate a complete capture of public institutions. Instead, each episode results in a confrontational dynamic that can be seen as a zero-sum game: some policy measures are delayed or fail to be implemented due to business opposition, while the State remains steadfast in continuing its initiatives.

One of the key components of the policy is the governance framework surrounding lithium. Broadly, governance can be understood as a style of government based on cooperation between governmental and non-governmental actors in the formulation and management of public policies (Zurbriggen, 2011). This governance perspective assumes a certain level of equivalence among actors in influencing the process (Maillet & Carrasco, 2019). However, in countries like Chile, business actors have historically played a privileged role in shaping public policies (Madariaga, 2020). In contexts marked by power asymmetries between business and state actors, bureaucratic autonomy becomes crucial for ensuring that institutions are not merely symbolic (Orihuela et al., 2021). Thus, even when business actors have not been central to policy formulation, they can still influence outcomes through their opposition (or support) to institutional rules.

This dynamic highlights a specific aspect of the role of business actors in lithium policy processes. The possession of privileged information creates an initial asymmetry that can lead to the exercise of business power (Busemeyer & Thelen, 2020). This is compounded by the reluctance of business actors to include new participants who could engage in research and development (R&D). Industrialization processes, such as those outlined in Bachelet's policy, require greater private sector investment, the inclusion of new actors, increased state oversight, and environmental compensations. These requirements undoubtedly pose short-term disadvantages for established actors who have the capacity to maintain high-profit margins due to the growing international demand for lithium (Martin et al., 2017). Despite these challenges, the State has successfully implemented concrete measures to add value to the production process, promote research and development, and generate significant revenues from high taxes imposed on lithium companies (which are proportionally much higher than those on copper).

This situation is exemplified by the case of SQM. For years, the company financed political campaigns for various figures, produced much of the technical information on lithium, and established both formal and informal networks with political actors (Matamala, 2015). SQM leveraged its institutional position and expertise, which, combined with various mechanisms, allowed the company to circumvent certain established policy rules without facing significant repercussions on its operations in the past. However, the State's newly strengthened role in lithium governance has led SQM to contribute to the industrialization of lithium in several ways: by funding research, providing financial contributions to the state and local communities, and selling lithium at low prices for the production of complex goods.

Theoretically, my argument is that when external circumstances shift—toward increased state control over lithium and a growing public discourse advocating for a different approach to the mineral—business actors begin to resist new provisions that conflict with their immediate interests. Nevertheless, the development of state capacities can counteract these dynamics, demonstrating the potential to advance the complexity of the lithium value chain within the national framework. In extractive contexts like lithium, the so-called "resource curse" is not inevitable; rather, developmental challenges stem from an "institutional curse" (Menaldo, 2016). As long as state institutions remain strong, progress can be made in selective policies that promote industrialization and the development of green technologies linked to lithium. The counterfactual argument here is that with business support for these measures, it would be possible to advance frontier policies that would enable the creation of ecosystems and pioneering companies in the production of lithium-based products. This would significantly boost the sector by adding value through the manufacturing of complex lithium-based products. Figure 6.3 illustrates the causal mechanism derived from this analysis.

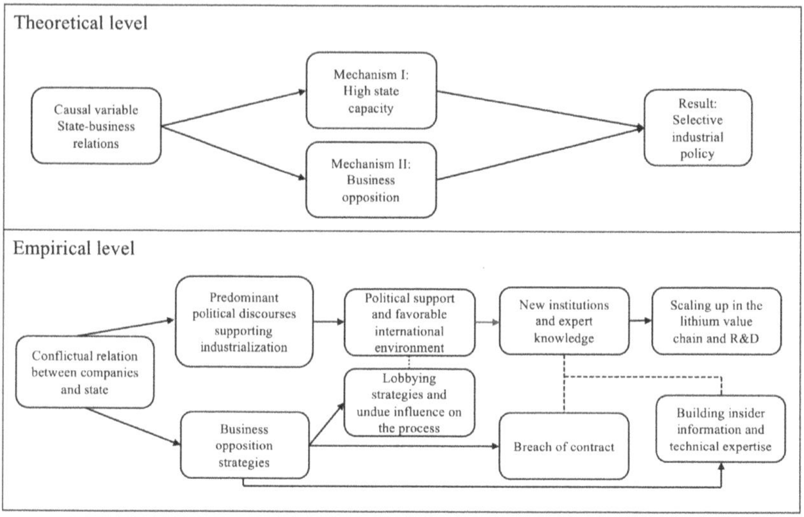

Fig. 6.3 Causal narrative explaining the establishment of lithium policy in Chile. *Source* Own Elaboration

CHAPTER 7

Closing the Lithium Triangle: Public Policies in Argentina and Bolivia

Introduction

The analysis of the Chilean case, presented in the preceding chapters, has illustrated a confrontational dynamic between businesses and the state. On one side, the State successfully developed ad hoc capacities to implement lithium policy; on the other, business actors opposed various measures through different strategies, resulting in a selective industrial policy. This chapter aims to complement the analysis of the Chilean case by examining Argentina and Bolivia as comparative cases. It is important to remember that these three countries form the lithium triangle and are key players in lithium industrialization in Latin America, despite pursuing divergent trajectories in their respective projects..

Argentina and Bolivia play a significant methodological role in this research, as they serve as cases that empirically validate the proposed typology. In simpler terms, the central argument is that each of the cases under analysis corresponds to a distinct configuration within the proposed typology, as illustrated in Table 7.1. It is noteworthy that no case has been identified with the characteristics required to fit into the frontier policies category, which poses a challenge for future research.

In the Argentine case, I demonstrate that although there have been attempts to advance toward greater vertical industrialization, these efforts have not prospered. Instead, extractive activities have intensified, leading to a significant increase in investment projects focused on lithium

S. Carrasco, *From (De)regulation to Industrialization?*, Latin American Political Economy, https://doi.org/10.1007/978-3-031-77130-9_7

Table 7.1 Typology of state–business relations, types of industrial policy and cases

State capacity	*Business role*	
	Business support	*Business opposition*
High state capacity	Frontier Industrial Policy	Selective Industrial Policy (Chile)
Low state capacity	Stagnant Industrial Policy (Bolivia)	Non-Industrial Policy (Argentina)

Source: Own elaboration

extraction, perpetuating more liberal policies regarding lithium. In fact, Argentina is expected to become the world's leading lithium exporter in the coming years. In contrast, Bolivia has established a state-led industrial policy. In this country, lithium is regarded as a central strategic resource for Bolivia's development model, as well as for its extraction and industrialization. Consequently, a state-owned company (YLB) was created to oversee the process. Despite these efforts, the expectations for lithium exploitation have not been met, resulting in pilot production processes with marginal extraction volumes compared to those in Chile and Argentina. While there has been some support from companies in this process, the weakness of the State has allowed for the development of certain conditions that facilitate the functioning of pilot programs. This has led to a stagnant industrial policy.

Based on this general characterization, the chapter is structured as follows. First, the Argentine case is analyzed, focusing on lithium policy and the political, governmental, and business dynamics that have shaped its current policy framework. Similarly, the Bolivian case is analyzed, with an emphasis on its industrialization process, the challenges faced, and the role of various governmental actors in this context. In this case, it is argued that while Bolivia had the political will to transform its lithium policy, it has not been able to build the necessary capacities to achieve this. The companies that sought to participate in this process supported Bolivia's efforts, although their direct involvement did not materialize.

The Argentine Case

Argentina is currently the world's fourth-largest producer of lithium, with only two projects in operation (Lendoiro, 2021). However, it is anticipated that once all rhe 20 projects in its portfolio are fully operational, the country could export 120,000 tons of lithium carbonate (LCE). By 2024, this scenario had shifted favorably for Argentina, with 50 projects in the pipeline, 4 in operation, and 6 under construction (Zamarin, 2024). This development positions Argentina to become one of the leading global exporters of lithium, potentially surpassing Chile's production. Additionally, 66% of Argentina's lithium exports are destined for China, followed by 13% for the United States and 10% for South Korea (Roca, 2024). The regulatory and reform challenges faced by Bolivia and Chile have created disincentives for investment in those countries, presenting an opportunity for the Argentine market, which has seen a dramatic increase in lithium extraction projects in recent years.

The government of Alberto Fernández (2019–2023) expressed a strong interest in developing the sector (Lewkowicz, 2021), aiming to advance toward greater industrialization. However, initiatives in this area have been relatively marginal, while extractive activities surrounding lithium have intensified. In this section, I argue that this dynamic is driven by the State's limited technical capacity to advance industrialization, coupled with a decentralized political structure that fragments decision-making regarding lithium. Furthermore, private actors have actively promoted the liberalization of lithium-related policies, resulting in extractive projects with low levels of R&D integration.

These factors have led to the establishment of a horizontal policy framework that, in practice, focuses on implementing policy instruments designed to streamline lithium extraction processes, while also delivering short-term economic benefits to subnational governments. This approach has hindered the development of a comprehensive industrial policy, reinforcing an extractivist model of lithium exploitation. The consequences of this model are evident in its impact on the environment, local communities, and the unmet promises of green growth.

Lithium Exploitation in Argentina: A Contextual Analysis

Lithium extraction in Argentina occurs within a specific legal and institutional context. Unlike Bolivia or Chile, lithium in Argentina is not subject to special regulation but is governed alongside other mining activities (Pascuini & Obaya, 2020), as noted by an interviewee:

> "—Lithium is regulated by the mining code, so it is just another element of the mining code. Unlike Chile, it is not considered a strategic resource. This means that it can be tendered... licenses for exploitation can be granted to private entities without any issues. That is a key difference" (Interview 25—International Expert).

The governing legislation is the Mining Code, Law No. 1919, which classifies lithium as a first-category mineral. However, it has been noted that there is no specific legal framework regulating lithium extraction. The salt flats, where lithium is extracted, are privately owned, and agreements are made with international companies, resulting in minimal financial returns for the Argentine state. Additionally, resource exploiters can request rights over the resource, but this does not grant ownership of the land itself; they only pay royalties to the province and a fee to the landowners, who are often indigenous communities (UNLP, 2019). The Constitution establishes the federal nature of mining activities, granting provinces the authority to enact regulations governing economic activities (Pascuini & Obaya, 2020).

One of the primary criticisms of Argentina's regulatory framework is that it fosters speculation with projects. Companies often purchase concessions only to later sell them for profit. Additionally, the Mining Investments Law and the Mining Code allow the import of equipment without tariffs, set royalties at 3% of exports, and include tax exemptions and fiscal stability. However, they lack mechanisms for establishing social dialogue with local communities (Lewkowicz, 2021). Another major critique, based on the gathered evidence, is that Argentina does not have a specific lithium policy, unlike Bolivia and Chile (UNLP, 2019).

The industry has also faced environmental conflicts, as discussed in the previous chapter, with water being the primary point of contention. Lithium mining consumes significant amounts of water for its production. Unlike the progress seen in the Olaroz salt flat and in Catamarca, several projects in Salinas Grandes—a basin between Salta and Jujuy with 33 communities—were halted, and there is no corporate presence. Protests have been driven by demands for the recognition of indigenous rights, the requirement for prior consultations, and the provision of information regarding the projects' impact on biodiversity (Lewkowicz, 2021).

The origins of Argentina's lithium production model are linked to the United States, which in 1953 commissioned large quantities of lithium hydroxide for the production of the H-bomb. This demand spurred the expansion of two American companies: Foote Minerals Company [now Albemarle] and Lithium Corp. of America [now FMC]. The Mining Code, implemented in 1980 under the military dictatorship, was crucial for the future privatization of the project at the Salar del Hombre Muerto. Furthermore, legal and institutional reforms driven by the World Bank through the Argentine Mining Sector Support Project (PASMA) established a sectoral regime favorable to mining corporations. Additionally, Article 124 of the Constitution was amended to grant provinces ownership of natural resources, which meant that environmental reports would fall under the jurisdiction of local mining authorities (Nacif, 2020).

During Alberto Fernández's administration, there was a marked interest in developing the lithium extraction sector, driven by the ongoing transition in the automotive market toward electric vehicles and battery production. It is estimated that Argentina holds 9% of the world's total lithium reserves (Lewkowicz, 2021). In 2021, the Fernández government explored the possibility of a legislative project to create a public lithium company, alongside a commission with scientific, technical, commercial, and industrial expertise. This commission would include participation from various levels of government [national and provincial], as well as indigenous communities and universities. Additionally, a new agency aimed at promoting the scientific development of lithium was proposed, all within an eight-year strategic framework (Lewkowicz, 2021).

In 2022, Argentina announced the establishment of YPF Litio, a state-owned company with ambitions to oversee the entire value chain, from exploration to battery production (Barragán, 2022). The battery plant was inaugurated in Buenos Aires province, in collaboration with Y-TEC, the technology business unit of YPF, aiming to foster projects with local suppliers (Barragán, 2023). However, the election of President Javier Milei, a libertarian, shifted the landscape for state-owned enterprises. Milei has expressed interest in deregulating the State and revising the legal framework for lithium to attract greater foreign investment (Ámbito, 2023). Furthermore, Milei has close ties with billionaire Elon Musk, who has shown significant interest in lithium, sourcing it from a deposit in the Salar del Hombre Muerto for the batteries used in Tesla electric vehicles (Rebossio, 2024).

Milei has undertaken diplomatic trips to various countries to attract investment and exploit natural resources, including lithium. In February 2024, he traveled with a delegation to Israel, securing a $100 million investment deal with the company XtraLit (Reventós, 2024). Another initiative under consideration for Congress is a project to promote electromobility, one aspect of which is to incentivize lithium industrialization. However, a major challenge for this project is that nearly all of the salt flats are already under concession (Lewkowicz, 2021), leaving the government with little room to maneuver. This dynamic is explored in the following section.

State Dynamics and Lithium Policies in Argentina

In the Argentine context, the state's role in lithium exploitation is heavily influenced by the structure of its political system. Argentina is a federal country, where a tension exists between the central government, which seeks national unity, and the provinces, which operate under the principle of autonomy (Bazan, 2013). Additionally, the provinces are heterogeneous, resulting in various "brown areas" (O'Donnell, 2004) where the state's capacity varies significantly. The literature suggests that, given these characteristics, establishing national regulations alone is insufficient for effective public policy implementation. There is also a need for the design of subnational rules to ensure policy implementation, as argued by Fernández and Garay (2020) in their analysis of native forest protection policy in Argentina's Chaco region. Consequently, political changes at the national level do not necessarily translate into shifts in subnational dynamics (Christel & Torunczyk, 2017).

The political dynamics arising from Argentina's federal structure significantly impact the relationship between the State and companies in the lithium sector. At the subnational level, provinces negotiate independently with corporations. These dynamics are particularly pronounced in the provinces where lithium is extracted. Provinces like Jujuy and others in the northern region generally exhibit lower levels of professionalization and state capacity, resulting in significant power asymmetries between local governments and the large, transnational corporations involved in lithium extraction, as illustrated by one interviewee:

> "The downside is that you're putting governments, which in Argentina's case are economically lagging provinces with minimal capacities and a very

small bureaucracy, in negotiations with large companies. This creates a significant power imbalance" (Interview 25—International Expert).

Furthermore, because lithium is extracted from multiple provinces in Argentina, this situation fosters competition among subnational entities to secure lithium investment projects that can increase their revenues through corporate tax payments. As noted:

> "What happens is that the provinces end up competing with each other in what the literature calls 'The Race to the Bottom,' meaning they lower standards to make themselves more attractive to foreign investment" (Interview 25—International Expert).

The federal structure, combined with the specific conditions of the lithium-producing provinces, creates short-term incentives for state actors in these regions to promote extractive activities to generate revenue. For example, in Jujuy, local activists with a worldview that deeply respects the environment argue that there is no place for lithium extraction, coining slogans like "lithium for today, hunger for tomorrow." Concerns have also been raised about the impact of lithium production on freshwater resources, as approximately 30,000 liters of freshwater are required to produce one ton of lithium carbonate. Communities have reported noticeable changes in their water supply since mining operations began (Pressley, 2019). In this context, the Environment and Natural Resources Foundation (FARN) has called for a halt to all new lithium production, invoking the precautionary principle of environmental law, which stipulates that if sufficient scientific information is lacking or the probable impacts are not well understood, the project should not proceed.

FARN's position was not well received by Miguel Soler, the Provincial Secretary of Mining in Jujuy, who dismissed the foundation's study linking mining operations to water issues. Soler argued that the provinces with lithium deposits are among the poorest in the country, resulting in economic dependency on lithium companies for employment. Additionally, provincial governments often lack the trained personnel necessary for effective monitoring (Pressley, 2019). The conflict in Jujuy underscores the provincial government's vested interest in developing mining activities. As Miguel Soler stated, "The government of Jujuy is fully open to dialogue... We respect the community, but at the same time, we must respect the law" (Pressley, 2019).

Moreover, these dynamics are further exacerbated by the role of business leaders in the context of Argentina's lithium policies. As noted by an interviewee, the presence of large companies engaged in extractive activities benefits the provincial elites—who are economically disadvantaged in the lithium-extracting provinces—by providing them with economic gains from these companies:

> "There is a local elite in these provinces, and what they do is prefer to coexist with large companies. They facilitate the establishment of these companies for various reasons; on one hand, due to the corruption involved, and on the other, because the landholdings are also in the hands of the local elite, but they are unable to exploit them due to a lack of sufficient capital" (Interview 24—International Expert).

The Role of State-Owned Enterprises (SOE)

Geographically, lithium is predominantly concentrated in the northern regions of Argentina, specifically in the provinces of Jujuy, Salta, La Rioja, and Catamarca. The state-owned company Jujuy Energía y Minería Sociedad del Estado (JEMSE) is a key player in promoting mining properties with potential for lithium production. JEMSE currently holds 10,500 hectares of mining properties in salt flats, facilitating strategic alliances for exploration through public tenders, joint ventures, or private initiative procedures. Specifically, JEMSE oversees the Agonic, Aguiliri, and Cibeles mines (JEMSE, n.d.).

Similarly, Catamarca Minera y Energética Sociedad del Estado (CAMYEN) has a contract for exploration with YPF Litio. This agreement pertains to the Chascuil mines located in the Salar Cazadero Grande, Tinogasta. CAMYEN also maintains a usufruct agreement with YPF, aiming to produce 20,000 tons of lithium per year (CAMYEN, n.d.). Recently, a proposal has emerged from the provinces to create a federal lithium company formed by the provinces to counteract the foreignization plans pursued by President Javier Milei (Ámbito, 2023). Although YPF Litio currently exists, Alejandro Rodríguez, Director of Instituto Consenso Federal and former National Deputy, has expressed concerns that libertarian plans might undermine it. He suggested that "several Argentine provinces, which own the lithium, could partner to form a state-owned enterprise." The proposal involves uniting JEMSE, CAMYEN, Energía y Minería Sociedad del Estado (EMSE de La Rioja), and REMSa S.A. (Recursos Energéticos y Mineros de Salta) to create a unified provincial block to resist central government measures.

YPF established YPF Litio S.A. to enhance the development and industrialization of lithium. Currently, it has a joint project with CAMYEN, focusing on activities from lithium deposit research and discovery to exploration and exploitation, aiming to expand mineral production and establish itself as a key player in the country's energy future (El Cronista, 2023).

Business Dynamics and Lithium Policies in Argentina

Economically, Argentina has adopted an aggressive investment incentive policy, including a legal guarantee of fiscal stability for 30 years. This policy has attracted substantial private investments over the past decade, particularly in around 20 development projects. Major lithium projects in Argentina include the Salar de Olaroz in Jujuy and the Salar del Hombre Muerto in Catamarca. Salta also stands out in this context (Vásquez, 2021). The largest lithium reserves are located in the northern provinces: Catamarca (Salar del Hombre Muerto and Salar de Antofalla), Salta (Salar del Rincón), and Jujuy (Salar de Olaroz and Salar de Cauchari) (UNLP, 2019). FMC Lithium (now Livent) began lithium extraction in the Salar del Hombre Muerto (Catamarca) in 1997, while Orocobre and Minera Exa entered the sector in recent years (UNLP, 2019).

Livent, an American company, operates the Salar del Hombre Muerto in Catamarca, with a production capacity of 20,000 tons per year, aiming to double this through an investment of 640 million USD. Livent is partnered with BMW. Conversely, Orocobre, an Australian firm, produces 17,500 tons annually and is associated with Toyota Tsusho (Japanese) and provincial company JMS. Sales Jujuy also supplies lithium to Toyota in Japan and to South Korean and Chinese firms for battery production (Lewkowicz, 2021). Another mining company, Minera Exar, a joint venture between Lithium Americas (Canadian) and Jiangxi Ganfeng Lithium (Chinese), plans to work in the Cauchari-Olaroz sector, expecting to reach a capacity of 25,000 tons upon project completion. The company has contracts with Tesla, Volkswagen, and BMW. French company Eramet, with projects in Salta's Salar de Centenario-Ratones, and South Korean company Posco, interested in Salta, have had their projects stalled due to the pandemic and macroeconomic uncertainty (Lewkowicz, 2021). Overall, it is estimated that between 50 to 60 firms hold most Argentine salt flat concessions. Exports in 2019 amounted to 184 million USD, while in 2020, they totaled 134 million USD for 31,500 tons. With the Cauchari-Olaroz project, national production is expected to reach 85,000 tons (Lewkowicz, 2021). The Cauchari-Olaroz project commenced operations in 2023 and, after one year, has achieved 70% of its designed capacity, with plans to increase annual production to 25,000 tons of lithium carbonate (De Vicente, 2024).

Despite being relatively few compared to traditional mining activities, lithium companies in Argentina have gained prominence in recent years, even leading national business organizations, demonstrating their cohesion. Notably, Franco Mignacco, President of the Mining Entrepreneurs Chamber, comes from the lithium sector. Minera Exac, investing 350 million USD in the Cauchari-Olaroz project, is significantly backed by the Chinese company Ganfeng. This indicates that cohesion among lithium entrepreneurs is a significant factor, differing from the organizational models in Chile and Bolivia.

Given the political and state dynamics surrounding lithium in Argentina, business actors have made Argentina their preferred investment destination within the lithium triangle in recent years (Interview 12—Albemarle Executive). Business leaders argue that Argentina's attractiveness lies in its clear regulatory framework, which facilitates and attracts private investment in lithium, as noted in the following citation. However, comparative analysis reveals that Argentina's regulations impose fewer restrictions than in the other two countries, allowing for continued extractivist practices similar to traditional mining, among other practical elements. For instance, Argentina imposes a much lower royalty than Chile and lacks clear obligations concerning the relationship between companies and communities. Evidence indicates that Argentine companies have developed various extraction strategies and community relations to sustain their economic activities with minimal social opposition (González & Snyder, 2021).

> "In contrast, Argentina is experiencing significant growth, with many projects and clear rules. One might wonder why Chile lacks clear rules while Argentina does. In Argentina, the rules are relatively clear, which is why new projects are underway—at least two or three are in construction, two projects are operational, and there are around 20 to 50 new projects in exploration, though I'm not sure of the exact number" (Interview 12—Albemarle Executive).

Efforts to industrialize lithium have advanced, such as research initiated a decade ago under the supervision of the National University of La Plata, leading to the establishment of the Lithium Working Group, involving various university bodies with a multidisciplinary approach (UNLP, 2019). One notable achievement in 2013 was the development of an electric tricycle that completed a long-distance journey, with the major milestone being the launch of the Ecobus Universitario, a 100% ecological transport for La Plata. However, these strategies remain peripheral to the broader dynamics of lithium value addition processes, which are currently dominated by a liberal extractivist perspective, difficult to reverse. Consequently, there has been a lack of industrial policies, with strategies focusing instead on market regulation, promoting competition, and increasing exploitation through market mechanisms, leaving the advancement of the lithium value chain primarily to the private sector.

The Bolivian Case

Lithium Policy in Bolivia

The institutional framework for lithium exploitation in Bolivia primarily revolves around Yacimientos de Litio Bolivianos (YLB), a decentralized state enterprise under the Ministry of Energy. YLB's objective is to "develop the basic chemistry processes of evaporitic resources with 100% state participation, for the production of lithium chloride, lithium sulfate, lithium hydroxide, lithium carbonate, potassium chloride, potassium nitrate, potassium sulfate, as well as derived and intermediate salts, and other products from evaporitic resources, encompassing the entire production chain from prospecting, exploitation, beneficiation, industrialization, and commercialization of value-added final products" (YLB, 2021).

Founded on April 27, 2017, YLB is designed as the entity to develop a comprehensive, national industrial lithium production project with its own investments and technologies. It aims to enhance research and production of derivative products, enabling Bolivia to position itself sustainably in the global market while driving a shift toward clean and alternative energy sources.

The history of Bolivia's lithium policy, however, began nearly a decade before YLB's establishment. On April 1, 2008, the Bolivian government enacted DS N°29.496, declaring the industrialization of the Salar de Uyuni a national priority for the productive, economic, and social development of the Department of Potosí. Subsequently, the Political Constitution of the State (CPE) recognized the "strategic and public interest character for the country's development" of natural resources (Article 348, Section II). Article 349 designates natural resources as property and direct, indivisible, and imprescriptible domain of the Bolivian people, with the state responsible for their administration in the collective interest. Thus, the institutional framework for lithium exploitation in Bolivia is primarily centered on YLB, a decentralized state enterprise under the Ministry of Energy (YLB, 2021).

Nevertheless, Article 2 of Law N° 928, which establishes YLB, stipulates that while the company will initially operate with 100% state participation in the basic chemistry processes of Bolivia's evaporitic resources, it may later partner with national or foreign private companies, provided that state participation remains majority. This provision led to the creation of the mixed company YLB-ACI in 2018, in partnership with the German firm ACI Systems, aimed at producing lithium salts from the residuals of YLB's original process. However, this project was canceled on November 2, 2019, through Supreme Decree 4060, due to dissatisfaction among communities adjacent to the salt flat (YLB, 2021).

In December 2023, after several years of pilot activities, Bolivia inaugurated its first industrial lithium carbonate plant as part of YLB's strategic plan, with a production capacity of 15,000 tons per year (Pizzoleo, 2023). However, this plant has recently encountered issues, as "YLB President Karla Calderón reported that the lack of raw material will prevent the newly inaugurated plant from reaching its maximum production level. She noted that this $111 million infrastructure was awarded to a Chinese company without considering the source of the lithium for processing" (Ruiz, 2024).

At the end of January 2024, YLB launched a second international call for proposals to continue the process of lithium industrialization, focusing on the exploitation of seven of its salt flats and attracting projects using direct lithium extraction (DLE) technology (Cooperativa, 2024). By mid-March of the same year, YLB received proposals from 38 companies from Argentina, Ireland, France, China, Germany, Russia, Brazil, and multinational consortia (Ibañez, 2024). This call aimed to implement pilot projects where companies would test their technology with Bolivian raw materials, at no cost to the Bolivian state.

State Capacity and Business Dynamics in Bolivia

The analysis reveals that there has been no significant opposition from business sector to Bolivia's industrialization project. On the contrary, over the years, various transnational business actors have shown interest in participating in the process. During Evo Morales's administration (2006–2019), efforts were made to establish conditions for multinational companies to ensure substantial control of the industry by the State, aiming to avoid repeating the extractivist history of Bolivian mining dominated by foreign companies. This approach led to several unsuccessful negotiations over time (Kazimierski, 2018). Under Luis Arce's administration (2020–2025), agreements were also made with companies from China and Russia (El Periódico de la Energía, 2023). However, skepticism has arisen concerning these agreements, with accusations of a lack of transparency on the part of the government (Sierra, 2024).

Bolivia is considered a high-risk destination compared to other regions, and investors express concerns about the return on their capital and profit margins (Millan, 2018). This context also raises questions about the productivity levels of the Bolivian industry, as the recovery rate at the pilot lithium carbonate plant in the Salar de Uyuni is significantly below 50%, while the global average is around 70% (Pascuini & Obaya, 2020). Thus, a major challenge has been finding an extraction technique that is effective, profitable, and sustainable enough to enable large-scale production (Fornillo, 2018). The promotion of state-owned enterprises (SOE) has faced various criticisms due to Bolivia's low level of industrialization, with doubts about the country's ability to maintain commercial mining operations. In response, YLB has sought to expand its commercial partnerships; recently, YLB's Director Karla Calderón traveled to Belgium and France to promote the second international call for the utilization of salar resources (El Periódico de la Energía, 2024).

Despite this, the Morales government was determined to capitalize on the growing global demand for rechargeable batteries, with the ultimate goal of transforming Bolivia into a manufacturer of these batteries (Millan, 2018). The core debate surrounding lithium revolves around two opposing positions: exporting lithium or advancing in the value chain (Fornillo, 2018). According to Juan Carlos Zuleta, former Executive Manager of YLB, the Morales government merely sold illusions in its rush to show progress on the lithium issue, but there were too many loose ends and secrecy (Millan, 2018). Conversely, indigenous communities and their union representatives have historically resisted the privatization of the Salar de Uyuni and have advocated for full state control over the lithium chain (Fornillo, 2018).

The empirical evidence indicates two main problems in Bolivia's industrialization process: one related to the country's bureaucratic capacities and the other to the technical expertise developed around lithium. Regarding the first issue, Bolivia experienced a lengthy process in establishing a lithium company. Although efforts to build capacities for lithium management began in 2010, it was not until 2017 that YLB was established to manage all aspects related to lithium, including its exploitation and productive linkages. This development allowed for a more dynamic management of lithium policy from the state sphere, highlighting the difficulty the state faced in developing these capacities. This challenge is viewed by some as a public management problem:

> "A significant issue has been the bureaucratic and management challenges associated with operations. Initially, this was under the jurisdiction of COMIBOL, and it was only in 2017 that a company was successfully established. Efforts to create such a company began in 2010 but failed due to regulatory processes in Potosí. By 2017, a company was successfully formed, providing a more dynamic management approach" (Interview 25—International Expert).

Secondly, a technical problem with the extraction of lithium from the Salar de Uyuni has emerged. The chemical processes involved in lithium extraction require specialized knowledge, which has been challenging for Bolivia to develop. This has prevented the industrial exploitation of lithium, resulting in a marginal level of production. As noted by an expert: "There has been a technical issue, which might have been underestimated, related to the high magnesium content in the brine of the Salar de Uyuni compared to other salars. This complicates the production of lithium carbonate with a high recovery rate under optimal conditions. This has caused significant delays. The project has been delayed for a long time, largely due to a lack of transparency in providing information on these matters" (Interview 25—International Expert).

Hernando Larrazábal, former Bolivian Director at the Inter-American Development Bank, observes that:

> "There is a significant frustration in Potosí, having been a symbol of wealth without development. The region has always felt neglected, so it is natural that they do not want to experience that again with lithium. Morales needs to balance his approach; if he focuses excessively on mineral wealth in Potosí, he should also address the needs of regions with gas" (Robinson, 2019).

Ströbele-Gregor (2015) argues that the architects of Bolivia's lithium project did not account for the global inequality affecting technological requirements and industrialization, nor the importance of international companies in controlling the value chains and lithium market (Ströbele-Gregor, 2015). However, some view this energy transition optimistically as a shift toward new development models and a means to integrate science and technology, achieving energy and ecological sovereignty (Kazimierski, 2018).

Lastly, Bolivia's political situation has undergone changes, with the governance crisis and the coup against Morales disrupting some negotiations between the Bolivian government and transnational companies, particularly those from China and Germany. There is speculation about the role of lithium in Morales's removal from office. When Bolivia was unable to finalize negotiations with Western firms, it opted to partner with Chinese companies, positioning Bolivia amidst the so-called new Cold War between the West and China. Despite these efforts, none of the initial objectives concerning the mineral have been fully achieved, leading some to view the experience as a failure: "It seems to me that it is a failed experience. The project was initially framed as a high degree of autonomy endeavor. The state controls the resource, exploits it, reserves it to avoid foreign companies, and aims to manage it locally" (Interview 25—International Expert). Regarding the governance crisis, actors such as Luis Arce and Morales suggested that the protests and political crisis were driven by the United States and transnational organizations aiming to control lithium, even referring to it as "The Lithium Coup" (Miranda, 2020).

In the political changes, Luis Arce, former Minister of Economy under Morales, assumed the presidency in 2020, continuing Morales's project but with modifications. The new president decided to shift focus, aiming to form strategic alliances with foreign private companies possessing the necessary technology (Barría, 2022). Contracts were signed between Bolivia and Russia, with the Russian group Uranium One investing approximately $450 million in a pilot lithium extraction project in Bolivia (Käufer, 2023). More recently, Luis Arce met with Russian President Vladimir Putin to launch a lithium battery production project (Calderón, 2024). Despite renewed efforts to advance the lithium industry, the outcomes remain uncertain, leaving open the question of which aspects of the industrialization process will ultimately materialize.

In terms of environmental management, Bolivia has struggled to establish effective regulations to protect the environmental aspects of lithium extraction. While there is a strong political discourse advocating for Mother Earth and her rights, this rhetoric is not significantly reflected in practice. Sager (2014) argues that there is insufficient government support for research and the promotion of more sustainable practices, as well as a lack of specific environmental legislation. Furthermore, there is a need to enhance awareness and understanding of Bolivia's legal pluralism in developing a new framework for environmental justice (Montaño, 2015). However, Bolivian environmental laws tend to be overly broad, attempting to address various interests but often failing to align with regional realities due to geographical, cultural, social, and economic differences. These laws frequently exhibit ambiguity, as they are sometimes formulated without clear connections to other regulations, leaving room for interpretation (Sager, 2014).

Overall, Bolivia's approach to lithium exploitation reveals an ongoing and incomplete process. Despite political intentions, the necessary administrative capacities were not adequately developed, leading the new administration to pursue an alternative approach though substantial results have yet to materialize. Despite interest from transnational companies to add value to the extraction processes, this support was hampered by Bolivia's limited state capacity. Consequently, while Bolivia aims to implement innovative policies to transform its development model, the measures taken so far have been relatively stagnant. These measures have included creating infrastructure for productive development, promoting the establishment of clusters in Uyuni, and developing communication and cooperation mechanisms between the state and private sector. However, they have not yet led to significant economic progress or commercial development.

In conclusion, the case of Bolivia's lithium industry highlights a complex interplay of political ambition, technical challenges, and environmental considerations, revealing both the potential and limitations of Bolivia's approach to lithium exploitation. Bolivia's strategy, initially marked by an assertive political vision and a desire for state-led industrialization, has faced significant hurdles in translating these ambitions into tangible outcomes. Bolivia's experience with lithium exploitation exemplifies the challenges faced by resource-rich countries in leveraging their natural assets for sustainable development. While Bolivia's aspirations to become a key player in the global lithium market are commendable, achieving these goals requires overcoming significant obstacles. The ongoing efforts to adapt and refine the country's approach to lithium extraction will be critical in determining whether Bolivia can successfully navigate the complexities of this emerging industry and achieve its long-term development objectives. For now, the Bolivian case can be understood as an example of a stagnant industrial policy.

Socio-Environmental Dynamics and Lithium Policy in the Triangle

The dynamics of socio-environmental conflicts are central to understanding state–business relations in lithium extraction. In previous chapters, I explored the intricacies of socio-environmental dynamics and their implications for community participation, highlighting the tensions these processes often generate. Building on these insights, the following section will delve deeper into the broader socio-environmental conflicts that frame state–business relations. I examine how these conflicts reflect not only local grievances but also the clash between central and peripheral interests. By exploring the evolving strategies of resistance, negotiation, and compromise, I aim to provide a more comprehensive understanding of how socio-environmental factors intersect with lithium policy in the lithium triangle.

Regarding public consultation processes, Escosteguy et al. (2022) contend that these processes frequently fail to meet minimum standards of participation and transparency, contrary to their intended goals. While acknowledging that these observations are often derived from case studies, the authors identify elements that enable broader generalizations. Escosteguy et al. assess the consultation conducted in 2021 for the project in Salar del Hombre Muerto, Argentina, characterizing it as biased due to restricted access to information and barriers to local participation. These shortcomings generated tensions and mistrust within the local community, where some individuals had access to negotiations over others. The authors argue that the issues observed in this consultation reflect pre-existing regional problems, including: (i) socio-economic, political, and environmental inequalities at the local level; (ii) procedural injustices stemming from the absence of Free, Prior, and Informed Consent (FPIC) and standardized consultation methodologies; (iii) alliances between provincial governments and involved companies; and (iv) fragmentation of community networks and communication channels (Escosteguy et al., 2022).

O'Faircheallaigh and Babidge (2023) argue that, despite the potential ineffectiveness of agreements and consultation processes, which may legitimize extractive activities, local communities can still secure various guarantees and benefits. The authors identify two strategies employed by the Atacameño communities in Chile to counteract the weak recognition of indigenous rights by the State during negotiations with mining companies: (i) advocacy strategies aimed at protecting territory and water resources essential for community subsistence; and (ii) strategies focused on securing direct benefits from mining activities through agreements with companies, such as funding to enhance basic infrastructure, including medical and educational centers. Although these agreements do not impose specific corporate obligations, they do grant communities a significant degree of local autonomy (O'Faircheallaigh & Babidge, 2023).

Similarly, González and Snyder (2023) offer a typology to define the terms of lithium extraction, which they apply to various mining projects in Argentina. In the Salar del Rincón (Salta) and the Salar del Hombre Muerto (Catamarca), extraction occurred without prior negotiation, allowing companies to impose conditions without making concessions to local communities or governments. In contrast, the Salar de Olaroz-Cauchari (Jujuy) witnessed negotiated projects that resulted in limited commitments to benefit local communities. Conversely, the project at Salinas Grandes-Guayatayoc (Jujuy) was ultimately canceled due to organized resistance that blocked access routes.

The authors highlight two crucial aspects for analysis. First, potential changes in negotiation modalities were observed in Catamarca. Second, despite being in the same province, the cases in Jujuy showed opposing outcomes (González & Snyder, 2023). This indicates that institutions and federal regulations are not the sole determinants of extraction methods. Rather, factors such as changes in local government leadership, coalition dynamics, levels of community organization, and the proximity of projects to settlements have a more substantial influence on outcomes. González and Snyder also acknowledge the limitations of this classification within a federal system like Argentina's. In contrast, Bolivia and Chile as unitary states, present different distributive effects. In Chile, centralization leads to greater influence by the central government, with environmental courts serving as formal channels for appeal and negotiation. In Bolivia, resistance to extraction by the state-owned company Yacimientos de Litio Bolivianos (YLB) reflects a conflict between central and peripheral interests over the distribution of benefits through negotiation processes and demonstrations. Therefore, while institutional factors may not have prominently influenced negotiations in Argentina, they may manifest differently in other contexts. As previously mentioned, in Chile, the focus is on the development of consultation processes.

While these local dynamics are highly relevant to lithium extraction methods, they remain subject to national public policies that set the overarching framework for how lithium is extracted and the degree of value-added achieved. Therefore, although variations between projects are observed, this does not undermine the broader argument regarding the configuration of lithium policies at the national level. Instead, it highlights the complexities in the relationships between the state and social actors when considering the multilevel dimension, as addressed in other studies on lithium (Carrasco et al., 2023).

CHAPTER 8

Divergent Trajectories of Lithium Policies: Some Conclusions

Revisiting the Argument: The Role of the State and Business in Shaping Lithium Policies

Advancement of Lithium Industrial Policies in Latin America

Since the mid-twentieth century, Latin American countries have engaged in significant development of industrial policies, reflecting the prevailing economic theories of modernization and industrial growth (Devlin & Moguillansky, 2013; Orihuela, 2018). However, the implementation of the Washington Consensus in the early 1990s marked a shift away from state involvement in the economy, favoring market liberalization and subordinating social policies to narrowly defined economic policies aimed at achieving macroeconomic stability (Williamson, 1990; Ocampo, 2006). This transition resulted in a predominance of liberal economic policies over recent decades, despite evidence that industrial policies have yielded successful outcomes in other contexts, particularly in certain Asian countries (Bulfone, 2022; Amsden, 2004).

Within this framework, the formulation of industrial policies has emerged as a significant challenge across Latin America, and particularly in Chile. Public policy in these contexts has been strongly influenced by (neo)liberal and elitist perspectives, which prioritize market efficiency as the primary solution to public issues (Maillet, 2015b; Olavarría, 2016). Consequently, efforts to advance national industrialization have often been marginal and, at times, ineffective (Bril-Mascarenhas & Madariaga,

S. Carrasco, *From (De)regulation to Industrialization?*, Latin American Political Economy, https://doi.org/10.1007/978-3-031-77130-9_8

2019). Notably, the lithium sector has generated new socio-technical imaginaries (Barandiarán, 2019) that have dominated the public and political discourse in the Andean countries, as explored throughout this book. This renewed focus on lithium policy has reintroduced discussions on industrial policy and a more proactive role for the State back into the political mainstream.

Despite this potential shift in Latin American policymaking, the policies surrounding lithium exhibit varied levels of industrialization. The Chilean case highlights how lithium policy has facilitated progress in certain areas of industrialization, including research, development, and enhancement of the lithium value chain. In contrast, Argentina's approach to industrialization remains relatively flat, characterized by regulatory measures and competition-promoting instruments, and is currently witnessing a surge of new extractive projects. Bolivia's experience, however, reflects a stagnant industrial policy, where state weaknesses have led to the establishment of a pilot plant and other supportive initiatives, but have fallen short of achieving the anticipated industrial processes.

A common feature across these countries is the impact of political transitions. Significant shifts in presidential administrations have disrupted the continuity of major projects. In Chile, the sequence of leadership has been Bachelet (left)–Piñera (right)–Boric (left). In Argentina: Fernández (left)–Milei (right). Bolivia has experienced transitions between Morales (left) and Arce (left). These changes underscore the lack of a broad national consensus regarding the role of lithium. In Chile, changes in government have led to the disbandment of participatory bodies or the initiation of new agendas, such as Boric's recent National Lithium Strategy. In Argentina, contrasting views on lithium mining have been evident, particularly in Milei's efforts to reduce regulation and attract additional foreign investment. Similarly, despite Arce's continuity with Morales' policies, Bolivia has opted to revise the strategy of his predecessor. These elements highlight the complexities of advancing governance in the Latin American context and illustrate that public policies are dynamic and subject to ongoing evolution. Consequently, the orientation of industrial policies will likely trend toward greater institutionalization over the long term, adapting to the evolving interactions between state and corporate actors within the lithium industry (Table 8.1).

This research has employed a hybrid theoretical approach to elucidate the configuration of lithium policies in Latin America. It demonstrates that political will, when combined with substantial state capacity, can

Table 8.1 Summary of changes in lithium actions and policies by government

Country	*Governments*	*Lithium policies during their administration*
Argentina	Alberto Fernández	- Promotion of a public lithium company
	Javier Milei	- Deregulation of lithium policies - Opening lithium projects to foreign investment
Chile	Michelle Bachelet	- Development of lithium policy and governance of salt flats
	Sebastián Piñera	- Lithium auction under the Special Lithium Operation Contracts (CEOL) model - Increased competition and the invitation of private companies
	Gabriel Boric	- National Lithium Strategy
Bolivia	Evo Morales	- Enhancing national capacity for the entire lithium value chain
	Luis Arce	- Building agreements with other States and foreign companies

Source: Own elaboration

drive public policy reforms beyond the dominant perspectives focused on liberal policy instruments. This necessitates the mobilization of state resources, the creation of specialized institutions within the bureaucracy to lead policy efforts, expert advisory, and the provision of studies and information aimed at advancing technological and industrial development in the lithium sector. However, given the central role of business in industrial policies, the outcomes of public policy configuration are mediated by the influence of these actors. The Chilean case illustrates how opposition from business actors—activated once the policy is implemented—creates a confrontational dynamic between the State and corporations. This results in an implementation that straddles the line between liberal and frontier policies, a phenomenon we refer to as Selective Industrial Policy.

In contrast, Argentina and Bolivia exhibit different dynamics between the State and business entities. In Bolivia, despite strong political will to advance a lithium industry, there is a mismatch between: 1) the level of specialized technical knowledge required for extraction and subsequent production processes; and 2) the State's limited capacity to drive these industrial policies and the challenges in establishing them in the short term. Although there has been no opposition from companies—indeed, several international firms have sought to collaborate in policy implementation—the fundamental weakness of the State results in a low-intensity relationship, leading to the establishment of weak industrial policy instruments.

Conversely, in Argentina, the federal structure of the State and the significant autonomy of provinces in managing mining activities (including lithium) complicate the implementation of central-level political directives concerning lithium. This issue is exacerbated by Argentina's precarious economic situation, where the crisis has intensified extractive activities, particularly in poorer provinces that use the proceeds to fund short-term policies aimed at increasing public welfare. Additionally, the influence of companies and their opposition to industrializing projects mean that the relationship surrounding lithium is dominated by business interests, with political actors benefiting in the short term. Consequently, traditional extractives logic persists, focusing on regulatory measures and the promotion of competition rather than advancing industrial development.

Therefore, the analysis of public policies at a comparative level highlights the variations between countries, the specific emphases of each, and the predominant role of the relational dynamics between the State and businesses at the sectoral level, beyond the national focus that typically dominates the debate on state capacity. While the processes of energy transition in Europe and, more broadly, in the Western world often assume the state's capabilities to carry out these processes, the study shows that this is not a given. The analysis of Chile in particular, and of the countries in the lithium triangle in general, reveals the challenges in building the necessary capacities to promote public policies, especially the difficulty in fostering collaborative relationships with business actors whose interests do not necessarily align with those of the government. After all, the short- and long-term incentives of businesses often differ with those of the State, particularly in emerging sectors of the economy, such as lithium, which have gained increased importance in recent years.

Finally, the book indirectly raises a debate regarding development models and the possibilities for advancing toward so-called green development models. The central question in this regard is about the coalitions and conditions necessary to advance toward new green growth models (Nahm, 2022) in the global periphery, and whether such progress is feasible. A less explored dimension in this regard, which could pave the way for future research, is the extent to which these dynamics are shaped by global structures and the international dynamics of businesses and countries involved in lithium acquisition to advance up the value chain. Furthermore, the extent to which these interests align or conflict with the interests of Latin American countries, within the framework of global capitalism, remains a relevant backdrop that has not been extensively addressed in this book but opens the door for further discussions and research in the field.

Lithium Policy and Capitalist Dynamics

In the lithium battery value chain, lithium extraction is merely one component among many required for the production of electric vehicles and other energy storage devices. From this perspective, the countries within the Lithium Triangle, situated in the Global South, are distanced from the production processes associated with electromobility. Industrial organization in this sector is highly specialized and concentrated, with only a few companies dominating battery manufacturing. Moreover, recent market trends indicate that electric vehicle manufacturers are increasingly taking on battery production themselves and even engaging in extraction through acquiring companies or shares. This trend toward consolidation within global corporations significantly reduces the scope for states to advance value-added processes in battery manufacturing and its components.

Given this context, we must question the potential for Lithium Triangle countries to develop industries without repeating the extractivist patterns and resource curse typical of Latin America (Ross, 2015). If lithium is indeed a unique mineral, contributing to energy transition processes and addressing climate change (Fornillo, 2018), it is crucial to examine whether its modes of extraction, production, and innovation are also distinctive. More broadly, these considerations lead us to a discussion about the dynamics of the Lithium Triangle within the framework of global capitalist systems. Specifically, this economic field—the market surrounding lithium—with its ultimate political-environmental objective (the energy transition), echoes Streeck's (2011) discourse on the potential for effective political management of democratic capitalism.[1]

[1] One of the pioneers of the concept of democratic capitalism is Michael Novak. In his book "The Spirit of Democratic Capitalism," Novak (1982) outlines that this system is composed of the interplay of three central elements: 1) an economic system based on free

The expansionist logic of capitalism leads to overproduction of goods (Sewell, 2008). As supply increases, prices fall, companies implement cuts leading to unemployment, and consequently, higher debt among those without work (Sewell, 2008). Additionally, capitalist expansion has turned the environment into a prime object of commodification, transforming environmental concerns into consumer goods (Carrasco & Madariaga, 2022).[2] The development of transformative production processes and rethinking development models in Latin American countries are central to the discourse on lithium. In this regard, public policies must encapsulate and channel these dynamics, moving beyond mere industrialization to encompass green industrialization policies. Some initiatives by Lithium Triangle countries have begun to reflect this direction; for instance, recent cooperation agreements between Argentina and Bolivia aim to jointly advance lithium exploitation with a focus on value addition, technological innovation, and research. While these initiatives are still in their nascent stages, and have not yet transformed lithium extraction methods, they signal necessary international cooperation dynamics to address challenges in lithium industrialization.

Finally, a crucial element within capitalism is the construction of imaginaries, which play a significant role in the lithium case. As Beckert (2016) posits, capitalist development is closely tied to imaginaries about the future, with the expectations of key actors, influencing capitalist dynamics. The temporal order of capitalism is essential (Sewell, 2008), as various actors shape their activities based on imagined future economies distinct from the present (Beckert, 2016). Consequently, the configuration of

markets, where economic incentives guide individual behavior; 2) a political system that functions within the framework of representative democracy; and 3) a cultural system that promotes pluralism.

[2] From an economic history perspective, William Sewell argues that the development of modern capitalist economies is underpinned by expansive and cyclical dynamics (Sewell, 2008). Specifically, Sewell posits that capitalism operates on an expansive economic trajectory, both geographically and by extending into other spheres of social life—such as technological development—resulting in concentration. Additionally, capitalism exhibits repetitive rhythms, commonly referred to as the business cycle, which are characterized by alternating periods of economic prosperity and crisis that arise from its own mechanisms (Sewell, 2008). Throughout history, governments have attempted to implement policies to address the challenges posed by these dynamics. However, achieving this requires effective political management of capitalism (Keynes, 1965). This is particularly challenging, as the pervasive nature of capitalism's dynamics influences economic and social development globally (Beckert, 2016).

expectations regarding mineral use is likely to impact current extraction dynamics and public policy decisions surrounding lithium. Ultimately, the futures imagined regarding lithium may also reshape the relationship between capitalism and democracy within the context of lithium industry development.

Contributions to the Academic Literature.

This study seeks to advance theoretical inquiries into how public policy processes can be understood through institutionalist perspectives while proposing an original theoretical framework. The central argument focuses on the interaction between the State and businesses in shaping public policy, suggesting that neither institutionalist approaches nor those emphasizing business power alone are sufficient to fully explain the development of industrial policies. By integrating both perspectives, the study provides a form of analysis that is less frequently employed in comparative research. In the case of lithium, some analyses approach the issue from a governance perspective that assumes equality among political, social, and business actors—an assumption that this study challenges (Obaya & Pascuini, 2020; Obaya, 2019; Poveda, 2020; León et al., 2020).

While literature on state capacity tends to be state-centric and often overlooks other actors, studies on business power tend to portray the State as a static entity, merely facilitating business interests. This work bridges these literatures by analyzing state–business relations to explain green industrialization policies in developing countries. It accounts for the significant influence businesses exert on industrial policy while acknowledging the varying degrees of strength and weakness within state institutions and the diverse capacities of their agents. Consequently, the study contributes to the theoretical refinement of these fields by developing an original typology of state–business relations within the context of green industrial policy formation.

Moreover, the research engages with the discussion on green industrial policy from a political economy perspective. Debates surrounding industrial policies are often dominated by neoclassical economic views that tend to overlook the political dimensions structuring these processes. While elements like efficiency, profit maximization, and incentives are essential for understanding economic decision-making, green industrial policies specifically aim to foster the development of a particular green industry (Lewis, 2021). In some cases, these emerging markets lack clarity regarding supply and demand, as well as the availability and distribution of inputs required to advance the value chain. In this context, political decisions, the state's ability to absorb high initial costs, and the imaginaries shaping sectoral development are crucial (Barandiarán, 2019). This book makes a significant contribution to the literature by analyzing green industrial policy as an outcome of political and economic interactions.

In addition, the book situates this phenomenon within the Latin American context, where there is a growing scholarly interest in exploring new development models that incorporate technological innovations and strategic sector growth. However, for developing countries, advancing these models poses specific challenges. While there are important exceptions (e.g., Hochstetler, 2020), developing countries remain understudied in the political economy literature. This work refines the analysis of public policy from a Global South perspective, offering a more nuanced view of green industrialization and related policies.

Specifically, in the case of lithium, most social science research has focused on the socio-environmental conflicts generated by mineral extraction. While this study acknowledges the social dimensions involved, it argues that decisions regarding the lithium industry and its value chain, although shaped by socio-environmental factors, are ultimately driven by the state's role and its relative influence vis-à-vis business groups. From a political economy perspective, public policies on economic issues are shaped by the ideas, interests, and institutions (Madariaga, 2018) of the actors involved in political decision-making. Given the recent importance of the lithium industry, this study provides a detailed analysis of these dynamics, particularly the influence of State and business actors in shaping green industrial policy.

The book also offers a substantial contribution to the study of value chains and upgrading in economic activities through the lens of public policy, presenting a theoretical framework that integrates state–business relations. This approach provides a clearer understanding of how public policies influence the development of strategic sectors such as lithium in Latin America, highlighting the essential role of state intervention in building industrial and technological capacities. By comparing the cases of Chile, Argentina, and Bolivia, the book sheds light on how political dynamics—such as government transitions and partnerships with private actors—affect progress within value chains.

While value chains and upgrading are inherently complex, the book seeks to model these dynamics analytically, allowing for a simplified understanding of social realities. In doing so, it provides a conceptual tool for examining how public policies can foster the development of key industries and promote value addition. This analytical approach offers valuable insights for scholars and policymakers into how public policies influence state–business relations and determine the success or failure of industrialization and upgrading processes in sectors like lithium extraction and production.

Lastly, this study broadens the understanding of public policy by emphasizing its fluid and evolving nature. Contrary to traditional analyses that treat public policy as static, the book demonstrates that policies, particularly in the lithium sector, are continually reconfigured in response to changing state-business dynamics. Drawing from Hacker and Pierson's (2011) assertion that policies evolve even when designed to maintain the status quo, this research encourages scholars to conceptualize public policy as a dynamic process, shaped by shifting incentives, interests, and ideas over time. This approach challenges static interpretations of policy outcomes and opens new avenues for analyzing the role of state–business relations in shaping industrial and green policy agendas.

Implications for Decision-Making Processes and Public Policies

Based on the research conducted, several key lessons can be drawn for public policy processes within the context of the Lithium Triangle countries. Three main takeaways were identified: 1) the inherently political nature of the discussion surrounding industrial policies must be acknowledged; 2) the political role of businesses and the importance of their inclusion in decision-making processes must be recognized; and 3) public policies should be understood as dynamic processes that adapt to the pressures of various factors.

First, it is crucial to consider political variables in public policy discussions related to lithium and its industrialization. Ultimately, the debate over whether to advance a particular type of industrial policy is tied to broader discussions on development models, wherein different perspectives compete, especially in light of the current climate crisis (Carrasco & Madariaga, 2022). Therefore, before delving into the specifics of policy instruments, there must be a reflection on the medium- and long-term objectives of these actions. In public debates on industrialization, this perspective often becomes overshadowed by technical and technological considerations. However, any of these choices carry significant implications for social justice, environmental damage, economic growth, and inequality, among other issues, which necessitate a political lens for holistic management.

The development debate presents significant dilemmas on how to reconcile economic growth with environmental considerations (Carrasco & Madariaga, 2022). In recent decades, various alternatives to development have been proposed, such as the Green New Deal, which advocates for a more active role of the state in coordinating the economy (Aldana & Riofrancos, 2020), or degrowth, which seeks to abandon capitalist production and accumulation logics to transition toward new ways of life and consumption that are compatible with environmental sustainability (Haberl et al., 2020). Although not explicitly stated, the discussion surrounding lithium policies touches on broader debates about development models and the potential role of this industry in facilitate the energy transition. Thus, the lithium debate is not merely technical but fundamentally political, with state and corporate actors serving as pivotal agents in green industrial policy.

Second, the central role of businesses in industrial policies must be acknowledged, as they are the primary targets of state intervention in this context (Bulfone, 2022). Moreover, businesses possess various power resources that can be leveraged to shape the field of public policy (Fairfield, 2015). Therefore, public policies aimed at transforming development models must consider the expectations of businesses and seek the necessary support to implement them. Otherwise, the evidence presented in this book shows that the degree of business opposition can be a critical variable in the effectiveness of industrial policy. More broadly, the economy should be understood as a system deeply embedded in society, meaning its configuration depends on the social and political processes that build and shape its institutional framework (Polanyi, 2017; González & Madariaga, 2018). Thus, public policies can direct economic dynamics, as seen in the case of lithium.

The research also has implications for understanding institutional design. Historical institutionalism has largely focused on demonstrating how initial decisions have long-term consequences for institutional trajectories (Pierson, 2000). While this research acknowledges the importance of historical trajectories, it places special emphasis on the dynamic nature of public policy configurations, where the relative position of state and corporate actors continually shapes public policy. Additionally, this research points to a broader discussion about the possibility of achieving effective political management of contemporary capitalism (Streeck, 2011). After all, in capitalist democracies, public policy outcomes are heavily influenced by the relationship between the state and capital (Haggard et al., 1997). Therefore, this study has examined the intersection of state capacity and business dynamics in shaping lithium policies in Latin America, highlighting challenges in policy implementation and the evolving state-business relationship. The aim is to refine theoretical perspectives on state-business relations, public policies and capitalist dynamics, while contributing to the broader analysis of public policy.

Appendix 1. List of Interviews

N°	*Profession*	*Organization*	*Sector*
1	Industrial Civil Engineer	National Lithium Commission	Public/Political sector
2	Master in Governance	CORFO	Public/Political sector
3	PhD in Economics	CORFO	Public/Political sector
4	BA in Economics	NGO	Civil Society Organization
5	Lawyer	National Lithium Commission	Public/Political sector
6	Geographer	Albemarle	Business
7	Lawyer	National Lithium Commission	Academic
8	PhD in Political Economy	National Lithium Commission	Public/Political sector
9	BA in Economics	Ministry of Mining	Public/Political sector
10	Lawyer	CORFO	Public/Political sector
11	Civil Engineer	Albemarle	Business sector
12	Lawyer	Albemarle	Business sector
13	Civil Engineer	CORFO	Public/Political sector
14	Accountant	Ministry of Mining	Public/Political sector
15	Economist	Civil Service	Public/Political Sector
16	Civil Engineer	Consultant	Business sector
17	PhD in Economics	University of Chile	Academic and business sector

(continued)

S. Carrasco, *From (De)regulation to Industrialization?*, Latin American Political Economy, https://doi.org/10.1007/978-3-031-77130-9

(continued)

N°	*Profession*	*Organization*	*Sector*
18	Union leader	SQM	Business sector
19	Industrial Civil Engineer	Lithium Committee CORFO	Public/Political sector
20	Industrial Civil Engineer	CChNC	Public/Political sector
21	Civil Engineer	USM	Academic and business sector
22	Civil Engineer	CODELCO	Business sector
23	PhD in Social Sciences	UBA	Academic
24	PhD in Social Sciences	UNSAM	Academic
25	Civil Engineer	Consultant	Business sector
26	PhD	OPSAL	Civil Society
27	PhD in Engineering	Antofagasta University	Academic
28	Civil Engineer	SQM	Business sector
29	Geologist	Consultant	Business sector
30	Economist	COCHILCO	Public/Political sector
31	Architect	CORFO	Public/Political sector
32	Lawyer	Environmental Superintendency	Public/Political sector
33	Lawyer	Chilean Chamber of Mines	Business sector
34	Geologist	UDD	Academic
35	Anthropologist	CODELCO	Public/Political sector
36	Political Scientist	Consultant	International organization
37	Economist	Asociación de Vehículos Eléctricos de Chile A.G	Public/Political sector
38	Political Scientist	Ministry of Mining	Public/Political sector
39	Economist	SQM	Business sector
40	PhD	NGO	Civil Society

Appendix 2. Key Characteristics of Major Companies in the Lithium Industry

Company	*Country*	*Year operation began*	*Role in the value chain*	*Level*	*Public or private*
Albemarle	Chile	1984	Extraction	Multinational	Private
SQM	Chile	1994	Extraction	National	Private
YLB	Bolivia	2017	Responsible for activities across the entire value chain: prospecting, exploration, extraction, beneficiation, installation, implementation, commissioning, operation, and management of evaporitic resources, inorganic chemistry complexes, industrialization, and commercialization	National	Public

(continued)

S. Carrasco, *From (De)regulation to Industrialization?*, Latin American Political Economy, https://doi.org/10.1007/978-3-031-77130-9

(continued)

Company	*Country*	*Year operation began*	*Role in the value chain*	*Level*	*Public or private*
JEMSE	Argentina	2011	Holds an 8.5% equity stake in companies operating in the salt flats, participating in lithium carbonate production, with the right to priority purchase of 5% of the produced lithium carbonate	Federal	Public
Camyen	Argentina	2012 (established)	Shareholder and promoter of the lithium industry	Federal	Public
YPF (lithium)	Argentina	2021 (subsidiary)	Exploration and extraction for lithium carbonate and hydroxide production	National	Public
Eramine	Argentina	2024	Lithium extraction from salar brine and processing into battery-grade lithium carbonate	Multinational	Private
NewCo	Argentina	2024	Lithium extraction from salar brine and processing into battery-grade lithium carbonate	Multinational	Private
Minera Exar	Argentina	2023	Lithium carbonate development and production at the Cauchari-Olaroz deposit	Multinational	Private
Livent	Argentina	1998	Lithium extraction	Multinational	Private
Orocobre	Argentina	2015	Lithium extraction from salar brine and processing into battery-grade lithium carbonate	Multinational	Private
Eramet	Argentina	2024	Lithium extraction and production of lithium carbonate	Mutlinational	Private

(continued)

(continued)

Company	*Country*	*Year operation began*	*Role in the value chain*	*Level*	*Public or private*
Allkem	Argentina	2021	Lithium extraction from salar brine and processing into battery-grade lithium carbonate	Multinational	Private

Source Own elaboration based on empirical analysis

References

Abdel-Latif, A., & Schmitz, H. (2009). State-business relations and investment in Egypt. *IDS Research Reports, 2009*(61), 1–105. https://doi.org/10.1111/j.2040-0217.2009.00061_2.x

Acemoglu, D. (2002). Technical change, inequality, and the labor market. *Journal of Economic Literature, 40*(1), 7–72. https://doi.org/10.1257/jel.40.1.7

Adolph, C. (2013). Bankers, bureaucrats, and central bank politics: The myth of neutrality. *Cambridge University Press*. https://doi.org/10.1017/CBO9781139506762

Aguilera, C. (2009). *Un análisis de las Comisiones Asesoras Presidenciales del Gobierno de Michelle Bachelet: documento de trabajo, Programa de Gobernabilidad*. Flacso.

Agusdinata, D. B., Liu, W., Eakin, H., & Romero, H. (2018). Socio-environmental impacts of lithium mineral extraction: Towards a research agenda. *Environmental Research Letters, 13*(12), Art. 12. https://doi.org/10.1088/1748-9326/aae9b1

Akchurin, M. (2020). Mining and defensive mobilization: Explaining opposition to extractive industries in Chile. *Sociology of Development, 6*(1), 1–29. https://doi.org/10.1525/sod.2020.6.1.1

Aklin, M., & Mildenberger, M. (2020). Prisoners of the wrong dilemma: Why distributive conflict, not collective action, characterizes the politics of climate change. *Global Environmental Politics, 20*(4), 4–27. https://doi.org/10.1162/glep_a_00578

Aldana, D., & Riofrancos, T. (2020). Latin America's green new deal. *NACLA Report on the Americas, 52*(2), 117–121.

S. Carrasco, *From (De)regulation to Industrialization?*, Latin American Political Economy, https://doi.org/10.1007/978-3-031-77130-9

Allain, M., & Madariaga, A. (2020). Understanding policy change through bricolage: The case of Chile's renewable energy policy. *Governance, 33*(3), Art. 3. https://doi.org/10.1111/gove.12453

Altenburg, T., & Rodrik, D. (2017). Green industrial policy: Accelerating structural change towards wealthy green economies. In *Green industrial policy: Concept, policies, country experiences*. UN Environment.

Alvarez (2019). Las siete propuestas que recibió Corfo para el Instituto de Tecnologías Limpias. *La Tercera*. https://www.latercera.com/pulso/noticia/las-siete-propuestas-recibio-corfo-instituto-tecnologias-limpias/664568/

Álvarez, R. (2015). *Gremios empresarios, política y neoliberalismo. Los casos de Chile y Perú (1986–2010)*. LOM Ediciones.

Ambec, S. (2017). Gaining competitive advantage with green policy. In *Green industrial policy: Concept, policies, country experiences*. UN Environment.

Ámbito. (2023). Advierten que Javier Milei quiere extranjerizar el litio y proponen la creación de una empresa federal. *Ámbito*. https://www.ambito.com/politica/advierten-que-javier-milei-quiere-extranjerizar-el-litio-y-proponen-la-creacion-una-empresa-federal-n5907121

Amengual, M. (2016). *Politicized enforcement in Argentina: Labor and environmental regulation*. Cambridge University Press.

Amengual, M., & Dargent, E. (2020). The social determinants of enforcement: Integrating politics with limited state capacity. In D. M. Brinks, S. Levitsky, & M. V. Murillo (Eds.), *The politics of institutional weakness in Latin America* (pp. 161–182). Cambridge University Press. https://doi.org/10.1017/9781108776608.007

Amsden, A. (2004). La sustitución de importaciones en las industrias de alta tecnología: Prebisch renace en Asia. *Revista De La CEPAL, 82*, 75–90.

Amsden, A. H. (1991). Diffusion of development: The late-industrializing model and greater East Asia. *The American Economic Review, 81*(2), 282–286.

Ansell, C. (2000). The networked polity: Regional development in Western Europe. *Governance, 13*(2), 279–291. https://doi.org/10.1111/0952-1895.00136

Andrews, J. P. (2021). Senado debate sobre asignación de fondos de Corfo para el Instituto de Tecnologías Limpias: parlamentarios denuncian irregularidades en licitación. *La Tercera*. https://www.latercera.com/nacional/noticia/senado-debate-sobre-asignacion-de-fondos-de-corfo-para-el-instituto-de-tecnologias-limpias-parlamentarios-denuncian-irregularidades-en-licitacion/TR2W5ZNR5FBK5I4ZOXN5UP3RIA/

Argento, M., & Zícari, J. (2017). Las disputas por el litio en la Argentina: ¿materia prima, recurso estratégico o bien común? *Prácticas De Oficio, 1*(19), 37–49.

Argento, M., & Zícari, J. (2018). Políticas públicas y conflictos territoriales en torno a la explotación del litio en Salta: el caso de Salinas Grandes.

Andes, 29(1), 00. http://www.scielo.org.ar/scielo.php?script=sci_arttext&pid=S1668809020180001000l0&lng=es&tlng=es
Arnstein, S. R. (1969). A Ladder of citizen participation. *Journal of the American Institute of Planners, 35*(4), 216–224. https://doi.org/10.1080/01944366908977225
Arsel, M., Hogenboom, B., & Pellegrini, L. (2016). The extractive imperative and the boom in environmental conflicts at the end of the progressive cycle in Latin America. *The Extractive Industries and Society, 3*(4), 877–879. https://doi.org/10.1016/j.exis.2016.10.013
Balchin, N., Booth, D., & te Velde, D. W. (2019). *How economic transformation happens at the sector level: Evidence from Africa and Asia* [Research Report]. ODI Report. https://www.econstor.eu/handle/10419/206741
Barandiarán, J. (2019). Lithium and development imaginaries in Chile, Argentina and Bolivia. *World Development, 113*, 381–391. https://doi.org/10.1016/j.worlddev.2018.09.019
Barragan, F. (2022). El Gobierno incentiva a la minería y lanza empresa estatal de litio. *Ámbito.* https://www.ambito.com/economia/litio/el-gobierno-incentiva-la-mineria-y-lanza-empresa-estatal-n5523817
Barragan, F. (2023). Planta de baterías de litio: se inaugura en septiembre y tendrá 50% de integración local. *Ámbito.* https://www.ambito.com/economia/planta-baterias-litio-se-inaugura-septiembre-y-tendra-50-integracion-local-n5785642
Barría, C. (2022). Qué resultados tuvo la nacionalización del litio en Bolivia (y por qué AMLO pidió su asesoría para hacerlo en México). *BBC News.* https://www.bbc.com/mundo/noticias-america-latina-61185238
Beach, D., & Pedersen, R. (2019). *Process-tracing methods: Foundations and guidelines.* University of Michigan Press. https://doi.org/10.3998/mpub.10072208
Beckert, J. (2016). *Imagined futures: Fictional expectations and capitalist dynamics.* Harvard University Press.
Bell, S., & Hindmoor, A. (2015). Taming the city? Ideas, structural power and the evolution of British banking policy amidst the great financial meltdown. *New Political Economy, 20*(3), 454–474.
Bentley, A., Lewis, J., & Oatley, T. (2021). Green industrial policy and the global transformation of climate politics. *Global Environmental Politics, 21*(4), 1–19. https://doi.org/10.1162/glep_a_00640
Blair, J. Balcázar Morales, R, Barandiarán, J. & Maxwell, A. (2022). *Agotado: cómo evitar que la minería del litio agote el recurso hídrico, drene los humedales y perjudique a las comunidades en América del Sur.* CalPoly-Ponoma, Observatorio Plurinacional de Salares Andinos, UC Santa Barbara, NRDC.

Blatter, J., & Blume, T. (2008). In search of co-variance, causal mechanisms or congruence? Towards a plural understanding of case studies. *Swiss Political Science Review*, *14*(2), Art. 2. https://doi.org/10.1002/j.1662-6370.2008.tb00105.x

Blatter, J., & Haverland, M. (2012). *Designing case studies: Explanatory approaches in small-n research*. Palgrave Macmillan.

Block, F. (2008). Swimming against the current: The rise of a hidden developmental state in the United States. *Politics & Society, 36*(2), 169–206. https://doi.org/10.1177/0032329208318731

Block, F. (2011). Crisis and renewal: The outlines of a twenty-first century new deal. *Socio-Economic Review, 9*(1), 31–57. https://doi.org/10.1093/ser/mwq017

Bolin, B. (2007). *A history of the science and politics of climate change: The role of the Intergovernmental Panel on Climate Change*. Cambridge University Press. https://doi.org/10.1017/CBO9780511721731

Braconier, H., Nicoletti, G., & Westmore, B. (2014). *Policy challenges for the next 50 years*. OECD. https://doi.org/10.1787/5jz18gs5fckf-en

Brady, H. E., & Collier, D. (Eds.). (2004). *Rethinking social inquiry: Diverse tools, shared standards*. Rowman & Littlefield.

Breetz, H., Mildenberger, M., & Stokes, L. (2018). The political logics of clean energy transitions. *Business and Politics, 20*(4), 492–522. https://doi.org/10.1017/bap.2018.14

Bril-Mascarenhas, T., & Madariaga, A. (2019). Business power and the minimal state: The defeat of industrial policy in Chile. *The Journal of Development Studies*, *55*(6), Art. 6. https://doi.org/10.1080/00220388.2017.1417587

Bril-Mascarenhas, T., & Maillet, A. (2019). How to build and wield business power: The political economy of pension regulation in Chile, 1990–2018. *Latin American Politics and Society*, *61*(1), Art. 1. https://doi.org/10.1017/lap.2018.61

Bril-Mascarenhas, T., Maillet, A., & Mayaux, P.-L. (2017). Process tracing. Inducción, deducción e inferencia causal. *Revista de Ciencia Política (Santiago)*, *37*(3), Art. 3. https://doi.org/10.4067/S0718-090X2017000300659

Brinks, D. M., Levitsky, S., & Murillo, M. V. (Eds.). (2020). *The politics of institutional weakness in Latin America*. Cambridge University Press. https://doi.org/10.1017/9781108776608

Brion, F. (2018a). Corfo sella pacto con SQM y triplica cuota de extracción de litio del Salar de Atacama. *La Tercera*. https://www.latercera.com/noticia/sqm-corfo-sellan-acuerdo-salar-atacama-tras-largo-arbitraje/

Brion, F. (2018b). Eduardo Bitran, vicepresidente Ejecutivo de Corfo: "SQM es demasiado estratégica para que su venta no pase por una consulta previa". *La Tercera*. https://www.latercera.com/negocios/noticia/eduardo-bitran-vicepresidente-ejecutivo-corfo-sqm-demasiado-estrategica-venta-no-pase-una-consulta-previa/94233/#

Bulfone, F. (2022). Industrial policy and comparative political economy: A literature review and research agenda. *Competition & Change*. https://doi.org/10.1177/10245294221076225

Busemeyer, M. R., & Thelen, K. (2020). Institutional sources of business power. *World Politics*, *72*(3), Art. 3. https://doi.org/10.1017/S004388712000009X

Buur, L., & Whitfield, L. (2013). Industrial policy and state-business relations: Towards a heuristic approach. In D. W. te Welde (Ed.), *State-Business Relations and Industrial Policy: Current policy and research debates*. DFID-ESRC Growth Research Programme.

Calderón, V. (2024). El presidente de Bolivia, Luis Arce, anuncia proyecto para producir baterías de litio con Rusia en reunión con Putin. *CNN Español*. https://cnnespanol.cnn.com/2024/06/06/bolivia-luis-arce-proyecto-baterias-litio-rusia-putin/

Calvo, E. (2017). Procesos de extracción de litio de sus depósitos en salares argentinos. In E. J. Baran (Ed.), *Litio: un recurso natural estratégico desde los depósitos minerales a las aplicaciones tecnológicas* (pp. 69–83). Academia Nacional de Ciencias Exactas, Físicas y Naturales.

de Diputados, C. (2021). *Informe de la Comisión Especial Investigadora de los Actos de la Corfo y de Otras Autoridades en Relación con su Intervención en el Proceso de Licitación para la Creación de un Instituto de Tecnologías Limpias*. Biblioteca del Congreso Nacional.

Campanini, J. (2021). Los devenires del litio en Bolivia. In R. Morales (coord.). *Salares Andinos, ecología de saberes por la protección de nuestros salares y humedales*. Observatorio Plurinacional de Salares Andinos.

Campanini, J. (2022). El litio en Bolivia: antecedentes, desafíos e inconsistencias. In A. Aleida (coord.). *Litio en América Latina: Demanda global contra daño socioambiental*. Secretaría de Medio Ambiente y Recursos Naturales, México.

Campanini, O. (2013). Agua y minería en Bolivia. *Cartilla Pueblo y Soberanía*, 3. Centro de Documentación e Información Bolivia.

CAMYEN. (s/f). Minería. https://camyen.catamarca.gob.ar/mineria/

Carrasco, S. & Madariaga, A. (2022). El desarrollo que queremos: visiones, conflictos y participación. In Costa, E. y Belemmi, V. (Eds.), *Economía en tiempos de crisis: perspectivas para la transición socioecológica en Chile*. Santiago: Editorial FIMA.

Carrasco, S., Hernández, J., & Cariaga, V. (2023). The temporalities of natural resources extraction: Imagined futures and the spatialization of the lithium industry in Chile. *The Extractive Industries and Society, 15*, 101310.

Carruthers, D., & Rodriguez, P. (2009). Mapuche protest, environmental conflict and social movement linkage in Chile. *Third World Quarterly, 30*(4), 743–760.

Carter, N. (2018). *The politics of the environment: Ideas, activism, policy*. Cambridge University Press.

Castillo-Gallardo, M. (2016). Desigualdades socioecológicas y sufrimiento ambiental en el conflicto "Polimetales" en Arica. *Convergencia, 23*(72), Art. 72.

Centeno, M. A. (2015). *Blood and debt: War and the nation-state in Latin America*. Penn State University Press. https://doi.org/10.5325/j.ctv14gphb8

Christoff, P. (2005). Out of chaos a shining star? Towards a typology of green states. In J. Barry & R. Eckersley (Eds.), *The state and the global ecological crisis* (pp. 25–52). MIT Press.

Chua, A. L. (1995). The privatization-nationalization cycle: The link between markets and ethnicity in developing countries. *Columbia Law Review, 95*(2), Art. 2. https://doi.org/10.2307/1123231

Ciftci, M. M., & Lemaire, X. (2023). Deciphering the impacts of 'green' energy transition on socio-environmental lithium conflicts: Evidence from Argentina and Chile. *The Extractive Industries and Society*. https://doi.org/10.1016/j.exis.2023.101373

Cingolani, L. (2013). *The state of state capacity: A review of concepts, evidence and measures*. UNU-MERIT Working Papers. http://collections.unu.edu/view/UNU:40

Cisneros, P. (2020). A comparative study of the introduction of restrictions to large-scale mining in four Latin American countries. *Review of Policy Research, 37*(5), 687–712. https://doi.org/10.1111/ropr.12400

Cisternas, C., & Vásquez, J. (2018). Comisiones Asesoras Presidenciales en Chile. *European Review of Latin American and Caribbean Studies, 106*, 1–22.

Cofré, V. (2019). *Ponce Lerou: Pinochet, el litio, las Cascadas, las platas políticas*. Editorial Catalonia.

Cofré, V. & Aguilera, P. (2024). Tianqi concreta su amenaza y recurre a tribunales para frenar la alianza entre SQM y Codelco. *La Tercera*. https://www.latercera.com/pulso/noticia/tianqi-concreta-su-amenaza-y-recurre-a-tribunales-para-frenar-la-alianza-entre-sqm-y-codelco/W2UKAWXFXFCLXEY7ILDD3DH2UU/

Colgan, J. D., Green, J. F., & Hale, T. N. (2021). Asset revaluation and the existential politics of climate change. *International Organization, 75*(2), 586–610. https://doi.org/10.1017/S0020818320000296

Comunidades originarias la cuenca de Salinas Grandes y Laguna de Guayatóc, & Jujuy, Argentina. (2023). Manifiesto de la Mesa de Comunidades Originarias de la Cuenca de Salinas Grandes y Laguna de Guayatayoc. *Alter-Nativa*, (12), 148–149.

Conde, M., & Le Billon, P. (2017). Why do some communities resist mining projects while others do not? *The Extractive Industries and Society, 4*(3), 681–697. https://doi.org/10.1016/j.exis.2017.04.009

Cooperativa. (2024). Bolivia va por la industrialización del litio "a mayor escala". *Cooperativa*. https://cooperativa.cl/noticias/economia/materias-primas/litio/bolivia-va-por-la-industrializacion-del-litio-a-mayor-escala/2024-01-26/185632.html

Cooperativa. (2016). Presidenta Bachelet presento nueva política del litio: "Es un primer paso". *Cooperativa*. https://cooperativa.cl/noticias/economia/materias-primas/litio/presidenta-bachelet-presento-nueva-politica-del-litio-es-un-primer/2016-01-25/122620.html

Corbetta, P. (2007). *Metodología y técnicas de investigación social*. McGraw-Hill.

Crespi, G., Tacsir, E., & Vargas, F. (2014). *Innovation and productivity in services: Empirical evidence from Latin America*. Inter-American Development Bank.

Cuevas, R. (2021). Disputa por los fondos del litio: las zonas grises de la millonaria licitación del Instituto de Tecnologías Limpias. *Ciper Chile*. https://www.ciperchile.cl/2021/09/02/disputa-por-los-fondos-del-litio-las-zonas-grises-de-la-millonaria-licitacion-del-instituto-de-tecnologias-limpias/?fbclid=IwAR0mzYPZ00NQ2lamQ9IUEICVSLrjyXMnnIfiGNpdlVW2YEVyWFqYCADl-E0

Culpepper, P. D. (2015). Structural power and political science in the post-crisis era. *Business and Politics*, *17*(3), Art. 3. https://doi.org/10.1515/bap-2015-0031

Damonte, G. (2021). Limited state governance and institutional hybridization in alluvial ASM in Peru. *Resources Policy, 72*, 102118. https://doi.org/10.1016/j.resourpol.2021.102118

De Vicente, A. (2024). Argentina: Cauchari-Olaroz busca aumentar su producción de carbonato de litio a 25 mil toneladas. *Reporte minero & Energético*. https://www.reporteminero.cl/noticia/noticias/2024/08/cauchari-olaroz-busca-aumentar-prodoccion-carbonato-litio

Dechezleprâtre, A., Martin, R., & Mohnen, M. (2014). *Knowledge spillovers from clean and dirty technologies*. London School of Economics and Political Science.

Delamaza, G., Maillet, A., & Martínez Neira, C. (2017). Socio-territorial conflicts in chile: configuration and politicization (2005–2014). *ERLACS*, *0*(104), Art. 104. https://doi.org/10.18352/erlacs.10173

Denney, S., Southin, T., & Wolfe, D. A. (2023). Do winners pick government? How scale-up experience shapes entrepreneurs' assessments of innovation policy mixes. *Science and Public Policy, 50*(5), 858–870. https://doi.org/10.1093/scipol/scad030

Dente, B., & Subirás, J. (2014). *Decisiones públicas. Análisis y estudio de los procesos de decisión en políticas públicas*. Ariel.

Díaz Paz, W. F., Escosteguy, M., Seghezzo, L., Hufty, M., Kruse, E., & Iribarnegaray, M. A. (2023). Lithium mining, water resources, and socio-economic issues in northern Argentina: We are not all in the same boat. *Resources Policy*, 81, N.PAG. https://doi.org/10.1016/j.resourpol.2022.103288

Doner, R. F., & Schneider, B. R. (2016). The middle-income trap: More politics than economics. *World Politics, 68*(4), 608–644. https://doi.org/10.1017/S0043887116000095

Dorador, C., Fink, P., Hengst, M., Icaza, G., Villalobos, A. S., Vejar, D., Meneses, D., Zadjelovic, V., Burmann, L., Moelzner, J., & Harrod, C. (2018). Microbial community composition and trophic role along a marked salinity gradient in Laguna Puilar, Salar de Atacama, Chile. *Antonie van Leeuwenhoek, 111*(8), Art. 8. https://doi.org/10.1007/s10482-018-1091-z

Dorador, C., Molina, V., Hengst, M., Eissler, Y., Cornejo, M., Fernández, C., & Pérez, V. (2020). Microbial communities composition, activity, and dynamics at Salar de Huasco: A polyextreme environment in the Chilean Altiplano. In M. E. Farías (Ed.), *Microbial ecosystems in central Andes extreme environments* (pp. 123–139). Springer International Publishing. https://doi.org/10.1007/978-3-030-36192-1_9

Dorn, F. M., & Ruiz Peyré, F. (2020). Lithium as a strategic resource: Geopolitics, industrialization, and mining in Argentina. *Journal of Latin American Geography, 19*(4), 68–90. https://doi.org/10.1353/lag.2020.0101

Dowrick, S. (2004). Trade openness and growth: Who benefits? *Oxford Review of Economic Policy, 20*(1), 38–56. https://doi.org/10.1093/oxrep/grh003

Eckhardt, J., & Lee, K. (2018). Global value chains, firm preferences and the design of preferential trade agreements. *Global Policy, 9*, 58–66. https://doi.org/10.1111/1758-5899.12612

El Ancasti. (2020). "El Gobierno autorizó nuevas obras en el Río Los Patos, en Antofagasta de la Sierra". *Diario El Ancasti*. https://www.elancasti.com.ar/politica-economia/2020/6/14/el-gobierno-autorizo-nuevas-obras-en-el-rio-los-patos-en-antofagasta-de-la-sierra-436525.html

El Cronista. (2023). YPF Litio: cómo es la apuesta nacional para convertir a Argentina en un jugador clave. *El Cronista*. https://www.cronista.com/brand-strategy/ypf-litio-como-es-la-apuesta-nacional-para-convertir-a-argentina-en-un-jugador-clave/

El Periódico de la energía. (2023). Bolivia firma acuerdos con empresas de China y Rusia para extracción directa de litio. *El periódico de la energía*. https://elperiodicodelaenergia.com/bolivia-firma-acuerdos-empresas-china-rusia-extraccion-directa-litio/

El Periódico de la energía. (2024). Yacimientos de Litio Bolivianos (YLB) buscará socios en Bélgica y Francia para la industrialización de litio. *El Periódico de la energía*. https://elperiodicodelaenergia.com/yacimientos-litio-bolivianos-ylb-buscara-socios-belgica-francia-industrializacion-litio/

Escosteguy, M., Clavijo, A., Paz, W. F. D., Hufty, M., & Seghezzo, L. (2022). "We are not allowed to speak": Some thoughts about a consultation process around lithium mining in Northern Argentina. *The Extractive Industries and Society, 11*, 101134. https://doi.org/10.1016/j.exis.2022.101134

Etchemendy, S. (2011). *Models of economic liberalization: Business, workers, and compensation in Latin America, Spain, and Portugal*. Cambridge University Press. https://doi.org/10.1017/CBO9780511835223

Evans, P. (1996). El Estado como problema y como solución. *Desarrollo Económico, 35*(140), 529. https://doi.org/10.2307/3467372

Evans, P. B., Rueschemeyer, D., & Skocpol, T. (Eds.). (1985). *Bringing the state back*. Cambridge University Press. https://doi.org/10.1017/CBO9780511628283

Evans, P., & Rauch, J. E. (1999). Bureaucracy and growth: A cross-national analysis of the effects of "Weberian" state structures on economic growth. *American Sociological Review, 64*(5), 748. https://doi.org/10.2307/2657374

Fairfield, T. (2010). Business power and tax reform: Taxing income and profits in Chile and Argentina. *Latin American Politics and Society*, *52*(2), Art. 2. https://doi.org/10.1111/j.1548-2456.2010.00081.x

Fairfield, T. (2015). Structural power in comparative political economy: Perspectives from policy formulation in Latin America. *Business and Politics*, *17*(3), Art. 3. https://doi.org/10.1515/bap-2014-0047

Falkner, R. (2008). *Business power and conflict in international environmental politics*. Palgrave Macmillan UK. https://doi.org/10.1057/9780230277892

Farías, A. (2019). *Políticas sociales en Chile: Trayectoria de inequidades y desigualdades en distribución de bienes y servicios*. Universidad Alberto Hurtado.

FIMA. (2018). Admiten Recursos de Protección contra acuerdo Corfo – SQM en Salar de Atacama. *Fiscalía del medio Ambiente (FIMA)*. https://www.fima.cl/2018/02/21/admiten-recursos-de-proteccion-contra-acuerdo-corfo-sqm-en-salar-de-atacama/

Fornillo, B. (2015). Leyes sobre el litio: ¿recurso estratégico minero u oportunidad científico-industrial? *Realidad Económica, 295*, 5.

Fornillo, B. (2018). La energía del litio en Argentina y Bolivia: Comunidad, extractivismo y posdesarrollo. *Colombia Internacional*, *93*, Art. 93. https://doi.org/10.7440/colombiaint93.2018.07

Fornillo, B. (Ed.). (2019). *Litio en Sudamérica geopolítica , energía y territorios*. CLACSO. http://repositorio.uasb.edu.bo/handle/54000/1376

Fortin, J. (2010). A tool to evaluate state capacity in post-communist countries, 1989–2006: A tool to evaluate state capacity in post-communist countries. *European Journal of Political Research, 49*(5), 654–686. https://doi.org/10.1111/j.1475-6765.2009.01911.x

French-Davis, R. (2001). *Crisis Financieras en economías exitosas*. CEPAL.

Fuentes, A., & Pipkin, S. (2015). Self-discovery in the dark: The demand side of industrial policy in Latin America. *Review of International Political Economy, 23*(1), 153–183. https://doi.org/10.1080/09692290.2015.1104374

Gardini, G. L. (2006). Government-business relations in the construction of Mercosur. *Business and Politics, 8*(1), 1–26.

Geddes, B. (1994). *Politician's dilemma: Building state capacity in Latin America*. University of California Press.

Genovese, F., & Tvinnereim, E. (2018). Who opposes climate regulation? Business preferences for the European emission trading scheme. *The Review of International Organizations*. https://doi.org/10.1007/s11558-018-9318-3

George, A. L., & Bennett, A. (2005). *Case studies and theory development in the social sciences*. MIT Press.

Gerring, J. (2004). What is a case study and what is it good for? *American Political Science Review, 98*(2), Art. 2. https://doi.org/10.1017/S0003055404001182

Gerring, J. (2006). *Case study research: Principles and practices*. Cambridge University Press. https://doi.org/10.1017/CBO9780511803123

Godoy, C. (2022). Minería del litio en Chile y conflictividad social: una mirada sobre los aspectos político-comercial, geopolítico y socioambiental desde una perspectiva interméstica. *Estudios Avanzados, 3*, 6. https://doi.org/10.35588/estudav.v0i36.5650

Goldin, I. (2016). *The pursuit of development: Economic growth, social change and ideas*. Oxford University Press.

Gómez, S. (2022). Fractura metabólica a la acumulación por desposesión: minería del litio, imperialismo ecológico y despojo hídrico en el noroeste argentino. *Agua y Territorio, 20*, 23–40. https://doi.org/10.17561/at.20.5699

González, F. (2017). Codelco inicia búsqueda de socio para explotar litio. *La Tercera*. https://www.latercera.com/noticia/codelco-inicia-busqueda-socio-explotar-litio/

González, L. I., & Snyder, R. (2020). Modes of lithium extraction in Argentina: Mining politics in Catamarca, Jujuy, and Salta. In *Natural resources and policy choices in Latin America*. Konrad Adenauer Foundation. https://ri.conicet.gov.ar/handle/11336/157541

González, L. I., & Snyder, R. (2023). Modes of extraction in Latin America's lithium triangle: Explaining negotiated, unnegotiated, and aborted mining projects. *Latin American Politics & Society, 65*(1), 47–73. https://doi.org/10.1017/lap.2022.32

González-Bustamante, B., Olivares, A., Abarca, P., & Molina, E. (2016). Servicio civil en Chile, análisis de los directivos de primer nivel jerárquico (2003–13). *Revista De Administração Pública, 50*, 59–80.

Green, J. F. (2021). Does carbon pricing reduce emissions? A review of ex-post analyses. *Environmental Research Letters, 16*(4), 043004. https://doi.org/10.1088/1748-9326/abdae9

Grumbach, J. M. (2015). Polluting industries as climate protagonists: Cap and trade and the problem of business preferences. *Business and Politics, 17*(04), 633–659. https://doi.org/10.1515/bap-2015-0012

Gudynas, E. (2009). Diez tesis urgentes sobre el nuevo extractivismo. Contextos y demandas bajo el progresismo sudamericano actual. In *Extractivismo, política y sociedad* ISBN 78-9978-51-024-7

Gundermann, H., & Göbel, B. (2018). Comunidades Indígenas, Empresas Del Litio Y Sus Relaciones En El Salar De Atacama. *Chungará (Arica), ahead*, Art. ahead. https://doi.org/10.4067/S0717-73562018005001602

Haberl, H., Wiedenhofer, D., Virág, D., Kalt, G., Plank, B., Brockway, P., Fishman, T., Hausknost, D., Kraus-mann, F., Leon-Gruchalski, B., Mayer, A., Pichler, M., & Schaffartzik, A., Sousa, T., Streecky J., & Creutzig, F. (2020). A systematic review of the evidence on decoupling of GDP, resource use and GHG emissions, part II: Synthesizing the insights. *Environmental Research Letters, 15*(6), 065003.

Hacker, J. S., & Pierson, P. (2002). Business power and social policy: Employers and the formation of the American welfare state. *Politics & Society, 30*(2), Art. 2. https://doi.org/10.1177/0032329202030002004

Hacker, J. S., & Pierson, P. (2011). Drift and democracy: The neglected politics of policy inaction. In Working Group on Institutional Change

Haggard, S., Kang, D., & Moon, C. I. (1997). Japanese colonialism and Korean development: A critique. World Development, 25(6), 867–881.

Hall, P. A. (1993). Policy paradigms, social learning, and the state: The case of economic policymaking in Britain. *Comparative Politics*, 275–296.

Hall, P. A., & Soskice, D. W. (Eds.). (2001). *Varieties of capitalism: The institutional foundations of comparative advantage*. Oxford University Press.

Hart, O. (2009). Regulation and Sarbanes-Oxley. *Journal of Accounting Research, 47*(2), Art. 2.

Haslam, P. A., & Tanimoune, N. (2016). The determinants of social conflict in the Latin American mining sector: new evidence with quantitative data. *World Development, 78*, 401–419. https://doi.org/10.1016/j.worlddev.2015.10.020

Hernández, J. (2018) Estrategias Organizacionales, Competencia y Colusión en una Economía de ¿Libre Mercado? En Madariaga, A. y González, F. *La constitución social, política y moral de la economía chilena*. RIL Editores

Hochstetler, K., & Kostka, G. (2015). Wind and solar sectors in Brazil and China: Interests, state-business relations and policy outcomes. *Global Environmental Politics*. https://doi.org/10.1162/GLEP_a_00312

Hochstetler, K. (2020). *Political economies of energy transition: Wind and solar power in Brazil and South Africa*. Cambridge University Press. https://doi.org/10.1017/9781108920353

Holland, A. C. (2016). Forbearance. *American Political Science Review*, *110*(2), Art. 2. https://doi.org/10.1017/S0003055416000083

Holland, A. C. (2017). *Forbearance as redistribution: The politics of informal welfare in Latin America*. Cambridge University Press. https://doi.org/10.1017/9781316795613

Hughes, L., & Meckling, J. (2017). The politics of renewable energy trade: The US–China solar dispute. *Energy Policy*, *105*, 256–262. https://doi.org/10.1016/j.enpol.2017.02.044

Huntington, S. P. (1996). *Political order in changing societies*. Yale University Press.

Ibañez, R. (2024). YLB recibe propuestas de 38 empresas internacionales para el desarrollo del litio. *La Razón*. https://www.la-razon.com/economia/2024/03/07/ylb-recibe-propuestas-de-38-empresas-internacionales-para-el-desarrollo-del-litio/

Irarrázaval, F., & Carrasco, S. (2023). One step forward, two steps back? Shifting accumulation strategies in the lithium production network in Chile. *The Extractive Industries and Society*. https://doi.org/10.1016/j.exis.2023.101327

JEMSE. (n.d.). Minería. https://jemse.gob.ar/mineria/

Jenkins, J. D. (2014). Political economy constraints on carbon pricing policies: What are the implications for economic efficiency, environmental efficacy, and climate policy design? *Energy Policy*, *69*, 467–477. https://doi.org/10.1016/j.enpol.2014.02.003

Jerez Henríquez, B. (2018). *Impacto socioambiental de la extracción de litio en las cuencas de los salares altoandinos del Cono Sur*. OCMAL.

Jerez, B., Garcés, I., & Torres, R. (2021). Lithium extractivism and water injustices in the Salar de Atacama, Chile: The colonial shadow of green electromobility. *Political Geography*, *87*, 102382. https://doi.org/10.1016/j.polgeo.2021.102382

Kalazich, F., Yager, K., Prieto, M., & Babidge, S. (2019). "That's the problem with that lake; it changes sides": Mapping extraction and ecological exhaustion in the Atacama. *Journal of Political Ecology*, *26*(1), Art. 1. https://doi.org/10.2458/v26i1.23169

Kattel, R., & Lember, V. (2010). Public procurement as an industrial policy tool: An option for developing countries? *Journal of Public Procurement, 10*(3), 368–404. https://doi.org/10.1108/JOPP-10-03-2010-B003

Katzenstein, P. J. (1985). *Small states in world markets: Industrial policy in Europe*. Cornell University Press.

Käufer, T. (2023). La carrera por el litio: Moscú y Pekín avanzan en Bolivia. *DW*. https://www.dw.com/es/la-carrera-por-el-litio-mosc%C3%BA-y-pek%C3%ADn-llevan-la-delantera-en-bolivia/a-67845331

Kazimierski, M. A. (2018). Almacenamiento energético frente al inminente paradigma renovable: El rol de las baterías ion-litio y las perspectivas sudamericanas. *Letras Verdes. Revista Latinoamericana de Estudios Socioambientales, 23*, Art. 23. https://doi.org/10.17141/letrasverdes.23.2018.3055

Kim, I. S., Milner, H. V., Bernauer, T., Osgood, I., Spilker, G., & Tingley, D. (2019). Firms and global value chains: Identifying firms' multidimensional trade preferences. *International Studies Quarterly*. https://doi.org/10.1093/isq/sqy055

Krueger, A. O. (1974). The political economy of the rent-seeking society. *The American Economic Review, 64*(3), 291–303.

Lall, S. (2001). Competitiveness indices and developing countries: An economic evaluation of the global competitiveness report. *World Development, 29*(9), 1501–1525. https://doi.org/10.1016/S0305-750X(01)00051-1

Landman, T. (2017). *Issues and methods in comparative politics: An introduction*. Routledge, Taylor & Francis Group.

La Tercera. (2012a). Las claves de la controversial explotación del litio, el denominado "combustible del futuro". *La Tercera*. https://www.latercera.com/noticia/las-claves-de-la-controversial-explotacion-del-litio-el-denominado-combustible-del-futuro/

La Tercera. (2012b). Codelco reitera que no necesita postular a licitación para participar en el negocio del litio. *La Tercera*. https://www.latercera.com/noticia/codelco-reitera-que-no-necesita-postular-a-licitacion-para-participar-en-el-negocio-del-litio/#

La Tercera. (2012c). Codelco reitera que no necesita postular a licitación para participar en el negocio del litio. *La Tercera*. https://www.latercera.com/noticia/codelco-reitera-que-no-necesita-postular-a-licitacion-para-participar-en-el-negocio-del-litio/#

La Tercera. (2012d). SQM se adjudicó primera licitación de contratos para explotación de litio en Chile. *La Tercera*. https://www.latercera.com/noticia/sqm-se-adjudico-primera-licitacion-de-contratos-para-explotacion-de-litio-en-chile/

La Tercera. (2012e). Ministerio de Minería decreta inválida la licitación del litio a la empresa SQM. *La Tercera*. https://www.latercera.com/noticia/ministerio-de-mineria-decreta-invalida-la-licitacion-del-litio-a-la-empresa-sqm/

La Tercera. (2012f). Lagos Weber: "Lo ocurrido con el litio es un bochorno internacional". *La Tercera*. https://www.latercera.com/noticia/lagos-weber-lo-ocurrido-con-el-litio-es-un-bochorno-internacional/#
La Tercera. (2016). Consejo de Corfo aprueba acuerdo con Rockwood para aumentar producción de litio en el Salar de Atacama. *La Tercera*. https://www.latercera.com/noticia/consejo-corfo-aprueba-acuerdo-rockwood-aumentar-produccion-litio/
La Tercera. (2018). Tianqi: feliz con participación sin control en SQM. *La Tercera*. https://www.latercera.com/pulso/noticia/tianqi-feliz-participacion-sin-control-sqm/194588/#
La Tercera. (2021). Ues cuestionan adjudicación del Instituto de Tecnologías Limpias a consorcio extranjero y senadora Provoste pide a Presidente revertir decisión. *La Tercera*. https://www.latercera.com/nacional/noticia/ues-cuestionan-adjudicacion-del-instituto-de-tecnologias-limpias-a-consorcio-extranjero-y-senadora-provoste-pide-a-presidente-revertir-decision/VYDVE7HH7VEV3NF32JIFEFAN7A/
Lavarello, P., & Sarabia, M. (2017). La política industrial en la Argentina durante la década de 2000. En *Manufactura y cambio estructural. Aportes para pensar la política industrial en la Argentina* (p. 330). CEPAL.
Leach, M., Scoones, I., & Stirling, A. (2010). *Dynamic sustainabilities: Technology, environment, social justice*. Routledge. https://doi.org/10.4324/9781849775069
Lebdioui, A. (2024). *Survival of the greenest: Economic transformation in a climate-conscious world*. Cambridge University Press.
Leiva, F. I. (2019). Economic elites and new strategies for extractivism in Chile. *European Review of Latin American and Caribbean Studies*. https://doi.org/10.32992/erlacs.10511
Lendoiro, F. (2021). Boom de litio: los 10 proyectos argentinos en los que se invierten US 4500 millones. *Cronista*. https://www.cronista.com/apertura-negocio/empresas/litio-l10-proyectos-con-us-4500-millones-de-inversion-que-esperan-arrancar-en-argentina/
León, M., Muñoz, C., & Sánchez, J. (2020). *La gobernanza del litio y el cobre en los países andinos*. 173.
Levitsky, S., & Murillo, M. V. (2010). Variación en la fortaleza institucional. *Revista De Sociología*. https://doi.org/10.5354/0719-529X.2010.14399
Lewis, J. I. (2021). Green industrial policy after Paris: Renewable energy policy measures and climate goals. *Global Environmental Politics, 21*(4), 42–63. https://doi.org/10.1162/glep_a_00636
Lewis, J. I. (2014). The rise of renewable energy protectionism: Emerging trade conflicts and implications for low carbon development. *Global Environmental Politics, 14*(4), 10–35. https://doi.org/10.1162/GLEP_a_00255

Lewis, J. I. (2023). Green industrial policy in comparative perspective: Supporting renewable energy industry development in emerging economies. *The Oxford Handbook of Comparative Environmental Politics*. https://doi.org/10.1093/oxfordhb/9780197515037.013.24

Lewkowicz, J. (2021). Argentina debate el futuro del desarrollo del litio. *Diálogo Chino*. https://dialogochino.net/es/actividades-extractivas-es/46818-argentina-debate-el-futuro-del-desarrollo-del-litio/

Li, C., & Csaszar, F. A. (2019). Government as landscape designer: A behavioral view of industrial policy. *Strategy Science*. https://doi.org/10.1287/stsc.2019.0080

Lindblom, C. E. (1982). The market as prison. *The Journal of Politics*, *44*(2), Art. 2. https://doi.org/10.2307/2130588

Liu, W., & Agusdinata, D. B. (2020). Interdependencies of lithium mining and communities sustainability in Salar de Atacama, Chile. *Journal of Cleaner Production, 260*, 120838. https://doi.org/10.1016/j.jclepro.2020.120838

López, A., Obaya, M., Pascuini, P., & Ramos, A. (2019). *Litio en la Argentina: Oportunidades y desafíos para el desarrollo de la cadena de valor*. Inter-American Development Bank.

Lunde Seefeldt, J. (2020). Lessons from the lithium triangle: Considering policy explanations for the variation in lithium industry development in the "Lithium Triangle" countries of Chile, Argentina, and Bolivia. *Politics & Policy, 48*(4), 727–765. https://doi.org/10.1111/polp.12365

Lunde Seefeldt, J. (2022). Water as property: Contention between indigenous communities and the lithium industry for water rights in Chile. *Latin American Policy, 13*(2), 328–353. https://doi.org/10.1111/lamp.12265

Madariaga, A. (2016). Mechanisms of neoliberal resilience: Comparing exchange rates and industrial policy in Chile and Estonia. *Socio-Economic Review*. https://doi.org/10.1093/ser/mww015

Madariaga, A. (2019). From 'Green Laggard' to regional leader: Explaining the recent development of environmental policy in Chile. *Bulletin of Latin American Research, 38*(4), 453–470. https://doi.org/10.1111/blar.12841

Madariaga, A. (2020). *Neoliberal resilience: Lessons in democracy and development from Latin America and Eastern Europe*. Princeton University Press.

Madariaga, A., & González, F. (2018). La constitución social, política y moral de la economía chilena. RIL Editores.

Madariaga, A., Maillet, A., & Rozas, J. (2021). Multilevel business power in environmental politics: The avocado boom and water scarcity in Chile. *Environmental Politics, 30*(7), Art. 7. https://doi.org/10.1080/09644016.2021.1892981

Maillet, A. (2015a). Más allá del "modelo" chileno: Una aproximación multisectorial a las relaciones Estado-mercado. *Revista de Sociologia e Política, 23*(55), Art. 55. https://doi.org/10.1590/1678-987315235504

Maillet, A. (2015b). Variedades de neoliberalismo. Innovación conceptual para el análisis del rol del Estado en los mercados. *Revista de Estudios Políticos, 169*, Art. 169. https://doi.org/10.18042/cepc/rep.169.04

Maillet, A., & Carrasco, S. (2019). Regulación y poder empresarial: El caso del transporte público en Santiago (2007–2017). *Revista De Administração Pública, 53*(5), 942–959. https://doi.org/10.1590/0034-761220180079

Maillet, A., Faure, A., & Carrasco, S. (2019). Organizaciones ciudadanas y coproducción de las políticas públicas. Ciudadano Inteligente, Espacio Público y la Agenda de Probidad en Chile. En *Los efectos de los procesos participativos en la acción pública* (1ª ed., pp. 17–50). Tesco.

Mann, M. (1984). The autonomous power of the state: Its origins, mechanisms and results. *European Journal of Sociology, 25*(2), 185–213. https://doi.org/10.1017/S0003975600004239

Marina, V., & Cueto, H. (2013). Bolivia's energy and mineral resources trade and investments with china: Potential socioeconomic and environmental effects of lithium extraction. *Latin American Policy, 4*(1), Art. 1. https://doi.org/10.1111/lamp.12007

Martin, G., Rentsch, L., Höck, M., & Bertau, M. (2017). Lithium market research—Global supply, future demand and price development. *Energy Storage Materials, 6*, 171–179. https://doi.org/10.1016/j.ensm.2016.11.004

Matamala, D. (2017). *Poderoso caballero. El pe$o del dinero en la política chilena*. Catalonia.

Mayka, L. (2019). *Building participatory institutions in latin america: reform coalitions and institutional change*. Cambridge University Press. https://doi.org/10.1017/9781108598927

Mazzucato, M. (2011). The entrepreneurial state. *Soundings, 49*(49), 131–142. https://doi.org/10.3898/136266211798411183

Mceachern, D., & Doyle, T. (2008). *Environment and politics*. Routledge.

Meckling, J. (2011). The globalization of carbon trading: Transnational business coalitions in climate politics. *Global Environmental Politics, 11*(2), 26–50. https://doi.org/10.1162/GLEP_a_00052

Meckling, J. (2015). Oppose, support, or hedge? Distributional effects, regulatory pressure, and business strategy in environmental politics. *Global Environmental Politics, 15*(2), Art. 2. https://doi.org/10.1162/GLEP_a_00296

Meckling, J., & Hughes, L. (2017). Globalizing solar: Global supply chains and trade preferences. *International Studies Quarterly, 61*(2), 225–235. https://doi.org/10.1093/isq/sqw055

Meckling, J., & Nahm, J. (2018a). When do states disrupt industries? Electric cars and the politics of innovation. *Review of International Political Economy, 25*(4), 505–529. https://doi.org/10.1080/09692290.2018.1434810

Meckling, J., & Nahm, J. (2018b). The power of process: State capacity and climate policy. *Governance, 31*, 741–757. https://doi.org/10.1111/gove.12338

Meckling, J., & Nahm, J. (2021). Strategic state capacity: How states counter opposition to climate policy. *Comparative Political Studies*. https://doi.org/10.1177/0010414021102430

Meckling, J., Kelsey, N., Biber, E., & Zysman, J. (2015). Winning coalitions for climate policy. *Science, 349*(6253), 1170–1171. https://doi.org/10.1126/science.aab1336

Millan, L. (2018). Bolivia's almost impossible lithium dream. *Bloomberg*. https://www.bloomberg.com/news/features/2018-12-03/bolivia-s-almost-impossible-lithium-dream?leadSource=uverify%20wall

Milmanda, B. F., & Garay, C. (2020). The multilevel politics of enforcement: Environmental institutions in Argentina. *Politics & Society*, *48*(1), Art. 1. https://doi.org/10.1177/0032329219894074

Minería Chilena. (2018). Se desata el arbitraje entre la Corfo y Albemarle: El conflicto es abordado por la fiscal de la estatal, María Elina Cruz. *Minería Chilena*. https://www.mch.cl/negocios-industria/se-desata-arbitraje-la-corfo-albemarle/

Miranda, B. (2020). Litio en Bolivia: por qué el país con las mayores reservas de este valioso recurso tiene tantos problemas para explotarlo. *BBC News*. https://www.bbc.com/mundo/noticias-america-latina-51666362

Montes, C. y Quezada, J. (2021). Adjudicación del Instituto de Tecnologías Limpias (ITL) genera molestia en consorcio de universidades chilenas. *La Tercera*. https://www.latercera.com/que-pasa/noticia/adjudicacion-del-instituto-de-tecnologias-limpias-itl-genera-molestia-en-consorcio-de-universidades-chilenas/PV53J44ZKJHZVBAUY26QL7A6VU/

Morales, R. (2021). Crisis y minería del litio en el Salar de Atacama. La necesidad de una mirada desde la Justicia Climática. In Morales, R. (coord.) *Salares Andinos, ecología de saberes por la protección de nuestros salares y humedales*. Observatorio Plurinacional de Salares Andinos, Fundación Tantí.

Moreno-Brieva, F., & Marín, R. (2019). Technology generation and international collaboration in the global value chain of lithium batteries. *Resources, Conservation and Recycling, 146*, 232–243. https://doi.org/10.1016/j.resconrec.2019.03.026

Murphy, D. D. (2002). The business dynamics of global regulatory competition. In *Dynamics of regulatory change: How globalization affects national regulatory policies*. University of California Press.

Nacif, F. (2020). *Litio en Argentina: dos décadas de explotación*. FARN: Fundación Ambiente y Recursos Naturales. https://investiga.unlp.edu.ar/especiales/litio-17104

Nahm, J., & Urpelainen, J. (2021). The enemy within? Green industrial policy and stranded assets in China's power sector. *Global Environmental Politics, 21*(4), 88–109. https://doi.org/10.1162/glep_a_00632

Nahm, J. (2022). Green growth models. In L. Baccaro, M. Blyth, & J. Pontusson (Eds.), *Diminishing returns: The new politics of growth and stagnation.* Oxford University Press.

Naudé, W. (2010). *Industrial policy: Old and new issues*. WIDER Working Paper. https://www.econstor.eu/handle/10419/54072

Newell, P. (2021). Power shift: The global political economy of energy transitions. *Cambridge University Press.* https://doi.org/10.1017/9781108966184

Nogales (24/01/2019). Humo blanco: Corfo y Albemarle llegan a acuerdo por precio preferente para productores que darán valor agregado al litio. *La Tercera.* https://www.latercera.com/pulso/noticia/corfo-albemarle-acuerdan-mecanismo-calculo-precio-preferente-industrializacion-del-litio/500032/

North, D. C. (1990). *Institutions, institutional change and economic performance.* Cambridge University Press.

Núñez, L. (2018). Bitrán revela que recibió "presiones de la Nueva Mayoría" para no sacar a Ponce de SQM. *Emol.* https://www.emol.com/noticias/Economia/2018/06/06/908807/Bitran-revela-que-recibio-presiones-de-la-Nueva-Mayoria-durante-negociaciones-para-sacar-a-Ponce-Lerou-de--SQM.html

O'Donnell, G. (1993). On the state, democratization and some conceptual problems: A Latin American view with glances at some postcommunist countries. *World Development, 21*(8), 1355–1369. https://doi.org/10.1016/0305-750X(93)90048-E

O'Faircheallaigh, C., & Babidge, S. (2023). Negotiated agreements, indigenous peoples and extractive industry in the Salar de Atacama, Chile: When is an agreement more than a contract? *Development & Change, 54*(3), 641–670. https://doi.org/10.1111/dech.12767

O´Ryan, F. (2019). Directorio de Codelco aprueba pasar a siguiente etapa del "Proyecto Litio". *La Tercera.* https://www.latercera.com/pulso/noticia/directorio-codelco-aprueba-pasar-siguiente-etapa-del-proyecto-litio/759515/

O´Ryan, F. (2020). Tesla ya tiene socio para el litio, mientras SQM aprueba dividendo eventual. *La Tercera.* https://www.latercera.com/pulso/noticia/tesla-ya-tiene-socio-para-el-litio-mientras-sqm-aprueba-dividendo-eventual/3LZQFLJN3ZDTNP4N72FFBW2J5I/

Obaya, M. (2021). *Una mirada estratégica sobre el triángulo del litio.* Fundar.

Obaya, M., & Céspedes, M. (2021). *Análisis de las redes globales de producción de baterías de ion de litio: Implicaciones para los países del triángulo del litio.* CEPAL. https://repositorio.cepal.org/handle/11362/46943

Obaya, M., & Pascuini, P. (2020). Estudio comparativo de los modos de gobernanza del litio en la Argentina, Chile y el Estado Plurinacional de Bolivia. In M. León, C. Muñoz, & J. Sánchez (Eds.) *La gobernanza del litio y el cobre en los países andinos*. CEPAL, Deutsche Gesellschaft für Internationale Zusammenarbeit (GIZ).

Obaya, M., López, A., & Pascuini, P. (2021). Curb your enthusiasm. Challenges to the development of lithium-based linkages in Argentina. *Resources Policy, 70*, 101912. https://doi.org/10.1016/j.resourpol.2020.101912

Olson, M. (1989). Collective action. In J. Eatwell, M. Milgate, & P. Newman (Eds.), *The invisible hand* (pp. 61–69). Palgrave Macmillan UK. https://doi.org/10.1007/978-1-349-20313-0_5

Orellana, G. (2018). Samsung, Molymet y firma china ganan licitación de litio e invertirán US$ 754 millones en el país. La Tercera. https://www.latercera.com/negocios/noticia/samsung-molymet-y-firma-china-ganan-licitacion-de-litio-e-invertiran-us-745-millones-en-el-pais/93385/#

Orellana, G. (2019a). *Fracasa licitación de valor agregado para el litio y Corfo evalúa llamar a nueva licitación*. La Tercera. https://www.latercera.com/pulso/noticia/fracasa-licitacion-valor-agregado-litio-corfo-evalua-llamar-nueva-licitacion/754832/#

Orellana, G. (2019b). *Participante de fallida licitación para industrializar el litio cuestiona rol de Corfo*. La Tercera. https://www.latercera.com/pulso/noticia/participante-fallida-licitacion-industrializar-litio-cuestiona-rol-corfo/768081/

Orihuela, J. C. (2013). How do "mineral-states" learn? Path-dependence, networks, and policy change in the development of economic institutions. *World Development, 43*, 138–148. https://doi.org/10.1016/j.worlddev.2012.10.004

Orihuela, J. C. (2018). One blueprint, three translations: Development corporations in Chile, Colombia and Peru. In A. Ferraro & M. Centeno (Eds.), *State and nation making in Latin America and Spain: The rise and fall of the developmental state* (pp. 107–133). Cambridge University Press.

Orihuela, J. C., & Paredes, M. (2017). Fragmented layering: Building a green state for mining in Peru. In E. Dargent, J. C. Orihuela, M. Paredes, & M. E. Ulfe (Eds.), *Resource booms and institutional pathways* (pp. 97–117). Palgrave Macmillan. https://doi.org/10.1007/978-3-319-53532-6_4

Orihuela, J., Mendieta, A., Pérez, C., & Ramírez, T. (2021). From paper institutions to bureaucratic autonomy: Institutional change as a resource curse remedy. *World Development, 143*, 105463. https://doi.org/10.1016/j.worlddev.2021.10546

Osorio Gonnet, C. (2019). A comparative analysis of the adoption of conditional cash transfers programs in Latin America. *Journal of Comparative Policy Analysis: Research and Practice, 21*(4), 385–401. https://doi.org/10.1080/13876988.2018.1491671

Pack, H. (2006). Is there a case for industrial policy? A critical survey. *The World Bank Research Observer, 21*(2), 267–297. https://doi.org/10.1093/wbro/lkl001

Pagés, C., Pierre, G., & Scarpetta, S. (2009). *Job creation in Latin America and the Caribbean: Recent trends and policy challenges*. World Bank Publications.

Paredes, M. (2018). La transnacionalización de la resistencia a la minería en Tambogrande Y Pascua Lama. *América Latina Hoy, 80*, 73–94. https://doi.org/10.14201/alh2018807394

Peña, N. (2014). Comisión propondrá a Bachelet crear empresa pública para explotar litio en salares. *La Tercera*. https://www.latercera.com/noticia/comision-propondra-a-bachelet-crear-empresa-publica-para-explotar-litio-en-salares/

Perez-Cueto, C. (2012). Las claves del negocio del litio: un mercado pequeño con gran potencial de desarrollo. *La Tercera*. https://www.latercera.com/noticia/las-claves-del-negocio-del-litio-un-mercado-pequeno-con-gran-potencial-de-desarrollo/

Perez-Cueto, C. (2014). Presidenta Bachelet firmó decreto que crea la Comisión Nacional del Litio. *La Tercera*. https://www.latercera.com/noticia/presidenta-bachelet-firmo-decreto-que-crea-la-comision-nacional-del-litio/

Pierson, P. (2000). Increasing returns, path dependence, and the study of politics. *American political science review, 94*(2), 251–267. https://doi.org/10.2307/2586011

Pizarro, C., Palacios, J., & Novoa, S. (2012). Codelco prepara ingreso al negocio del litio. *La Tercera*. https://www.latercera.com/noticia/codelco-prepara-ingreso-al-negocio-del-litio/

Pizzaro, G., & Ramirez, P. (2018). El entierro del Caso SQM: así se fraguó la impunidad para el financiamiento político ilegal. *CIPER*. https://www.ciperchile.cl/2018/04/16/el-entierro-del-caso-sqm-asi-se-fraguo-la-impunidad-para-el-financiamiento-politico-ilegal/

Pizzoleo, J. (2023). Bolivia inaugura primera planta industrial de litio. *Reporte Minero*. https://www.reporteminero.cl/noticia/noticias/2023/12/bolivia-inaugura-primera-planta-industrial-litio

Polanyi, K. (2017). *La gran transformación*. Los orígenes políticos y económicos de nuestro tiempo. Fondo de Cultura Económica.

Poulantzas, N. (1974). Internationalisation of capitalist relations and the Nation-State. *Economy and Society, 3*(2), 145–179. https://doi.org/10.1080/03085147400000008

Poveda R. (2020). *Estudio de caso sobre la gobernanza del litio en Chile*. Serie Recursos Naturales y Desarrollo. Comisión Económica para América Latina y el Caribe (CEPAL).

Prebisch, R., & Cabañas, G. M. (1949). El desarrollo económico de la américa latina y algunos de sus principales problemas. *El Trimestre Económico, 16*(63(3)), 347–431.

Prensa, P. M. (2021). AIE expresa «preocupación» por licitación del Instituto de Tecnologías Limpias. *Portal Minero*. https://www.portalminero.com/wp/aie-expresa-preocupacion-por-licitacion-del-instituto-de-tecnologias-limpias/

Pressley, L. (2019). Litio: la fiebre del "oro blanco", ¿fortuna o infortunio para Argentina? *BBC News Mundo*. https://www.bbc.com/mundo/noticias-50082466

Primi, A., & Peres Núñez, W. (2009). *Theory and practice of industrial policy: Evidence from the Latin American experience*. ECLAC. https://repositorio.cepal.org/handle/11362/4582

Pulso. (2018a). Wall Street Journal: SQM y Tianqi controlarían el 70% del mercado mundial de litio. La Tercera. https://www.latercera.com/pulso/wall-street-journal-sqm-tianqi-controlarian-70-del-mercado-mundial-litio/

Pulso. (2018b). Bitrán le baja el perfil a las acusaciones de presión que él mismo denunció. *La Tercera*. https://www.latercera.com/pulso/noticia/bitran-le-baja-al-perfil-las-acusaciones-presion-denuncio-anteriormente/204719/

Rangel-Padilla, M. (2021). State-business relations and industrial upgrading in the digital era: The cases of software and aerospace sectors in Mexico (2000–2012). *Business and Politics, 23*(3), 309–329.

Rebossio, A. (2024). Elon Musk en la Argentina: la mina que le provee litio secó tierras fértiles y se descarta que instale una fábrica. *El Diario AR*. https://www.eldiarioar.com/economia/elon-musk-argentina-mina-le-provee-litio-seco-tierras-fertiles-descarta-instale-fabrica_1_11286361.html

Rettberg, A. (2001). The political preferences of diversified business groups: Lessons from Colombia (1994–1998). *Business and Politics, 3*(1), 47–63.

Reventós, B. (2024). Milei busca inversiones para el litio frente a la resistencia de las comunidades indígenas. *El País*. https://elpais.com/argentina/2024-04-20/milei-busca-inversiones-para-el-litio-frente-a-la-resistencia-de-las-comunidades-indigenas.html

Riffo, J. (2024). Acuerdo SQM-Codelco: análisis critica falta de licitación, bajos beneficios y contrato hasta 2060. *Interferencia*. https://interferencia.cl/articulos/acuerdo-sqm-codelco-analisis-critica-falta-de-licitacion-bajos-beneficios-y-contrato-hasta

Robinson, A. (2019). La maldición del litio boliviano. *La Vanguardia*. https://www.lavanguardia.com/internacional/20191118/471704959499/bolivia-evo-morales-litio.html

Roca, M. (2024). El boom del litio: Argentina inauguró su cuarta planta de producción y hay otros 48 proyectos en carpeta. *DEF*. https://defonline.com.ar/energia-mineria/el-boom-del-litio-argentina-inauguro-su-cuarta-planta-de-produccion-y-hay-otros-48-proyectos-en-carpeta/

Rodríguez, I., Inturias, M., Frank, V., Robledo, J., Sarti, C., & Borel, R. (2019). *Conflictividad socioambiental en Latinoamérica. Aportes de la transformacion de conflictos socioambientales a la transformacion socio-ecologica*. Cuadernos de la Transformación, Friedrich-Ebert-Stiftung (FES)

Rodrik, D. (2009). Industrial policy: Don't ask why, ask how. *Middle East Development Journal, 1*(1), 1–29. https://doi.org/10.1142/S1793812009000024

Rodrik, D. (2014). Green industrial policy. *Oxford Review of Economic Policy, 30*(3), 469–491. https://doi.org/10.1093/oxrep/gru025

Romeo, G. (2019). Riesgo ambiental e incertidumbre en la producción del litio en salares de Argentina, Bolivia y Chile. In Fornillo, B. (coord.). *Litio en Sudamérica. Geopolítica, energía, territorios* (pp. 223–260). IEALC-Editorial El Colectivo-CLACSO.

Rosanvallon, P. (2012). *La sociedad de los iguales*. RBA Libros.

Ross, M. L. (2015). What have we learned about the resource curse? *Annual Review of Political Science, 18*(1), Art. 1. https://doi.org/10.1146/annurev-polisci-052213-040359

Ruiz, M. (2024). YLB reporta que la planta de litio tiene dificultades por falta de materia prima. *EJU*. https://eju.tv/2024/03/ylb-reporta-que-la-planta-de-litio-tiene-dificultades-por-falta-de-materia-prima/

San Juan, P. (2018) Agrupaciones indígenas y de regantes piden a la Corte Suprema anular acuerdo Corfo-SQM. *La Tercera*. https://www.latercera.com/pulso/noticia/agrupaciones-indigenas-regantes-piden-la-corte-suprema-anular-acuerdo-corfo-sqm/340311/

San Juan, P., & Gac, M. (2020). Anuncio de Musk para reducir dependencia del litio derriba acciones de SQM y bolsa chilena es la que más se contrajo en el mundo. *La Tercera*. https://www.latercera.com/pulso/noticia/anuncio-de-musk-para-reducir-dependencia-del-litio-derriba-acciones-de-sqm-y-bolsa-chilena-es-la-que-mas-se-contrajo-en-el-mundo/3OJPFVA2XFGAFA7TRVQ55C256A/#

San Juan, P. (2021). Gobierno fija meta de que al 2035 sólo se vendan autos eléctricos en Chile. *La Tercera*. https://www.latercera.com/pulso/noticia/gobierno-lanza-estrategia-de-electromovilidad-que-busca-que-al-2035-solo-se-vendan-autos-electricos-en-chile/IEX77BBVDNFHJBELRBJLHQVPDA/

Schneider, B. (2015). *Designing industrial policy in Latin America: Business-state relations and the new developmentalism*. Springer.

Schneider, B. R. (1995). El abrazo esquivo: Sinergia entre el sector privado y el Estado en los países de industrialización reciente. *Política y Gobierno, 2*(1), 5–41.

Schneider, B. R. (2009). Hierarchical market economies and varieties of capitalism in Latin America. *Journal of Latin American Studies, 41*(3), Art. 3. https://doi.org/10.1017/S0022216X09990186

Schorr, B. (2018). Oportunidades desiguales: Empresas y Estado en conflictos sobre la minería en Chile. *Estudios Atacameños, 57*, 239–255. https://doi.org/10.4067/S0718-10432018005000601

Schorr, B. (2021). Towards new rules for political transparency. Lessons from anti-corruption initiatives in Peru and Chile. In: Schorr, B. & Damonte, G. (Eds.), *Andean States and the Resource Curse* (pp. 142–157). Routledge.

Schorr, B., & Damonte, G. (2021a). A curse over the Andes? In G. Damonte & B. Schorr (Eds.), *Andean states and the resource curse* (pp. 3–35). Routledge. https://doi.org/10.4324/9781003179559-2

Schorr, B., & Damonte, G. (2021b). Institutional change in extractive economies. In G. Damonte & B. Schorr (Eds.), *Andean states and the resource curse* (pp. 251–267). Routledge. https://doi.org/10.4324/9781003179559-17

Schrank, A. (2013). Rewarding regulation in Latin America. *Politics & Society, 41*(4), 487–495. https://doi.org/10.1177/0032329213507549

Sen, K., & Te Velde, D. W. (2009). State business relations and economic growth in Sub-Saharan Africa. *Journal of Development Studies, 45*(8), 1267–1283. https://doi.org/10.1080/00220380902863307

Sewell, W. H. (2008). The temporalities of capitalism. *Socio-Economic Review, 6*(3), Art. 3. https://doi.org/10.1093/ser/mwn007

Sierra, Y. (2024). Bolivia: nuevos planes de gobierno para producción de litio despiertan incertidumbre ante falta de transparencia. *Mongabay*. https://es.mongabay.com/2023/05/produccion-de-litio-incertidumbre-falta-de-transparencia-bolivia/

Silva, E. (1996). Democracy, market economics and environmental policy in Chile. *Latin American Politics and Society, 38*(4), 1–33.

Silva, E. (2002). Capital and the Lagos Presidency: Business as usual? *Bulletin of Latin American Research, 21*(3), 339–357. https://doi.org/10.1111/1470-9856.00047

Silva, P. (2010). *En el nombre de la razón*. Ediciones Universidad Diego Portales.

Snyder, R. (2001). Scaling down: The subnational comparative method. *Studies in Comparative International Development, 36*(1), 93–110. https://doi.org/10.1007/BF02687586

Soifer, H. (2020). Shadow cases in comparative research. *Qualitative and Multi-Method Research*. https://doi.org/10.5281/ZENODO.4046562

Soifer, H. D. (2012). Measuring state capacity in contemporary Latin America. *Revista De Ciencia Política, 32*(3), 585–598.

Song, Y., Li, G., Wang, Q., Meng, X., & Wang, H. (2020). Scenario analysis on subsidy policies for the uptake of electric vehicles industry in China. *Resources, Conservation and Recycling, 161*, 104927. https://doi.org/10.1016/j.resconrec.2020.104927

Stein, E., & Tommasi, M. (2006). La política de las políticas públicas. *Política y gobierno*, *13*(2), Art. 2.
Sticco, M., Scravaglieri, P. y Damiani, A. (2019) *Estudio de los recursos hídricos y el impacto por explotación minera de litio. Cuenca Salinas Grandes y Laguna Guayatayoc - Provincia de Jujuy*. FARN.
Stigler, G. J. (1971). The theory of economic regulation. *The Bell Journal of Economics and Management Science*, *2*(1), Art. 1. https://doi.org/10.2307/3003160
Subirats, J., Knoepfel, P., Larrue, C., & Varone, F. (2008). *Análisis y gestión de políticas públicas*. Ariel.
Svampa, M. (2013). «Consenso de los Commodities» y lenguajes de valoración en América Latina. *Nueva Sociedad*, *244*, 30–46.
Svampa, M. (2019). *Las fronteras del neoextractivismo en América Latina: Conflictos socioambientales, giro ecoterritorial y nuevas dependencias*. Bielefeld University Press. https://doi.org/10.14361/9783839445266
te Velde, D. W. (2013). *State-business relations and industrial policy. Current policy and research* debates DEGRP.
UNLP (2019). Litio: un tesoro escondido en la Puna Argentina. *Investiga. Ciencia y Tecnología UNLP*. https://investiga.unlp.edu.ar/especiales/litio-17104
UPI. (2012). Senador Girardi pide a gobierno detener proceso de licitación del Litio. *La Tercera*. https://www.latercera.com/noticia/senador-girardi-pide-a-gobierno-detener-proceso-de-licitacion-del-litio/
Valenzuela-Fuentes, K., Alarcón-Barrueto, E., & Torres-Salinas, R. (2021). From resistance to creation: Socio-environmental activism in Chile's "Sacrifice Zones". *Sustainability*, *13*(6), Art. 6. https://doi.org/10.3390/su13063481
Vásquez, P. (2021). Litio en Argentina: hay que saber aprovechar el momento. *El Economista*. https://eleconomista.com.ar/economia/litio-argentina-hay-saber-aprovechar-momento-n45055
Vaughan, D. (1982). Transaction systems and unlawful organizational behavior. *Social Problems*, *29*(4), Art. 4. https://doi.org/10.2307/800026
Villa María Vivo. (2014). En la Puna, el litio se consume millones de litros de agua. https://villamariavivo.com/preocupa-en-punajujena-explotaciones-de-litio-que-consumen-millones-de-litrosde-agua/
Voskoboynik, D. M., & Andreucci, D. (2022). Greening extractivism: Environmental discourses and resource governance in the 'Lithium Triangle'. *Environment and Planning E: Nature and Space*, *5*(2), Art. 2. https://doi.org/10.1177/25148486211006345
Wagner, L., & Walter, S. (2020). Cartografía de la conflictividad minera en Argentina (2003–2018): Un análisis desde el Atlas de Justicia Ambiental. *Ciccus*, *3*, 247–278.

Warwick, K. (2013). Towards a new stage in Norway's science, technology and innovation system: Improving the long-term plan for research and higher education. *OECD Science, Technology and Industry Policy Papers*. https://doi.org/10.1787/ce07b7c3-en

Weber, M. (2016). Bureaucracy. In W. Longhofer & D. Winchester (Eds.), *Social theory re-wired*. Routledge.

Weiss, L. (1998). *The myth of the powerless state: Governing the economy in a global era*. Polity.

Whitfield, L., & Therkildsen, O. (2011). *What drives states to support the development of productive sectors? Strategies ruling elites pursue for political survival and their policy implications*. Dansk Center for Internationale Studier og Menneskerettigheder. DIIS Working Paper, 15.

Willem te Velde, D. (2003). *Foreign direct investment and income inequality in Latin America*. Instituto de Investigaciones Socio-Económicas (IISEC), Universidad Católica Boliviana. https://ideas.repec.org/p/ris/iisecd/2003_004.html

World Bank Group. (2017). The growing role of minerals and metals for a low carbon future. *World Bank*. https://doi.org/10.1596/28312

Yoguel, G., Lugones, M., & Sztulwark, S. (2007). *La política científica y tecnológica Argentina en las últimas décadas: Algunas consideraciones desde la perspectiva del desarrollo de procesos de aprendizaje*. CEPAL.

Zamarin, F. (2024). Chile sigue liderando en la región: proyectos de litio en Argentina tropiezan ante derrumbe de precios. *Radio Biobio*. https://www.biobiochile.cl/noticias/economia/actualidad-economica/2024/08/25/chile-sigue-liderando-en-la-region-proyectos-de-litio-en-argentina-tropiezan-ante-derrumbe-de-precios.shtml

Zícari, J., Fornillo, B., & Gamba, M. (2019). El mercado mundial del litio y el eje asiático. Dinámicas comerciales, industriales y tecnológicas (2001–2017). *Polis (Santiago)*. https://doi.org/10.32735/S0718-6568/2019-N52-1376

Index

A
Administrative capacities, 47, 112, 120, 168
Albemarle, 5, 86, 98, 126, 133
Arce, Luis, 165, 167

B
Bachelet, Michelle, 5, 96, 102, 129
Bargaining power, 43
Boric, Gabriel, 147
Brown areas, 158
Bureaucracy, 53
Bureaucratic autonomy, 34, 54
Bureaucratic capacities, 166
Bureaucratic institutions, 7
Bureaucrats, 51
Business actors, 175
Business cohesion, 57
Business(es), 49, 165
Business interests, 6, 61, 176
Business power, 9, 150, 179
Business preferences, 124
Business strategies, 37

C
Capitalist expansion, 178
Carbon pricing, 22
Case study, 13
Catamarca Minera y Energética Sociedad del Estado (CAMYEN), 160
Chilean Lithium Society, 126
Civil society, 53
Climate change, 23, 69, 71
Climate change risks, 37
CODELCO, 6, 95, 143
Coercive capacity, 46
Collective action, 23
Commodities boom, 5, 41
Communities, 42, 103, 156
Consensus, 174
Co-opted, 43
Corporación de Fomento de la Producción (CORFO), 95, 96
Corporatism, 52, 53

D
Demand shocks, 62

S. Carrasco, *From (De)regulation to Industrialization?*, Latin American Political Economy, https://doi.org/10.1007/978-3-031-77130-9

Demobilization, 51
Deregulation, 36
Developmental states, 11
Discursive power, 56
Distributive effects, 55, 171

E
Ease of Doing Business Index, 81
Electromobility, 2, 71, 77
Embedded autonomy, 34
Empresa Nacional de Minería (Enami), 148
Energy transition, 5, 7, 71
Entrepreneurs, 7, 9, 49, 54
Environmental complexity, 62
Environmental conflicts, 156
Environmental institutions, 83
Environmental law, 159
Evo Morales, 165
Externalities, 22
Extractivism, 41

F
Facilitative policies, 29
Federal, 158, 159, 171
Fernández, Alberto, 155, 157
Financial sector, 56
Fiscal capacity, 46
FMC Lithium, 87
Forbearance, 48
Free-market, 41
Frontier policies, 29, 151, 175

G
Global value chain, 26, 64
Green growth, 23
Green industrial policy, 27, 29, 32, 179
Green New Deal, 182

H
Horizontal coordination, 52
Horizontal policies, 29

I
Imaginaries, 8, 33
Incentives, 22
Indigenous communities, 87, 165
Industrial capacity, 47
Industrialization, 12
Industrialization processes, 150
Informal practices, 6
Institute of Clean Technologies (ITL), 103
Institutional business power, 140
Institutional curse, 151
Institutions, 50
Instrumental power, 56, 57, 129
Interest groups, 23, 50

J
Jujuy Energía y Minería Sociedad del Estado (JEMSE), 160

L
Labor market, 78
Legal capacity, 47
Legislators, 51
Liberal policy, 175
Lithium extraction, 74
Lithium policy, 147
Lithium Policy and Salar Governance framework, 148
Lithium Policy and the Governance of Salars, 102, 116
Lithium Triangle, 9, 74, 153, 177

M
Macroeconomic policies, 35

Market failures, 36
Market liberalization, 36
Market regulation, 6
Middle-income trap (MIT), 10
Milei, Javier, 157
Mining Code, 94, 156
Mobilization, 51

N
National budget, 145
Nationalist public policies, 7
National Lithium Commission, 112, 116
Negotiation, 169
Neoextractivism, 41
Non-concessionable, 102
Non-Metallic Mining Committee, 102, 118, 143

O
Opposition, 135, 143, 165, 175

P
Paris Agreement, 110
Peru, 38
Piñera, Sebastián, 102, 106, 125
Pluralism, 52
Pockets of efficiency, 63
Policy stability, 62
Political capacities, 110
Political discourse, 168
Political interests, 49
Political scandals, 129
Political system, 158
Political transitions, 174
Political will, 174
Presidential Advisory Commissions, 112
Presidential systems, 65
Privatization process, 98, 99
Process of "publicization", 104
Process tracing, 15
Productivity learning, 63
Public consultation, 169
Public discourse, 104
Public opinion, 60, 105
Public policy, 7

R
Rents, 4
Rent-seeking, 65
Resource curse, 11, 35, 151
Royalty, 133, 162
Ruling coalition, 63
Ruling elites, 63

S
Selective Industrial Policy, 12, 175
Shadow study, 14
Social conflicts, 5
Sociedad Chilena del Litio (SCL), 97
Sociedad Minera Salar de Atacama (Minsal), 97
Sociedad Química y Minera de Chile (SQM), 2, 5, 57, 84, 98, 126, 150
Socio-ecological inequalities, 5
Socio-environmental conflicts, 84, 169
Socio-environmental impacts, 83
South America, 2
Special Contract for Lithium Operation (CEOL), 143
Special Lithium Operation Contracts (CEOL), 102, 126
Speculation, 156
State-business relations, 7, 34, 179
State-business relationships, 11, 148
State capacity, 9, 12, 46, 66, 80, 121, 150, 168, 174
State-led industrial policy, 6, 154
State-owned company, 6

State-owned enterprises, 165
State power, 49
Status quo, 61
Strategic capacity, 50
Structural, 56
Structural power, 56, 140
Supply shocks, 62

T
Technical capacity, 155
Technical expertise, 166
Technical knowledge, 175
Technology sector, 5
Territorial capacity, 47
Tesla, 1, 27
Third-order change, 104
Trade-off, 53
Trade policy, 64
Typological theory, 14

U
Unitary, 171
United States, 2

V
Value-adding, 12
Value chain, 75
Vertical coordination, 52
Vertical industrialization, 153

W
Washington Consensus, 24, 36, 173
Water stress, 84
Winning coalitions, 51
World Bank, 10

Y
Yacimientos de Litio Bolivianos (YLB), 89, 163
YPF Litio, 157

The manufacturer's authorised representative in the EU is Springer Nature Customer Service Centre GmbH, Europaplatz 3, 69115 Heidelberg, Germany. If you have any concerns regarding our products, please contact ProductSafety@springernature.com

Printed and bound by CPI Group (UK) Ltd, Croydon, CR0 4YY

30/09/2026

02225591-0004